Via Car Love Northern California

Via Corsa Travel Guidebooks

A new way to look at your love of the automobile. Authoritative and comprehensive, these Guidebooks are a must for any car lover!

Via Corsa, Ltd.
P.O. Box 13803
Scottsdale, Arizona 85267-3803
Email: *info@viacorsa.com*
Web address: *www.viacorsa.com*

ISBN-10: 0-9825710-2-X
ISBN-13: 978-0-9825710-2-6

Library of Congress Control Number:
2013911384

This guidebook is the third release in our travel book series for car lovers.

Author - Ron Adams
Editing - Alan Krome and Sabu Advani
Principal Photography - Ron Adams
Cover Photos & Back Cover Photos -
Ron Adams
Original Cover Design - Vince Martinez
California Map - Map Resources
Open Street Maps data was used in the
creation of all city and location maps.

Main cover photo: *1955 OSCA MT4 Morelli Spyder at the 2009 Pebble Beach Concours d'Elegance, Monterey, CA*

Now in Print
Via Corsa Car Lover's Guide to Southern Germany
ISBN-13: 978-0-9825710-1-9

Coming soon
Via Corsa Car Lover's Guide to Southern California

Our books are exclusively distributed by Motorbooks International and Quayside Publishing
www.motorbooks.com or
www.qbookshop.com/motorbooks.com

For wholesale or phone orders, contact Motorbooks International at (800) 458-0454.

Inset front page photos, left to right:
Hot Rods at Goodguys Hot Rod Week
1936 Duesenberg Model SJ Convertible at the Blackhawk Museum
Lamborghini Gallardos at Concorso Italiano
1969 Porsche 917 K takes on "The Corkscrew" at Mazda Raceway Laguna Seca

Back cover photos from top to bottom:
Mario Andretti at his Andretti Winery, The California Mille on Highway 1
Opposite: *Pierce Arrow at the 2009 Pebble Beach Concours d'Elegance, Monterey, CA*

Table of Contents

Table of Contents

Welcome to the Via Corsa Guidebook Series! We are an independent publishing company dedicated to writing guidebooks covering the hot spots of car activity in the United States and Europe. Each book is a comprehensive guide covering every aspect of the automobile—be it car museums, race tracks, factory tours, car shows, or drives. In other words, this is a book for people who love cars. **"Via Corsa Car Lover's Guide to Northern California"** is our third title and our next step towards writing and producing guidebooks that will eventually cover most of Europe and the United States. Here at Via Corsa we love cars. We have been around them for decades and want to share our knowledge and insight gained in the process. No matter what your passion, there is something in this book for you, and if you enjoy this guide, please tell us!

Family Fun

As the years go by, it has become increasingly important to me as a parent to look for better ways to travel with children. While many places pose challenges for a family, many welcome them with open arms. Using your best judgement will avoid many possible problems—such as bringing along a youngster to a wine tasting. But often enough there are some hidden surprises out there to delight children of all ages. Look for these blue sidebar boxes for some of those such places or activities.

About Ron Adams

Ron is the principal author and photographer of *Via Corsa Car Lover's Guides*. Before graduating from high school in Colorado, Ron Adams had travelled to 6 of the 7 continents; including China, Peru, Zimbabwe, and the Australian Outback. After college, he moved to Munich, Germany to live. He has raced on Mugello, Hungaroring, and Salzburgring in Europe and has raced Road America, Lime Rock, Mazda Raceway Laguna Seca, Infineon Raceway, Road Atlanta, VIR, PIR, and several other tracks in the United States. He won the 1998—1999 Arizona Regional SCCA Championship in Formula Mazda and placed 1st in the 2000 Ferrari Challenge Endurance Series and 4th in the Ferrari Sprint series. Ron currently lives in Paradise Valley, Arizona with his wife and two children.

Introduction to Via Corsa Car Lover's Guide to Northern California

At first glance, Northern California presents a number of unique challenges for a guidebook series such as this. My first impression was that, other than the spectacular scenery, there was not a whole lot there. Sure, there are a few great car museums, but nothing like the large number I saw in Germany. There were also no manufacturers or factory tours.

Monterey Classic Car Week turns the Monterey peninsula into a destination spot for roughly one week a year. While Monterey is a great place to visit all year around, it is this week that we will focused.

But Northern California did not disappoint. Take Napa and Sonoma Counties. Wine Country. Everyone knows this and there are many books written about the area, but this is the first one covering it for the car enthusiast.

There are eight sections in this book and each section is further broken down into spreads. Each spread includes in-depth coverage of that site's history, current events, or exhibitions. This guidebook does not use the traditional guidebook format of listing sites by region.

▶ The eight sections cover **Museums, Wineries, Race Tracks, Driving Experiences and Schools, Monterey Car Week, Hot Rods & Hot Spots, Movie Locations**, and **Rally Routes**.

▶ The **Rally Route** section is a collection of routes driven by the California Mille organized by the late Martin Swig who was kind enough to allow us to sort through a decade of rallies and present our readers the very best of Northern California.

▶ The **Appendix** lists a few extra sites to see and general travel information.

Want to comment?
Email: *info@viacorsa.com*

Did we make a mistake?
Email: *corrections@viacorsa.com*

Join us on Facebook at
www.facebook.com/ CarLoversGuidebooks

or Twitter at www.twitter.com/viacorsa

Retail Orders
Our guidebooks are available through Motorbooks International

Phone orders
(800) 826-6600 or (715) 294-3345

Internet orders
www.motorbooks.com
or
www.amazon.com

Location Maps, Directions, and Phone Numbers

Location Maps and Directions

From **Monterey:** *(<- starting point)*
▶ Federal Interstates and U.S. Highways are in **BLUE**
▶ Highway exit ramps are white with a **BLUE** or **GREEN** border.
▶ California State highways are **DARK GREEN**
▶ Roads are **BLACK**
▶ The end destination is in **RED**
▶ Some adjacent roads are deleted
▶ Interstate signs are BLUE with white numbers. State highway signs are GREEN with white numbers.
▶ Most maps are not to scale

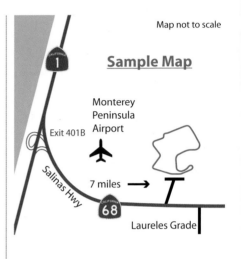

Photo Tips

Throughout this book, I offer readers a few tips. This consists of either restrictions for photographers (such as the use of tripods) or thoughts on creating better photos on your journeys. Hopefully, my tips may be used by any level of photographer.

Quick Stats

▶ If you would like a brief overview of a site or topic without having to read an entire spread, please refer to our **"Quick Stats."** These answer the most frequent questions asked and provide a brief overview of that site.

A Note About My Travel Pictures

My goal with each successive *Car Lover's Guidebook* is to personally take almost all the pictures. I set this goal as a way to personally experience any given site firsthand and so be able to offer first hand advice through both photos and text including tips and advice on taking better photographs.

"Journal Entries"

A Guidebook can be an impersonal place. Usually they seems little more than collections of facts, figures, and photos. While these are important, also look for a few of my personal stories from over the years with "Journal Entries."

✍ *Ron Adams*

Each section of our guidebook is denoted by an easy-to-identify icon. These icons are placed at the top corner of each page. The introduction to the guidebook, as well as the appendix and index, do not have icons and some pages with photographs will also not have an icon.

Museums

The few museums in Northern California host some of the best collections in the world.

Wineries

Each winery we cover has a unique connection to the car enthusiast through either automobile racing or collecting.

 ## Race Tracks

There are three road courses, four drag strips, seven asphalt ovals, and seventeen dirt track ovals in Northern California.

Driving Experiences & Schools

With every great racetrack, there is usually a great way to experience it safely and with professionals.

 ## Monterey Peninsula

For more than a week, the entire Monterey Peninsula and Pebble Beach become a mecca for car lovers worldwide.

Hot Rods & Hot Spots

Home to hot rod event promoter Goodguys, the Hot Rod scene in Northern California is rich with service shops and dealers

 ## Movie Locations

Two of the greatest car movies ever made were filmed in Northern California, *American Graffiti* and *Bullitt*. See where they were shot!

Rally Routes

Ride with the California Mille Rally as it cruises along the coast and through the Redwoods and Wine Country.

 ## Exclusive Interviews

We have several exclusive interviews and Question and Answer sessions with many notable figures involved in Northern California.

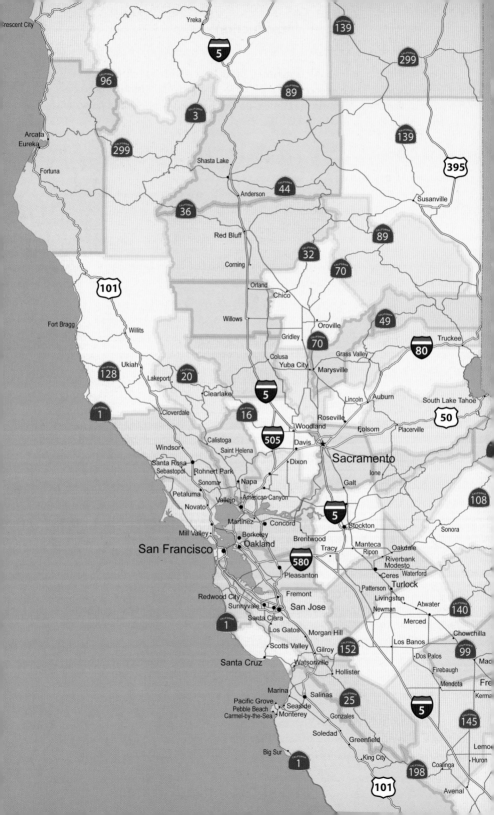

Map of Northern California

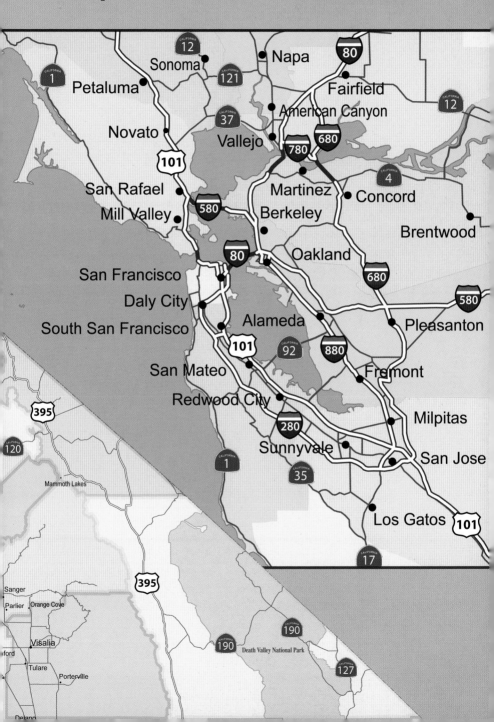

Map of San Francisco

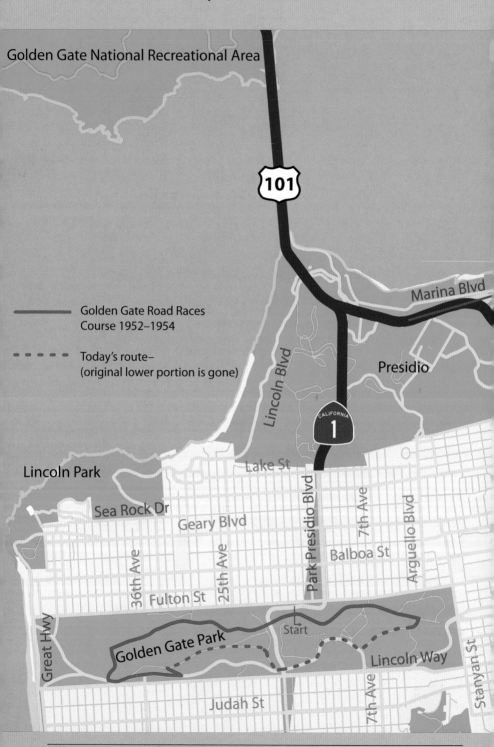

Golden Gate National Recreational Area

101

Marina Blvd

Presidio

Golden Gate Road Races
Course 1952–1954

Today's route–
(original lower portion is gone)

Lincoln Blvd

CALIFORNIA
1

Lake St

Lincoln Park

Sea Rock Dr

Geary Blvd

Park Presidio Blvd

7th Ave

Arguello Blvd

36th Ave

25th Ave

Balboa St

Great Hwy

Fulton St

Golden Gate Park

Start

Lincoln Way

Stanyan St

7th Ave

Judah St

Map of San Francisco

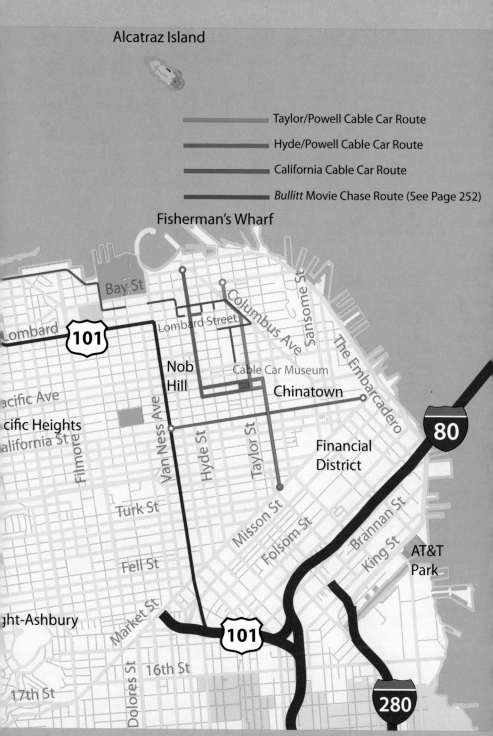

Alcatraz Island

Taylor/Powell Cable Car Route

Hyde/Powell Cable Car Route

California Cable Car Route

Bullitt Movie Chase Route (See Page 252)

Fisherman's Wharf

Bay St

Lombard

101

Lombard Street

Columbus Ave

Sansome St

The Embarcadero

Nob Hill

Cable Car Museum

Chinatown

Pacific Ave

Pacific Heights

California St

Filmore

Van Ness Ave

Hyde St

Taylor St

Financial District

80

Turk St

Misson St

Folsom St

Brannan St

King St

AT&T Park

Fell St

Haight-Ashbury

Market St

101

Dolores St

16th St

17th St

280

Know Before You Go

As you prepare for your trip to Northern California, there are a few things to know before you go and during your trip.

General Statistics

▶ September is the warmest month for both Monterey and San Francisco. July is the warmest month for Napa Valley.

▶ The wettest months for all Northern California are January and February.

▶ According to the Bay Area Census, the San Francisco Bay Area is home to over 7 million people, and the total population of all of Northern California exceeds 13 million.

When to Go

There is no bad time to visit Northern California, but there are some busy periods. Grape harvest in the fall brings tourists to wine country and, of course, the third weekend in August is full house for Monterey.

What to Take

Visitors between October and March need a raincoat, and the Monterey Car Week visitors need good walking shoes. For those driving the back roads or coastal roads, bring spares, extra coolant, and an AAA card.

Getting There by Car

I-5 is the main N/S route with US 101 and SR 1 the coastal routes. E/W is I-80 from Reno, I-15 from Las Vegas, and I-10 from Phoenix.

Getting There by Air

The major airports in the San Francisco Bay Area are **San Francisco International Airport** (SFO) *www.flysfo.com*, **Oakland International Airport** (OAK) *www.flyoakland.com*, and **San Jose International Airport** (SJC) *www.flysanjose.com*. Visitors to Sacramento fly into **Sacramento International Airport** (SMF) *www.sacramento.aero*, and Monterey visitors may fly into **Monterey Regional Airport** (MRY) *www.montereyairport.com*.

Driving in California

If you don't drive into California with a car, chances are you will be renting one anyway. So read on. . .

Speed Limits

Interstates, U.S. Highways, and State Routes have a maximum speed limit of 70 mph with two-lane undivided highways limited to 55 mph. Business and residential areas are limited to a speed of 25 mph unless otherwise noted.

Alcohol Limits

The California Driving Under the Influence law defines the blood alcohol percentages (BAC) as the following.

▶ 0.08% or higher if 21 years old or older operating a regular passenger vehicle.

▶ 0.04% or higher when operating a commercial vehicle.

▶ 0.01% or higher if younger than 21 years old.

Traffic Congestion

To check current highway conditions, call 1 (800) 427-7623 or visit *www.dot.ca.gov/cgi-bin/roads.cgi* and enter the highway number. Traffic around the San Francisco Bay Area may be checked at *www.sfgate.com/traffic* or at *511.org*.

Seat Belt Law/ Helmet Law

Drivers and passengers must wear a seat belt at all times, and motorcyclists must wear helmets at all times. This is a "primary enforcement" law, so police may stop a vehicle for only these violations.

Car Seats

As of January 1, 2010, children under the age of eight must be secured in a car seat or booster seat in the back seat unless they are over 4'9", in which case they are required to use a seat belt in the backseat. Children over the age of eight must wear a seat belt. See *www.chp.ca.gov*.

Cell Phones & Texting

As of January 1, 2009, it is illegal to talk on a cellular telephone or read or write a text message. For those over the age of 18, a Bluetooth device may be used with a cell phone. The first offense is $20 and the second offense $50, and police actively enforce these laws. The ticket does not count as points, but will appear on a drivers license record.

Contact California Highway Patrol

Call 911 for emergencies or 1 (800) 835-5247 for non-emergencies.

Smoking

This little-known law prohibits an adult from smoking a pipe, cigar, or cigarette in a car if a minor is present. This is a secondary offense. In other words, you cannot be pulled over just for smoking.

Gas Prices

California often ranks in the top three or four states for the highest price for gasoline in the country. The high price of gas in California may be partially explained by high taxes, as the state's excise tax rate is the third highest in the nation at 36 cents per gallon.

Photo Radar

Photo radar is in full force in California. The current system requires a photo of both your face and the license plate.

General Rules of Thumb

▶ California drivers ignore their blinkers, so expect them to change a lane right in front of you without warning.

▶ There is no "fast lane" on the Interstate, so expect slow drivers on the far left with people speeding in the far right lane.

▶ If you are alone, do not cheat and use the car pool lane. This law is actively enforced.

▶ Move over to the side of the road when you see the red and blue flashing lights of an emergency vehicle, but also the amber lights of a Caltrans vehicle.

Introduction to Northern California

Defined as the counties from Monterey by the Pacific Ocean to Inyo and Death Valley at the south up to the state border with Oregon, Northern California is diverse in everything from climate and temperature to the people living here. Of course for car enthusiasts, Northern California offers its own diversity of car-related sights and activities ■

Via Corsa Car Lover's Guide to Northern California

San Francisco

The city of San Francisco is a major tourist destination and draws 16.5 million visitors year-round to see the popular tourist destinations such as **Chinatown**, **Alcatraz**, and **Fisherman's Wharf**. That means an average of 40,000 people a day, with summer weekends seeing crowds swell to several hundred thousand.

San Francisco has been inhabited for at least the last 10,000 years with the Ohlone people the first to live here. Spaniards moved into the bay in 1776 and founded the first **Presidio Army Base**, but it was the **Gold Rush** of the late 1840s that first drew large numbers of settlers. On April 18, 1906, an earthquake (estimated to be 8.0) and the ensuing fire killed thousands and nearly destroyed the city.

Today, the city of San Francisco is the fourth most populous city in California, after Los Angeles, San Diego, and San Jose. The neighborhoods that were once ravaged by the fires following the 1906 earthquake have been rebuilt and today reflect a city with 21st Century architecture with a little bit of a Victorian influence. Car enthusiasts over the last decades have seen road races in **Golden Gate Park**, countless movies filmed here, and enjoy a peppering of hot rod shops. While racing is no longer held inside the city limits, everything an enthusiast would want is within an hour or so drive.

Opposite: The Golden Gate National Recreation Area overlooking Golden Gate Bridge and San Francisco in the distance.

San Francisco Bay Area

Locals simply call it the "Bay Area" and tourists generally think the whole thing is called "San Francisco." The San Francisco Bay Area comprises nine to twelve counties, depending on whom you ask (*bayareacensus.ca.gov*).

East Bay

Alameda County
Major cities are Oakland (county seat), Alameda, and Berkeley.

Contra Costa County
Major cities are Concord, Oakley, and Martinez (county seat).

North Bay

Marin County
Major cities are Mill Valley, Novato, and San Rafael (county seat).

Sonoma County
Major cities are Petaluma, Sonoma, and Santa Rosa (county seat).

Napa County
Major cities are Calistoga, Napa (county seat), and Yountville.

Solano County
Major cities are Fairfield (county seat) and Vallejo.

The Peninsula

San Mateo County
Major cities are Daly, Menlo Park, and Redwood City (county seat).

Santa Clara County
Major cities are Cupertino, Milpitas, and San Jose (county seat).

San Francisco City and County
San Francisco is the only city/county in California.

Sacramento

Sacramento was founded in 1848 by **John Sutter** using a fortune made during **The California Gold Rush** and became the capital of California in 1854. Today, the city is an "off-the-beaten-path" tourist attraction for car enthusiasts coming from both Reno and the Bay Area. The Sacramento area is home to the **California Auto Museum** (see page 30) and a number of hot rod shops (see page 232); the **Heidrick Ag History Center** (see page 36) is in the nearby town of Woodland. Other attractions include the **California State Railroad Museum** (*www.csrmf.org*), the **Croker Art Museum**, (*www.crockerartmuseum.org*), and of course you should tour the **State Capital Building and Museum** (*www.capitolmuseum.ca.gov*).

Wine Country

The counties of Napa and Sonoma are technically part of the San Francisco Bay Area but these two counties are a world away from the bustling city at the core of the Bay Area. Each county offers an amazing array of wineries and car collections for even the most hard to please enthusiast. While all the wineries we cover (see page 61) want visitors to appreciate them for their wine above all else, they are all worth visiting for their car collections. In all seriousness, many wineries included in this guidebook specifically wanted us to point out that their car collections are a great bonus for their already fantastic winery.

Monterey Peninsula

For one week a year, car enthusiasts descend on the Monterey Peninsula to attend many of the dozens of events planned each year in August. Not surprisingly, Monterey is a great place to visit the other 51 weeks of the year. Over the course of the calendar year, Monterey and Pebble Beach host wine festivals, beer festivals, jazz festivals, rodeos, the **AT&T Pebble Beach Pro-Am** golf tournament (*www.pebblebeach.com*), whale watching, and the **Red Bull U.S. Grand Prix** (*www.redbullusa.com*) at **Mazda Raceway Laguna Seca** (*www.mazdaraceway.com*). But honestly, the best reason to return to the Monterey area is to come off-season and check into one of the resorts with a spa and just relax. Just kidding—take a Skip Barber class instead (*www.skipbarber.com*).

Northern Coast

For the car enthusiast, the Northern Coast of California is peppered with great drives. This underrated area is predominately served by California State Route 1 starting at the Golden Gate Bridge and running 215 miles to the north until it merges with US 101 north of Fort Bragg.

Above: *North of San Francisco on SR 1*

Sierra Nevada

This mountain range (which is *not* in Nevada) was the last hurdle for the pioneers wishing to migrate to California for the Gold Rush of the 1850s and many, like the infamous Donner Party, didn't make it. Today the Sierra Nevadas offer yet another bastion of great drives, skiing, boating, and other recreational sports. Reno is worth a visit to see the ex-Bill Harrah Collection and the **National Automobile Museum** (see page 54) as are Lake Tahoe, and **Yosemite National Park** (*www.nps.gov/ yose*). Visitors to Yosemite even have the chance to drive a Ford Model A (*tinlizzieinn.com*)

Death Valley

There are many reasons to visit **Death Valley National Park** (*www.nps.gov/ deva*), but few of them are in summer. During the winter and spring, visitors can stargaze, hike, and photograph one of the most diverse and picturesque national parks in the country. So why would anyone want to visit the hottest, driest, lowest place on earth? To photograph the latest automotive manufactures prototypes, of course. See our chat with spy photographer extraordinaire **Brenda Priddy** as she answers questions on working in Death Valley in summer (see page 238).

Top: Yosemite Falls and Half Dome in Yosemite National Park

Right: The Powell-Hyde Cable Car line reaches Fisherman's Wharf as the northern turnaround point (outbound) and the Powell Station at the intersection of Powell Street and Market Street as the southern turnaround point (inbound).

Highway One

California State Route 1 (typically called "Highway 1") is a mostly undivided north/south road that runs along the Pacific Ocean from Dana Point south of Los Angeles to Fort Bragg up north. The most famous section is the over-the-top scenic 133-mile stretch between San Luis Obispo and **Carmel-by-the-Sea**. This much written about drive is everything and more than its fans have said. In fact, if there is one drive to take in all of Northern California, this is it. There are a few tips I have learned over the years. Leave with a full tank of gas, avoid weekends, and if you happen to be heading to the **Monterey Car Week** towing your sports car with an underpowered 6-cylinder SUV, take US 101 instead.

Automotive Introduction to Northern California

Martin Swig, founder of the **California Mille** (see page 260), summed it up best when he said *"I was 12 years old, and my family moved here from northern New Jersey in late 1946. I knew I was in the land of the automobile and, having always been an auto nut, I would read national magazines like* **Life Magazine** *about these things called Hot Rods in California. And I remember thinking that this was the best thing that had ever happened to me."*

After the Second World War, *America's Greatest Generation* set out to both redefine and improve the quality of their lives. Cities around the country saw an exodus to the suburbs and California became the center of the car enthusiast world.

Hot Rods

The origins of the hot rod can be traced back to the Southern California of the 1930s, but the idea of modding the family Ford didn't really take off until the late 1940s. **Alex Xydias** founded his **So-Cal Speed Shop** in Burbank in 1946 to sell parts to the Hot Rodders, but it all really took off in 1948 with the first hot rod exhibition at the Los Angeles Armory and with the publication of *Hot Rod Magazine* by **Robert E. Petersen**. From there, the hot rod craze spread like wildfire across all of California and the rest of the country.

Drag Racing

A natural side effect of having all these hot rods cruising about was the dawn of the back road drag race. In 1951 and after only a few years as the first editor of *Hot Rod Magazine*, **Wally Parks** founded the **National Hot Rod Association (NHRA)** to provide a legal and safer way to race. Today, several of the drag strips built during these formative years are still scattered around California.

Road Races

Back in the early 1950s, there were no road race tracks in California. While many loved to drag race their hot rods, others wanted to take to a road course in their newly acquired European sports cars. In the 1950s, the **Sports Car Club of America** (SCCA) started organizing races for drivers wishing to campaign their Alfa Romeos, Allards, MGs, Triumphs, and Ferraris. The solution, albeit temporary, was to hold races on blocked-off streets in both Pebble Beach (see page 210) and Golden Gate Park in San Francisco. For three years, 90,000 spectators lined the streets of Golden Gate Park to watch the race and attend a concours at the Polo Grounds. The last running of the race in 1954 was billed as "Ferrari vs. Allard" with **Bill Pollack** in his Allard J2 edging out a still unknown **Phil Hill** in his Ferrari 212.

Car Manufacturing

Not many people may remember that **Milt Brown** founded his automobile company **Apollo Design Works** (see opposite page) in Oakland, but most enthusiasts know that **Tesla Motors, Inc.** is a Northern California-based manufacturer with their headquarters in Palo Alto.

Chat with Milt Brown

Back in the early 1960s, Milt Brown founded his own car company in Oakland, California, and built the critically acclaimed but often overlooked **Apollo 3500 GT**.

Via Corsa: How did it all begin?

Milt Brown: I always wanted to build a sports car, so I made contact with body manufacturers and finally found **Carrozzeria Intermeccanica** (still in business and located in Vancouver, Canada - *www.intermeccanica.com*). He (**Paul Reisner**) was just starting out, and he built a custom bodied coupe, and he wanted to expand. A friend I went to high school with put up the money for the prototype. We built the first car and got some investors in 1961.

VC: When was the first car made?

MB: The first prototype was made in 1961 and then the first production car was in 1962. The prototype was aluminum but none of the car dealers wanted an aluminum-bodied car and so then we switched to steel. It actually weighed 200 lb more than a steel body because the aluminum body needed all that supporting structure

Above: Milt Brown, Founder of the International Motor Cars, Inc. and Apollo Design Works.

Right: Apollo 3500 GT #1005 (2nd built)

and subframe. So the steel-bodied car was self-supporting and it was cheaper to build. We then started setting up dealers and our most well-known customer was **Pat Boone**. He owned the Apollo for five years.

VC: And at this point how many cars had you sold?

MB: We had made 39 cars from 1962 to 1964. But the reason that did us in is that the investors wanted us to build more cars and make more money. We doubled production without increasing the operating capital. We had a slow month and the bank called in our loans and that was it. We sold the assets to a company in Pasadena (who continued to manufacturer Apollos for a few more years).

VC: What was your best car?

MB: The best one was the convertible. **Franco Scaglione** (who also designed the **Alfa Romeo 33 Stradale**) did the convertible design, and many authors say it is one of the undiscovered masterpieces. It is beautiful.

VC: Do you own an Apollo now?

MB: Nope. You know what, people think that. I would rather build cars and work on them, and there are enough around here that any time I want to drive one, I just phone the owner up and take it out for a free checkup!

Automobile Museums

Compared to other parts of the world, Northern California might be a little light on the number of world-class collector car museums. But the ones that are here are spectacular and are some of the best in the world. What also sets the museums in Northern California apart from the rest of the world is the diversity of the collections and the dedication of the enthusiasts and volunteer docents to maintain and educate the public about the automobiles and their history ■

Car-Related Museums

Museum	City	Time to see Museum
Blackhawk Automotive Museum	Danville	3–6 hours
California Automobile Museum	Sacramento	1.5–6 hours
Heidrick Ag History Center	Woodland	2–4 hours
Hiller Aviation Museum	San Carlos	2–4 hours
Monterey Museum of Automotive Arts	Monterey	TBA
Oakland Museum	Oakland	2–6 hours
San Francisco Cable Car Museum	San Francisco	1–2 hours
National Automobile Museum	Reno	1 day

Additional Museums

The museums below aren't really museums in the traditional sense. They may not have polished showrooms or be open to the public on a full-time basis, but each covers a niche of history important to Northern California.

San Jose Fire Truck Museum

Not open to the public, but available to be toured by appointment. The museum contains 27 pieces of firefighting gear, including a 1905 Cadillac, 1923 American LaFrance, and a 1931 Mack Type 19 Pumping Engine. For more information, visit *www.sanjosefiremuseum.com*.

Opposite Page: *1953 Ferrari 250 MM Vignale-bodied Spyder Series 1. Personally owned by Phil Hill and driven by him to a win at the 1953 road race at Pebble Beach. On display at the Blackhawk Collection.*

Pacific Bus Museum

This "rolling" museum of buses offers the public a chance to ride one of 25 vintage buses on select Sundays in the Niles district of Fremont. The museum also works in conjunction with the **Niles Canyon Railway** (*www.ncry.org*) to provide transportation for their train passengers from downtown to the station. The museum is hoping to one day find a permanent home.
See *www.pacbus.org*.

Dan Rouit Flat Track Museum

Open by appointment, this museum is dedicated to preserving the history of flat track racing. The museum has posters, helmets, trophies, and motorcycles on display, including Harley Davidson, Honda, Yamaha, and Triumph. Call (559) 291-2242 or see *www.vft.org/rouit.html*.

Blackhawk Automotive Museum

The Blackhawk Automotive Museum has become one of the premier automotive museums in the world and a must-see for anyone visiting the San Francisco area. One of the best times to visit is during their annual Open House following the Pebble Beach Concours d'Elegance in August.

History

The museum was founded by **Ken Behring** in 1998 as the **Behring Auto Museum** in the Blackhawk Plaza Shopping Center. The museum later changed the name to the Blackhawk Automotive Museum.

Today

Today the Blackhawk Automotive Museum is one of the premier museums in the world and the collector cars inside are some of the best cars on the planet. The museum also focuses on education, history, and community events.

The Collection Theme

Think of the cars inside the museum as "rolling sculptures." While the museum sets the cars up as an art object to be admired under carefully placed lights, each and every car runs and to some extent is driven. Many are displayed at car shows around the world, including the **Pebble Beach Concours d' Elegance** (See page 209). Most of the cars are on loan to the museum and are rotated out, so if you are looking to see a particular car, feel free to contact the museum to check availability. The museum has placed the rarer and concept cars on the top of its two main galleries, and the cars in both galleries range in years from roughly 1906 to the early 1960s.

Must-See

The trio of Alfa Romeo BATs. The 1953 BAT 5, 1954 BAT 7, and 1955 BAT 9 are the result of a collaboration between Alfa Romeo and the Italian car designer Bertone.

Directions

From **US-101/Monterey by car:**

- ▶ North on US-101
- ▶ North on I-680 (35 miles)
- ▶ Exit 36 onto Crow Canyon Road.
- ▶ Follow Crow Canyon Rd. (4 miles)
- ▶ Right on Camino Tassajara (100 feet)
- ▶ Left into Blackhawk Plaza Shopping Center
- ▶ Park in mall parking lot.

Opposite Page: *Entrance to the Blackhawk Automotive Museum in the Blackhawk Plaza*

Top Right: *1955 Alfa Romeo BAT 9 on display at the Concorso Italiano in 2009*

Quick Stats

- ▶ Plan on spending 3–6 hours
- ▶ Over 90 pristine collector cars
- ▶ Over 70,000 sq ft
- ▶ Be sure to visit the temporary exhibit in the other building to the north of the main exhibition halls (Currently "Jukebox Saturday Night: Selections from the Golden Age of the Jukebox")

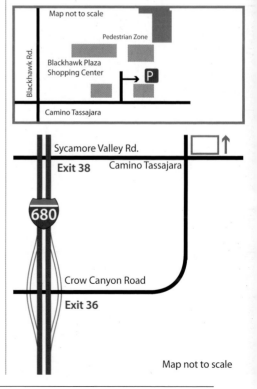

Exhibition Galleries

The main part of the museum consists of two different 25,000 sq ft galleries. The highlight cars and concept cars are on the upper level and temporary exhibits in the northern-most building.

The Cars

Here are some highlights

- ▶ 1886 Benz Patentwagen
- ▶ 1906 Cadillac Tulip Tourer
- ▶ 1926 Daimler ex-Gulab Singh
- ▶ 1926 Mercedes-Benz K Torpedo
- ▶ 1930 Bentley Corsica Coupe
- ▶ 1930 Bucciali TAV 8 Roadster
- ▶ 1931 Chrysler CG Imperial 8
- ▶ 1931 Isotta Fraschini Type 8A
- ▶ 1931 Packard Model 745
- ▶ 1932 Bugatti Type 50T Profilée
- ▶ 1932 Hispano-Suiza Model J-12
- ▶ 1932 Horch V-12 Type 670
- ▶ 1933 Alfa Romeo 8C Figoni
- ▶ 1934 Delage D8SS Cabriolet
- ▶ 1934 Duesenberg J Murphy
- ▶ 1936 Auburn Cabriolet
- ▶ 1936 Mercedes-Benz 540K
- ▶ 1937 Bentley 4¼ Litre Carlton
- ▶ 1937 Mercedes-Benz 540K
- ▶ 1937 Rolls-Royce Phantom III
- ▶ 1938 Bugatti Type 57SC Vanden Plas Tourer (1 of 1 built)
- ▶ 1939 Alfa Romeo 6C 2500
- ▶ 1939 Frazer Nash/BMW 328
- ▶ 1939 Lagonda V-12 Drophead
- ▶ 1948 Cadillac 62 Saoutchik
- ▶ 1949 Healey Silverstone

Top Left: *Nardi Blue Ray and Alfa Romeo concept cars in front of the 1924 Hispano-Suiza "Tulipwood"*

Middle Left: *a 1953 Cadillac Series 62 in front of a red 1954 Aston Martin DB 2/4*

Bottom Left: *The Rolls-Royce Phantom III Pebble Beach 2008 winner - First in Class*

- 1950 Ferrari 195 Sport Touring
- 1951 Jaguar C-Type
- 1952 Lancia Aurelia B42 Vignale
- 1952 Ferrari 212 Export
- 1952 Ferrari 342 America Vignale
- 1952 Lancia Aurelia B52 Vignale
- 1953 Delahaye Model 235
- 1953 Ferrari 250 MM Vignale Spyder (see page 22)
- 1954 Dodge Firearrow IV
- 1954 Ferrari 375 MM Ghia Cpe
- 1954 500 Ferrari Mondial
- 1955 Alfa Romeo 1900 SS Zagato
- 1955 Alfa Romeo B.A.T. 9
- 1955 Nardi Blue Ray 1
- 1955 Pegaso Tipo Z-102B
- 1956 Ferrari 625 Le Mans Spyder
- 1958 Ferrari 250 PF Series 1 Cab
- 1958 Nardi Blue Ray II
- 1960 Aston Martin DB4 GT
- 1960 Maserati 3500GT Vignale
- 1961 Jaguar/Cunningham XK-E
- 1962 Lincoln—JFK Fleet
- 1962 Maserati 5000 GT Allemano
- 1963 Ford Thunderbird "Italien" Concept Car

Top Right: *1936 Duesenberg Model SJ Convertible behind the 1929 Duesenberg Model J Torpedo Convertible*

Middle Right: *1955 Ferrari 750 Monza in front of a 1956 Jaguar D-Type*

Bottom Right: *The 1947 Delahaye Type 135MS, Guilloré Roadster Paris Salon Car*

Photo Tips

The Blackhawk Automotive Museum can be a challenge to photograph because of their black walls, ceiling, and floor—and even more difficult with a camera without high ISO capabilities. I did not use a flash and shot at 1,600 ISO using a 24-70mm f2.8 lens. Tripods are not allowed, but flash photography is permitted. Any commercial photography or videotaping must be pre-approved.

Events

Through out the year, the Blackhawk Automotive Museum offers the public a number of events. Admission varies by event. Some highlights include:

- ▶ **Blackhawk 500 Pinewood Derby**
  For more than a decade, each Spring scouts have come to race their hand-made cars.

- ▶ **Father's Day**
  Enjoy this annual car show with music, children's activities, food, and drinks.

- ▶ **Annual Open House**
  (see opposite page)

- ▶ **Old Blackhawk Magic**
  This annual Halloween costume party has been held at the museum for well over a decade and is a sellout event!

- ▶ **Holiday Model Railway Exhibit**
  In conjunction with the *European Train Enthusiasts* (ETE), a HO-scale model train exhibit is on display from roughly the end of November to the beginning of January.

- ▶ **Lecture Series**
  As part of their ongoing commitment to bring the very best to their museum patrons, the Blackhawk Automotive Museum provides lectures through out the calendar year.

Automotive Research Library

The library is open to the public and may be visited by appointment only. If you cannot visit the library in person, it is also possible to fax in a research request at the cost of $25 per hour.

Top Left & Below: *The Blackhawk Automotive Museum's main exhibition halls.*

Tours

There is a one-hour tour each weekend at 2:00 PM. This tour is free and part of your admission to the museum. The tours are led by museum docents and cover both the exhibition halls and temporary exhibits.

Cars & Coffee

Starting at 8:00 AM (and lasting until at least noon) on the first Sunday of the month, the Blackhawk Plaza and the museum host their own Cars & Coffee. No restrictions on types of cars, and park in front of the Anthropologie building.

Membership

Joining the museum as a member offers the chance to enjoy free admission, discounts, and more. Membership starts at $60.

Amenities

▶ Museum Library and Bookstore Open Friday–Sunday 10:00 AM to 5:00 PM

Admission

▶ Adults	$10
▶ Students (w/ valid ID)	$7
▶ Seniors (65 & older)	$7
▶ Children under 6	Free
▶ Active Military Personnel	Free

Hours

▶ Wednesday to Sunday 10:00 AM to 5:00 PM

▶ Closed New Year's Day, July 4, Thanksgiving, December 25

Contact Information

Blackhawk Automotive Museum
3700 Blackhawk Plaza Circle
Danville, CA 94506

Phone: (925) 736-2280
Fax: (925) 736-4818
Email: *museum@blackhawkmuseum.org*
www.blackhawkmuseum.org

For more on the Museum Guild call (925) 736-2277 x 651

the Blackhawk Automotive Museum is a 501(c)(3) nonprofit organization

Blackhawk Open House

For more than two decades, the Blackhawk Automotive Museum has opened up its doors to the public on the first Monday following the **Pebble Beach Concours d'Elegance** (See page 209).

This annual event is free to the public and offers the car enthusiast a chance to see some of the Pebble Beach show cars from the previous day, in addition to the 90 or so regular cars on display. Visitors need not RSVP and, in addition to the cars, the museum provides drinks and light snacks for all visitors on the lower level.

Above: *The Blackhawk Automotive Museum Open House*

California Automobile Museum

Often enough a museum becomes a static collection of objects set away from the public to enjoy at a distance. Not this museum. . . and it doesn't matter what your age may be. Children enjoy a number of hands-on activities ranging from sitting in and exploring vintage Fords to interacting with chassis and drivetrains, while the adults may enjoy sponsoring an individual classic car or meeting new friends at a variety of annual events. Plus, this museum offers the chance to drive a few of the museum's treasures!

History

As with most museums, the roots of the **California Automobile Museum** can be traced back to a single enthusiast. By the mid 1980s, Montana banker **Edward Towe** (rhymes with "plow") had collected several hundred classic Fords and even opened a museum in Deer Lodge (still open today as the **Montana Auto Museum** *pcmaf.org/auto.htm*). But in 1986, due to a number of factors, a large selection of cars were moved to Sacramento to help fill a museum founded by the **California Vehicle Foundation** (the **CVF** was founded in Sacramento in October 1983). The collaboration between the late Edward Towe and CVF made it possible for the museum to open to the public in May 1987 as the **Towe Ford Museum**. In 1997 the museum changed its name to the **Towe Auto Museum** and in 2009, to better reflect its mission, re-branded to become the **California Automobile Museum**.

Today

The California Automobile Museum (still operated by the CVF) is more than just classic cars lined up in rows, but rather a number of exhibits and displays designed to educate, interact, entertain, and help us understand the automobile and its influence on our lives today. There are 34 cars from the original Towe collection still in the museum.

Directions

From **San Francisco by car:**

▶ I-80 East to Sacramento
▶ Exit onto the I-80 Business Loop.
▶ Drive over the Sacramento River and stay right.
▶ Exit 4B onto 5th Street.
▶ Right/south on 5th Street
▶ Right/south on Broadway
▶ Right/north on Front Street
▶ Museum & parking to your left

Opposite Page: *The front entrance to the California Automobile Museum*

Top Right: *Not all the classic cars are parked inside the museum!*

Collection Theme

A visual display of the evolution of the automobile from 1900 to today with a look into the future. Several cars are placed inside themed displays to help set the context.

Quick Stats

- ▶ Plan on spending 1.5–6 hours
- ▶ Over 160 cars
- ▶ 72,000 sq ft
- ▶ Over 300 volunteers help run and operate the museum

Exhibition Hall

The museum is divided into eight main sections. Rather than line cars up in a line, the museum tries to portray the feel of the cars in the time period when they were manufactured. The best way to tour the museum is to start in the "Early 1900s" and walk clockwise.

Left Top: *1931 Chrysler CD Roadster in front of a 1930 Marquette Coupe*

Left Bottom: *"Phil's Garage" and a 1930 Studebaker FD Commander Roadster*

Opposite Top: *Floor plan of the Museum*

Opposite Bottom: *From L to R: 1921 Ford Model T Snowmobile, 1918 Grand 6 Touring, 1917 Ford Model T "Form A Truck" Conversion, 1912 Cadillac Model 30 Torpedo*

Photo Tips

The California Automobile Museum is a dark museum with tall, dark ceilings. This makes all photography a challenge. There are also several different types of light sources, so check your white balance to adjust for incandescent and fluorescent lights. I shot this museum at 2000 ISO and only used a flash for close-ups.

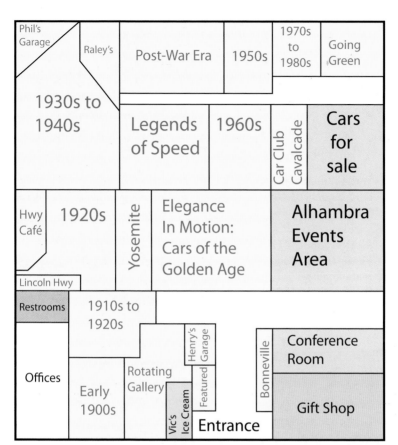

Phil's Garage

Raley's

Post-War Era

1950s

1970s to 1980s

Going Green

1930s to 1940s

Legends of Speed

1960s

Car Club Cavalcade

Cars for sale

Hwy Café

1920s

Yosemite

Elegance In Motion: Cars of the Golden Age

Alhambra Events Area

Lincoln Hwy

Restrooms

1910s to 1920s

Offices

Early 1900s

Rotating Gallery

Vic's Ice Cream

Henry's Featured Garage

Entrance

Bonneville

Conference Room

Gift Shop

Must-See

1932 Ford Deuce Coupe—**A.J. Foyt**'s first race car, 1911 Pierce-Arrow Model 48, 1987 Lamborghini Countach—**Malcom Forbes**

The Cars

Here are some highlights (but always subject to change)

- ► 1904 Ford C Runabout
- ► 1907 Ford Model K 6-40
- ► 1908 REO
- ► 1908 Cartercar Model H Touring
- ► 1910 Peerless Model 27
- ► 1911 Pierce-Arrow Model 48
- ► 1912 Metz Roadster
- ► 1914 Hupmobile Model 32
- ► 1915 Dodge Brothers Touring
- ► 1915 Ford Model T Coupelet
- ► 1923 Studebaker Model EL Six
- ► 1925 Franklin Model 10C
- ► 1927 Nash Coupe
- ► 1928 Willys Knight Coupe
- ► 1929 Hudson Super Six Roadster
- ► 1933 Hudson Essex Terraplane
- ► 1933 Ford "Popular" (English)

Events

Some highlights include

- ► **C.A.M. Car Cruise**
  Open to all makes and models, this annual event starts with a cruise through downtown Sacramento and ends with a huge car show.

- ► **Vettes for Vets**
  Now in its third year, each Memorial Day veterans are honored (and enter for free) with this annual showing of Chevrolet Corvettes.

Tours

If you wish to learn more about the museum, look for the docents in blue vests for a free tour. If you have 10 or more people, please contact the museum in advance.

Drive a Vintage Ford

Yes, it is possible to take a class and learn about and then drive a Ford Model A. Contact the museum for more information.

Facility Rental

There are a number of different areas open for event rental. The largest is their Alhambra Events Area (up to 500 seated) as well as a conference room and Vic's Ice Cream Parlor.

Memberships

A Museum "Gearhead" Membership starts at $50 per year for an individual with packages for companions, families, and car clubs. There is a 20% discount for seniors.

Amenities

The gift store that is open during museum hours. Vic's Ice Cream Parlor is open only for events and may be rented, however visitors to the museum is welcome to check it out!

Admission

- ▶ Adults $8
- ▶ Students $4
- ▶ Seniors (65+) $7
- ▶ Members   Free
- ▶ Discount admission on special occasions, see website.

Hours

- ▶ Open Daily
  10:00 AM to 6:00 PM
- ▶ Open late every third Thursday of the month until 9:00 PM (except December)
- ▶ Museum closes at 3:00 PM on Christmas and New Year's Eve and is closed Thanksgiving, Christmas, New Year's Day

Contact Information

California Automobile Museum
2200 Front Street
Sacramento, CA 95818

Phone: (916) 442-6802
Fax: (916) 442-2646
www.CalAutoMuseum.org
www.camcarsales.com
Email: *info@CalAutoMuseum.org*

California Automobile Museum is a 501(c)(3) nonprofit organization

Opposite Far Left: *1930 Vintage Drag Chevrolet "Hi Boy Roadster" by Dick Bertolucci with a Chevy 454 in front of the Michael Andretti 1985 March 85-C Indy Car*
Opposite Left: *1954 Chevrolet Corvette*
Below: *Ford Model T for all ages*

Family Fun

Taking young children to any museum can be hit or miss, even car museums. Fear not, here at the California Auto Museum, children are not just welcome, they are encouraged to interact with a number of displays and automobiles. There are several photo ready cars for children to climb on as well as "hand-on" displays such as a Ford Model A cutaway rear axle and other mechanical systems, all designed to entertain and educate your little ones!

Heidrick Ag History Center

If the idea of visiting an agriculture museum sounds a bit boring, you will be in for a big surprise. This is not a farm museum filled with dirt, cobwebs, and rusted out tractors, but instead a well planned and fascinating journey through the history of California Agriculture.

History

The History Center opened in 1997 to house the collection of **Fred Heidrick, Sr.** who had been collecting and restoring trucks and tractors for over 60 years. In the 1990s, his family persuaded him to donate his collection to a museum, but he went a step further and built the museum.

Today

The Heidrick Ag History Center is really a combination of two museums. The **Heidrick Antique Tractor Museum** offers visitors tractors, combines, and harvesters. The **Hays Antique Truck Museum** offers a historical look at fire trucks, military vehicles, and even a 1917 Wilton.

Collection Theme

If there is a common theme between the two museums, it is the history of California Agriculture dating back over 100 years with each collection expanding in depth on this theme.

The vehicles and their history are further explored with historically accurate displays. These displays are spread out between both museums and include farm settings, harvesting, winter and snow, a gas station, scale-model trucks, and a diner.

Quick Stats

- ▶ Plan on spending 2–4 hours
- ▶ Roughly 100 antique trucks and 100 antique tractors
- ▶ 130,000 sq ft
- ▶ Largest collection of its kind

Must-See

The handmade wooden pickup truck, 1919 Fageol Model 9-12 "Walking Tractor," 1953 REO "Eager Beaver" 2½-ton 6x6 military truck, and the Fordson Snowmobile.

Exhibition Halls

The Heidrick Ag History Center is actually two different museums in two buildings side by side, connected by a gallery. Each of the two museums—the **Heidrick Antique Tractor Museum** (closer to the entrance) and the **Hays Antique Truck Museum**, has a number of individual displays and exhibits pertaining to its respective themes.

Directions

From **Sacramento by car:**

- ▶ Head north on Interstate 5.
- ▶ Follow I-5 for roughly 16 miles.
- ▶ Take exit 536 North.
- ▶ Follow exit to Road 102.
- ▶ Merge onto Hays Lane west.
- ▶ Museum will be on left/south.

Opposite Page: *The front entrance to the Heidrick Ag History Center*

Top Right: *1908 William Galloway Co. ½-ton "GT Farm Wagon"*

Map not to scale

Heidrick Antique Tractor Museum

The tractor museum is next to the entrance and gift store. This museum features tractors by Holt, Best, and Caterpillar in one section with John Deere and Fordson in different sections. Highlights include

- ▶ 1915 Russel Model 8x10
- ▶ 1917 Holt 120 H.P.
- ▶ 1922 Waterloo Boy Model N
- ▶ 1924 Imperial Super Drive
- ▶ 1930 Oliver-Hart Parr 28-44

Hays Antique Truck Museum

The truck museum (named in honor of **Pop Hays**). Highlights include

- ▶ 1911 Randolph Model 14
- ▶ 1916 Packard Model D
- ▶ 1919 Oldsmobile Model T
- ▶ 1925 Ford Model T
- ▶ 1927 Chevrolet Series LM
- ▶ 1942 Dodge Weapons Carrier

Facility Rental

There are a number of areas open for event rental including the museum itself. Contact *events@aghistory.org*

Top Left: *1930 Chevrolet Model AD Roadster Pickup "Roadster Delivery"*
Middle Left: *1914 Selden Truck*
Bottom Left: *1917 Winton, Model22A*

Photo Tips

The Ag History Center has loads of indirect sunlight, thanks to dozens of skylights. A white ceiling and walls create well-lit trucks and tractors with few shadows. It may not be the prettiest to look at, but from a lighting standpoint, photography here is easy. I used 800 ISO, no flash, and a 24mm lens for most shots.

Membership

The various levels of membership begin at $55 for individuals.

Amenities

There is a gift store by the entrance.

Admission

- ▶ Adults (ages 13–61) $8
- ▶ Seniors (62+) $7
- ▶ Children (ages 5–12) $5
- ▶ Children under 5   Free
- ▶ Discounts for AAA members

Hours

- ▶ Open Wednesday–Sunday 10:00 AM to 5:00 PM
- ▶ Last admission 4:00 PM
- ▶ Check website for changes for summer and winter hours
- ▶ Museum closed on Easter, July 4, Thanksgiving, December 24, December 25, December 31, and January 1

Contact Information

Heidrick Ag History Center
1962 Hays Lane
Woodland, CA 95776

Phone: (530) 666-9700
Fax: (530) 666-9712
www.www.aghistory.org
Email: *aghistory@aghistory.org*

The Heidrick Ag History Center is a 501(c)(3) nonprofit organization

Top Right: *From L to R: 1944 Sterling 6x4, 1946 Kenworth 4x2, 1938 Fageol 3-5 ton*
Middle Right: *Caterpillar 60-Diesel 1C2*
Middle Right: *1957 recreation in wood*
Bottom Right: *Fordson Snowmobile nicknamed "Snow Devil"*

Hiller Aviation Museum

Most aviation buffs may not know the name Stanley Hiller, Jr. as a helicopter pioneer, but his legacy includes several functional and visionary inventions that helped cement Hiller as one of the three notable pioneers in vertical flight. All his work was based here in Northern California.

History

The museum only opened in 1998, but its history started being written long before. Its founder and bene- factor, **Stanley Hiller, Jr.,** started **United Helicopters** in 1949, when he was just 18 years old! His firm was later acquired by **Fairchild Aircraft** in 1964.

Today

The museum today reflects the birth and development of aviation in Northern California dating all the way back to the late 1800s. There is a strong focus on the history of the Hiller Aviation Company and its heli- copters. There are plenty of aircraft and a few automobiles on display.

Collection Theme

This aviation museum is focused on the history of flight as well as looking at new technologies and the future. The cars play a minor role in the museum and are overshadowed by its fascinating airplanes, helicopters, and aviation displays. This museum has several Hiller Aircraft helicopters on display.

Quick Stats

- Plan on spending 2 - 4 hours
- 40 aircraft and 2 Fords
- 27,600 sq ft of museum space and 8,490 sq ft atrium
- Largest indoor aviation museum in California

Must-See

It would be impossible to miss the HU-16 Grumman Albatross, so the must-see here is the ONR Hiller Flying Platform as well as all Hiller helicopters.

Directions

From **San Francisco by car:**

- South on US-101
- Take exit 411 (about 10 miles south of the San Francisco International Airport).
- Exit onto Holly Street/Redwood Shores Pkwy. and head East.
- Right/south onto Airport Way
- Right/west onto Skyway Road
- Museum will be on your left/east.

Opposite Page: *The front entrance to the Hiller Aviation Museum with a Rutan LongEZ on the roof.*

Top Right: *A 1928 Thaden T-1 Argonaut above the restoration shop.*

Exhibition Halls

The museum consists of the main museum gallery, an atrium, and a mezzanine. Inside the main gallery there are two large display areas detailing most of the museum's exhibits and aircraft. There are also a number of themed displays and a restoration shop in which visitors may see current projects.

Education plays a major role in the museum and its operation, and both the museum and areas inside the museum are geared towards this goal, such as the upper mezzanine and its flight simulators.

Direction
San Mateo Bridge
CA-92

101

Holly Street

Airport Way

Exit 411

San Carlos Airport

Skyway Road

P

Map not to scale

The Cars

▶ 1914 Ford Model T Station Wagon
▶ 1930 Ford Model A

The Airplanes

Here are some highlights

▶ 1883 Montgomery Glider replica
▶ 1910 Black Diamond
▶ 1928 Thaden T-1 Argonaut
▶ 1928 Travelair D4D
▶ 1929 Pietenpol
▶ 1931 Buhl Autogiro
▶ 1949 Hiller 360 helicopter
▶ 1952 Hiller YH-32-A
▶ 1955 HU-16 Grumman Albatross
▶ 1957 Hiller VXT-8 Coleopter
▶ 1969 Boeing 747 cockpit
▶ 1969 Lockheed YO-3A
▶ 1988 Boeing Condor spy plane
▶ 1992 Arnold AR-5 Sport Mono

Top Left: 1914 Ford Model T station wagon
Middle Left: *A 1930 Ford Model A sitting between the aircraft.*
Bottom Left: *Aero L39C "Albatross"*

Photo Tips

The Hiller Aviation Museum is well lit by massive fluorescent lights and easy to photograph (check your white balance). An upper level offers nice wide-angle shots of the museum floor.

Tours

Group tours (10 or more) are available to the public, last roughly 30 minutes and, are included in with the price of admission. To schedule one, contact the museum in advance. School tours call (650) 654-0200 extension x222; all other tours call extension x224.

Rentals

Available for day or evening events. The Atrium, Gallery, Mezzanine, or Conference Center may be rented.

Membership

Starting at $40 for seniors (age 65+), $55 for individuals, and $80 for the family. Annual benefits include free admission, free newsletter, a 10% gift store discount, and more.

Amenities

▶ Gift store with a large collection of aviation toys, books, flight wear, and more.

Admission

▶ Adults	$14
▶ Children ages 5 - 17	$9
▶ Seniors (65 & older)	$9
▶ Children under 4	Free

Hours

▶ Open 7 days a week
10:00 AM to 5:00 PM

▶ Closed Easter, Thanksgiving, and Christmas

Right: *Boeing 747-136, serial #20269 cockpit and upper fuselage.*

Contact Information

Hiller Aviation Museum
601 Skyway Road
San Carlos, CA 94070

Phone: (650) 654-0200
Fax: (650) 654-0220
Email: *museum@hiller.org*
www.hiller.org

The Hiller Aviation Museum is a 501(c)(3) nonprofit organization

Boeing 747

The museum's Boeing 747-136, serial #20269 first flew in March 1971 with British Airways and her final service flight was from New York's Kennedy Airport to London's Heathrow Airport. In 1998 she was sold to ARR Corporation for salvage and donated by ARR to the Museum in 1999.

Monterey Museum of Auto Arts

When I spoke to Morris Kindig, my first question was "What took so long?" He laughed and said that this is everyone's first question. Of course, we were talking about his bid to build the first car museum in the Monterey Peninsula. Expected to open sometime in 2015, Morris is the driving force behind the Monterey Museum of Automotive Arts. *"Our mission is to celebrate the historical significance of the automobile by sharing our passion for the cars and their legendary personalities with you. Honor the racing and concours history of the Monterey Peninsula by preserving these masterpieces and events for the future with the inspiring world-renowned Monterey Museum of Automotive Arts. We will conceive and build an associated Certified Education Curriculum in automotive restoration, and a restoration facility."*

Press Release by the Monterey Museum of Automotive Arts

Watch their website for updates, but as of now, this is what is proposed:

Experience the history of the automobile through its quest for speed and elegance of design. Learn about the men and their machines, the sweat and blood of those who raced them and the artistry of style and craftsmanship of those who built them.

Conceived to honor and recognize the undeniable relationship the automobile has with the Monterey Peninsula, the Museum will marquee the Pebble Beach Concours d' Elegance, Mazda Raceway Laguna Seca, and the legendary personalities that fostered, nurtured and sustained the passion for the automobile.

The proposed 150,000 sq ft venue is designed to house over one hundred of the world's finest automobiles within the Pebble Beach and Laguna Seca wings and main exhibition hall.

In addition, the facilities will include an active restoration area, theater, library, members club, restaurant, banquet facilities plus an art gallery, history and education center and retail store.

We believe the Monterey Peninsula is the best location in the world to build the Museum. Pebble Beach, Monterey, Carmel and Laguna Seca provide a rich tapestry of automotive histories and

Opposite & Above: *Conceptual models by the New School of Architecture & Design in San Diego, CA of the soon to be built Monterey Museum of Automotive Arts*

personalities in an endless story of challenges and successes. In addition it is a natural asset to the area, complementing other local destinations like the Monterey Bay Aquarium by providing a true, year-round destination for automotive enthusiasts, tourists, and community alike.

Follow the evolution and revolution of yesterday's technology and experience how it will influence personal transportation in the future.

The Monterey Museum of Automotive Arts will be independently operated and underwritten by the Automotive Heritage & Preservation Foundation, a non-profit 501(c)3 organization. It will be open year-round.

Contact Information

Automotive Heritage & Preservation Foundation
1118 Elko Drive
Sunnyvale, CA 94089
www.montereyautomuseum.com

Fund-raising & Sponsorship
Sally Shea—Development Director
(415) 753-2763
Email: *sls.museum@yahoo.com*

Oakland Museum

Nothing prepared us for the Oakland Museum of California. While there are some cars here, what really sets this museum apart from anything we have ever seen before are the themes and contexts in which the cars have been placed. The cars might be interesting, but what surrounds them is MORE interesting.

History

Opening in 1969 as a "Museum for the People," the Oakland Museum of California was a merger of three different museums that can be traced back to 1907 and the Oakland Public Museum and later the Oakland Art Gallery, and the Snow Museum.

Today

The museum visitors see today is part of a recent and expensive ($58 million) renovation covering all parts of the museum and galleries. This renovation was started in 2010 as a two-phase project that has only recently been completed with the reopening of the Nature Sciences Gallery.

Collection Theme

The overall museum theme is to explore the history and culture of Northern California, far beyond the scope of just motor vehicles. The exhibits we photographed are all part of "**Tools & Technology**" in the **History Gallery**.

Quick Stats

- ▶ Plan on spending 2–6 hours depending on galleries visited
- ▶ 6 or so vehicles of sorts
- ▶ 94,000 sq ft of gallery space on 7.7 acres covering four city blocks

Must-See

For vehicles, check out the 1951 Ford Victoria. But the real beauty of this museum isn't the cars but the displays and settings in which the cars have been placed.

Directions

From **San Jose by car:**

- ▶ North on Interstate 880
- ▶ Travel roughly 38 miles
- ▶ Exit 41A on to Oak Street
- ▶ Right/northeast on Oak Street
- ▶ Proceed 4 blocks to museum

From **San Francisco by car:**

- ▶ East on Interstate 80 over Oakland Bay Bridge
- ▶ Exit 8B and merge on to I-580 East, direction Stockton
- ▶ Exit 19C and merge with I-980
- ▶ Exit 1B, Jackson Street
- ▶ Merge onto 5th Street
- ▶ Left onto Oak Street

Opposite Page: *The Oakland Museum of California.*

Top Right: *1898 American LaFrance Steam Pumper, donated to the museum in 1968.*

Exhibition Galleries

The museum is divided into three floors, with the first floor housing the new **Nature Science Gallery** and Gardens. The second level houses the **History Gallery**, store, and Blue Oak Café. The third level houses the **Art Gallery**. Admission to the museum allows visitors entry to all three galleries, and each is well worth the time.

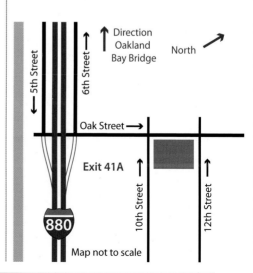

Map not to scale

Galleries

Natural Sciences Gallery

This gallery focuses on California as a biological hot spot. The collection also includes Chinese and Japanese Snuff Bottles (reopening 2013).

History Gallery

Chronological history of "Coming to California" with 2,500 artifacts and artworks. The **Tools and Technology** collection features everything from rare mining equipment to the early automobiles photographed here.

Art Gallery

Dating back to the early 1800s, the museum collection features over 70,000 works with significant examples of painting, sculpture, photography, and more.

Membership

Unlimited free admission for members, member exhibitions and events, discounts, and magazine subscription.

Docent Tours

▶ Highlight Tour on Fridays and Saturdays at 1:00 PM
▶ Gallery of California Art on Saturdays and Sundays at 2:00 PM
▶ Gallery of California History on Sundays at 3:00 PM
▶ Tour of the museum by Council of Architecture on first Sunday of the month at 1:00 PM

Top Left: *Early transportation such as this stagecoach are on display at the museum*

Bottom Left: *A Ford Model T displaying the hardships of travel on Route 66 during the Great Depression*

Amenities

- OMCA Store: 2,000 sq ft of California arts, crafts, and books. Store hours are 11:00 AM–5:00 PM, contact by calling (510) 318-8510
- Sculpture Gardens: 85 species of plants and more than 50 sculptures
- Blue Oak Café: open 11:00 AM to 4:30 PM
- Parking garage on levels one and two. Parking is available in the garage for a fee. Visitors receive a validation for a reduced rate.

Admission

- General $12
- Seniors $9
- Students w/ ID $9
- Children ages 9–17 $6
- Children ages 8 and under   Free

Bottom Left: *1913 Cadillac*

Bottom Right: *1951 Ford Victoria Hardtop customized by Joe Bailon in 1956. Nicknamed the "Mystery Car"*

Hours

- Wednesday to Sunday 11:00 AM to 5:00 PM except final Fridays April–October
- Friday 11:00 AM to 9:00 PM
- Closed Monday & Tuesday.
- Closed New Year's Day, 4th of July, Thanksgiving, and Christmas

Contact Information

Oakland Museum of California
1000 Oak Street
Oakland, CA 94607

Phone: (510) 318-8400
Toll free: (888) 625-6873
TTY: (510) 451-3322
Fax: (510) 451-3322
www.museumca.org

Membership Services
Email: *membership@museumca.org*

The Oakland Museum of California is a 501(c)(3) nonprofit organization

San Francisco Cable Car Museum

Have you ever thought about how a cable car moves? Or who is behind this unusual invention? Well, go to the San Francisco Cable Car Museum to see the cable cars, the Powerhouse and Barn, and the history behind the development of the system over a century ago. Then take a ride on one!

History

The San Francisco cable car dates back to the 1870s and was built up around San Francisco by eight cable-car companies, reaching a peak in the 1890s. Since then the system slowly deteriorated until the early 1980s, when renovations brought back the cable car.

Today

The Cable Car Museum was established in 1974 as a nonprofit educational facility and functions today as a museum of the history of cables cars in San Francisco. The museum covers the history of the cable car, as well as housing the powerhouse that runs cable cars today.

Collection Theme

The cable car is only one part of the system on display. The museum collection also covers the history of the men and companies that developed the technology behind the cable car system. Brakes, grips, sheaves, and more innovations are explored, as is the eventual demise of the cable car to other methods of transportation.

Quick Stats

- ▶ Plan on spending 1 - 2 hours
- ▶ Plan on spending a whole afternoon to RIDE the cable cars
- ▶ 3 antique cable cars
- ▶ There are four wire-rope loops pulling cable cars along three different routes.

Must-See

Be sure to head to the basement to see the Sheave Viewing Room.

Directions

From **San Francisco by car:**

- ▶ If you must drive a car (we don't recommend that), the museum is in the Nob Hill area and west of Chinatown. Parking is almost impossible even several blocks from the museum.

From **San Francisco by Cable Car**

- ▶ Board either the Powell/Hyde Street line (in red on this map) or the Powell/Mason Street line (green). Both have turnarounds on Market Street and Powell or to the north near Fisherman's Wharf.

Opposite: The San Francisco Cable Car Museum entry on Mason Street

Above: Explore the cable cars and the wheels (sheaves) that help move them.

Exhibition Galleries

There are two galleries on the mezzanine level, including antique cable cars and the Sheave Viewing Room in the bottom level. The mezzanine is a good place to view the powerhouse and barn with their giant white 14-foot wheels (sheaves) pulling the cables (wire rope) throughout the city and the cable cars currently in operation.

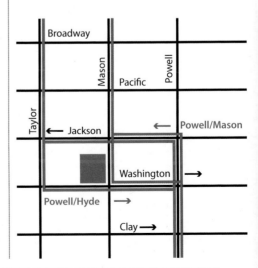

The Cable Cars

The museum houses three antique cable cars from the 1870s. The Sutter Street Railway Number 46 grip car, the Number 54 trailer, and the Clay Street Hill Railroad Number 8 grip car, the only surviving car from the Clay Street Hill Railroad.

The Sheave Viewing Room

On any given day, there are about two dozen cable cars gliding along downtown San Francisco at a constant 9½ miles per hour. Watch the "wire rope" enter the building from the streets outside, run through the sheaves and tensioners, and head back outside in a continuous loop.

Powerhouse

Originally built with coal-powered steam engines, these powerhouses once dotted the city. Today, the museum is the last powerhouse and barn pulling cable cars along the last four lines by electric motors.

Riding a Cable Car

There are three cable car routes in service, and two of them stop in front of the museum. The cable car routes are the Powell-Hyde line, the Powell-Mason line, and the California line. The Powell-Hyde and Powell-Mason lines stop at the museum, while the California line stops 3 blocks away near the **Fairmont Hotel**.

Cable Car Fare (prices for each-way)

- Adult & Youth $6
- Seniors $3
  (ages 65+) & Disabled before 7:00 AM and after 9:00 PM
- Seniors $6
  7:00 AM to 9:00 PM
- 1-day cable car pass $14

Cable Car Tips

Weekends are (of course) busy, and the crowds tend to line up at the turn-arounds. Try boarding a few stops up or down the line.

Amenities

The gift store offers a variety of cable car memorabilia, books, clothing, and even genuine cable car bells!

Museum Admission is Free

Hours

- ▶ April 1 though September 30
  10:00 AM to 6:00 PM
- ▶ October 1 through March 31
  10:00 AM to 5:00 PM
- ▶ Open every day except New Year's Day, Easter Sunday, Thanksgiving, and Christmas

Contact Information

San Francisco Cable Car Museum
1201 Mason Street
San Francisco, CA 94108

Phone: (415) 474-1887
www.cablecarmuseum.org

Opposite: *The power behind each cable car. Cables enter the powerhouse and barn from the street and wrap around the white sheaves in a figure eight.*

Top Right: *Each cable is actually a "wire rope" woven from steel wire and wrapped around a natural fiber core*

Bottom Right: *Sutter Street Railroad's #46 Grip Car from the 1870s is one of three historic cable cars on display*

Photo Tips

The San Francisco Cable Car Museum is one of the most difficult museums to photograph. There is direct sunlight at one end and displays under black ceilings and spot lights at the other end. Finding the correct exposure will take a few tries, and bracketing shots might be the best option.

National Automobile Museum

While most everyone loves "top ten" lists, some approach the idea with some skepticism. Make no mistake here, this museum belongs on anyone's "top ten" list of the best automobile museums. Good thing a lot of other media outlets think the same. Point being that this museum is a must-see.

History

The **Harrah Automobile Collection** opened in 1962 with 325 cars in Sparks, Nevada and blossomed to 1,400 by 1978. After the passing of Bill Harrah, 175 cars and all research material were donated to help found the museum, which opened to the public on November 5, 1989.

Today

The museum today is one of the best in the world. It has one of the finest horseless-carriage collections, an extensive collection of experimental and one-off vehicles, and celebrity-owned cars. *Autoweek* magazine named this "One of America's Five Greatest Automobile Museums."

Collection Theme

The goal of the museum is to educate the public and explore the history of automobiles and how it has shaped our lives as well as to perpetuate the legacy of **William "Bill" F. Harrah** as a renowned collector.

Before visitors even walk into the museum, they might notice that even the exterior reflects an automotive theme. The exterior is painted in "Heather Fire Mist," a popular 1950s car paint.

Quick Stats

- ▶ 105,000 square feet
- ▶ More than 200 vehicles
- ▶ Rated one of the best car museums in the world

Must-See

1907 Thomas Flyer, winner-of-the 22,000-mile 1908 New York-to-Paris race around the world. There are also a number of celebrity cars scattered around the museum, and they are worth hunting for.

Directions

From **San Francisco by car:**

- ▶ Interstate 80 east
- ▶ Follow for roughly 217 miles to Reno
- ▶ Take Exit 14/North Wells Road
- ▶ Right/south on N. Wells Road
- ▶ Right/west on Mill Street
- ▶ Right/north on Museum Drive
- ▶ Parking is located between Museum Drive and the museum to the west

Opposite: 1921 Rolls-Royce Silver Ghost built with Brockman Coachbuilders body
Above: 1914 Buick Touring on the "Turn of the Century" Street outside Gallery One

Exhibition Galleries

The museum is broken up into four distinct galleries separated by three period streets. Each gallery and street represent a different quarter of the 20th century. While the galleries contain the bulk of the cars, the street scenes are more interesting as they place the cars into a display to better give the mood of the time when that respective car was manufactured.

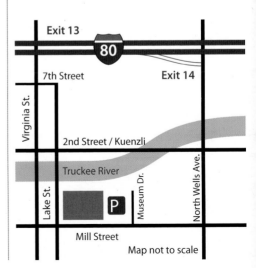

The Cars

There are so many cars worth mentioning that every list we may present would certainly do a disservice to those left off. Here are some ideas of groups of cars to see

▶ Celebrity cars: **John Wayne, Elvis Presley, Andy Griffith, James Dean**, and more.

▶ Horseless Carriages: Some of the best in the world are here!

▶ Prototypes and one-offs, such as the 1892 Philion Road Carriage

▶ Experimental cars such as the 1937 Airomobile Experimental Sedan

Banquet Rental

The diverse layout and design of the museum means that anything from an intimate party of 50 or up to 1,200 may be accommodated. The museum is up for just about any type of event, from theater presentations to weddings to period costume parties. Contact sales and marketing at (775) 333-9300.

Top Left: 1911 Pope-Hartford
Bottom-Left: 1950 Packard Series 2300 Super DeLuxe Eight on the "1950s Street"

Photo Tips

The National Museum offers just about every possible type of lighting known! Direct sunlight shines down through skylights or windows to dimly lit rooms with various types of light sources. While each room isn't difficult to shoot, it is the changes from one hall to another that will require your attention. Visiting on a cloudy day should help alleviate some problems.

Membership

Individuals may become museum members for $45 and may upgrade all the way up to the "Driving Force" level for $1,000. There is also an "Adopt-a-Car" program available.

Tours

Two self-guided audio tours are available in English or Spanish. Cost is free with the price of admission. Docents are also available at no extra cost to help visitors tour the museum.

Amenities

The museum has a gift store, automotive research library, and a theater. The gift store is open during museum hours, and the theater is open from 11:00 AM to 4:00 PM. With shows starting on the hour, the theater shows a 25-minute film about the museum and **William "Bill" F. Harrah**. The library is not open to the public but research requests may be granted for a fee.

Admission

Adults	$10
Seniors	$8
Children - ages 6-18	$4
Children under 6	Free

Top Right: *1955 Ferrari 625A*

Bottom Right: *1965 Lotus-Ford Indianapolis Race Car, ex-Dan Gurney and Dick Smothers inside Gallery Four.*

Family Fun

Despite the size of the museum, children should enjoy walking the scenic streets leading to each gallery. There are a number of places to sit down, and the theater is a good place for a family pit stop.

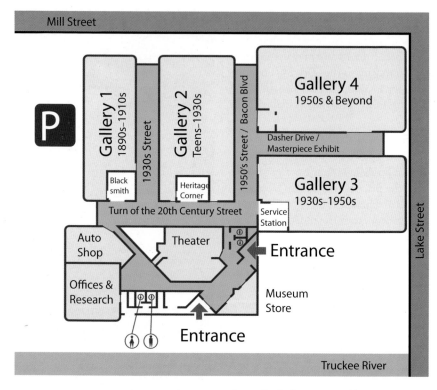

Mill Street

P

Gallery 1
1890s–1910s

1930s Street

Black smith

Gallery 2
Teens–1930s

Heritage Corner

1950's Street / Bacon Blvd

Gallery 4
1950s & Beyond

Dasher Drive / Masterpiece Exhibit

Gallery 3
1930s–1950s

Turn of the 20th Century Street

Service Station

Lake Street

Auto Shop

Theater

Entrance

Offices & Research

Museum Store

Entrance

Truckee River

Above: A map of the National Auto Museum

Below: (L) 1936 silver Mercedes-Benz 500K Special Roadster & (R) 1941 "Lana Turner" Chrysler Newport Dual Cowl Phaeton.

Opposite Below: The world-famous 1907 Thomas Flyer "35" New York-to-Paris race car and winner of the 22,000 mile 1908 New York to Paris automobile race.

Hours

- ▶ Monday - Saturday
  9:30 AM - 5:30 PM
- ▶ Sunday
  10:00 AM - 4:00 PM
- ▶ Closed Thanksgiving and
  Christmas

Contact Information

National Automobile Museum
The Harrah Collection
10 South Lake Street
Reno, NV 89501-1558

Phone: (775) 333-9300
Fax: (775) 333-9303
www.automuseum.org
Email: *info@automuseum.org*

Inquiries about membership may
be made through the main phone
number listed above.

The National Museum is a 501(c)(3)
Nonprofit Educational Organization

Top Right: *William "Bill" Fisk Harrah*

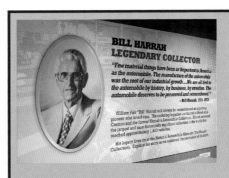

William "Bill" F. Harrah

William F. Harrah was born in 1911 in
Pasadena, California, and learned how to
run a business early when he purchased a
gaming company from his father in 1933.
When he moved to Reno, Nevada, he
founded a gaming business that would be
listed in 1973 on the NYSE as a publicly
traded company. Such success offered
him the chance to indulge his passion for
automobiles. After opening the Harrah
Automobile Collection in 1962, his collection blossomed to roughly 1,400 vehicles
by the time he passed away in 1978. Due
to public outcry, a selection of 175 automobiles were donated to help found the
National Auto Museum seen today.

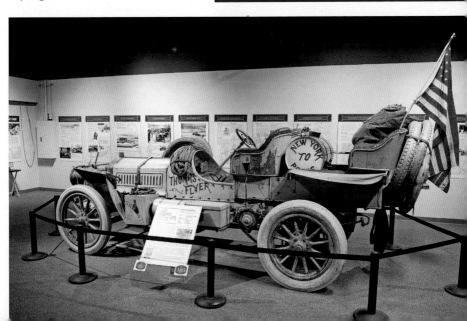

Northern California Wineries

Much to my delight, there are a healthy number of "car-related" wineries in both Napa and Sonoma County. I guess it shouldn't have come as a surprise, as both collecting or racing cars and running a winery often involves "passion," as Mario Andretti says. Good thing too, as the results are fantastic ■

Know Before You Go

Touring the Wine Country of Napa and Sonoma can be exciting, beautiful, and romantic. Even though it is more oriented towards those 21 year and older, there are a few child-friendly places (See *page 67*).

When to Go

The peak of the harvest is in October. This is an exciting time in both Napa and Sonoma, but book ahead!

What to Wear

Business attire is required at those nice Michelin-rated restaurants and many of the resort hotel restaurants require a suit jacket for men.

Reservations

Almost all restaurants take reservations, and many all but require them.

The restaurant **French Laundry** takes reservations two months in advance (*www.frenchlaundry.com*).

Costs

A meal for two at the French Laundry can cost upwards of $600 without wine and staying at a resort around Napa or Sonoma during the peak summer months or harvest season costs around $500 a night for double occupancy with suites costing into the thousands.

Weather

December is the coldest month, with an average high of 57°F and low of 37°F. The warmest month is July, with an average high of 83°F and an average low of 55°F. The maximum average precipitation occurs in February, with 5.54 inches falling on average.

Wine Aromas

Here are some popular ways to describe the aromas and flavors of varietal wines.

- **Cabernet Sauvignon**—berry, currant, bell pepper
- **Chardonnay**—butter, oak, vanilla, apple, fruity
- **Merlot**—berry, pepper, black cherry, chocolate
- **Pinot Noir**—cherry, blackberry, spicy
- **Riesling**—fruity, honey, apricot, floral
- **Sauvignon Blanc**—citrus, peach, grassy, fruity
- **Zinfandel**—pepper, spice, berry

Wine Country in a Classic

Forget the stretch limo. There is a far better way to visit wineries in Napa and Sonoma! Started in 1989 by **Tab Borge**, today **Classic Convertible Wine Tours** has a fleet of restored 1947 Packards available to groups up to 6 people. Rates start at $120 per hour for 5 plus hours. For more information, contact them at (707) 226-9227 or see *www.ccwinetours.com*.

Major Types of Wine

- **Cabernet Sauvignon**—Red wine derived from a crossing of Cabernet Franc and Sauvignon Blanc in the 1700s.
- **Chardonnay**—A white wine created from green grapes.
- **Merlot**—One of the most popular red wines is an offspring of Cabernet Franc.
- **Petite Sirah**—Petite, meaning small, refers to the smaller grapes of this red wine. This wine produces high tannins.
- **Pinot Grigio**—This dark blue/purple grape produces a white wine and, according to U.C. Davis, is a mutant variation of Pinot Noir.
- **Pinot Noir**—Despite being difficult to grow and ferment, this grape ("Noir" is French for black) is one of the most popular, producing some of the best red wines.
- **Riesling**—A white wine that dates back to 14th century Germany is now produced in California.
- **Sauvignon Blanc**—A white with a crisp or fruity aroma. This popular French wine is grown successfully around the world and in California.
- **Shiraz/Syrah**—Some call it Syrah, others call it Shiraz. This is another red wine that has migrated to California.
- **Zinfandel**—By the 19th century, this red wine was the most popular varietal in the United States.

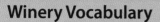

Winery Vocabulary

Words you may hear during a tour of a winery or vineyard.

- ▶ **Appellation**—An international legal definition of a wine region.

- ▶ **Acidity**—All wines have some acid, but it is the improper or unbalanced wines that taste sour.

- ▶ **Aging**—As a wine ages, the taste and color alter over time due to chemical reactions.

- ▶ **Aroma**—Scent derived from the grape variety.

- ▶ **American Viticultural Area (AVA)**—A wine region approved by the Bureau of Alcohol, Tobacco, and Firearms. Only used inside the United States.

- ▶ **Blends**—A bottle of wine that has been mixed with a number of different types of varietals.

- ▶ **Body**—Physical characteristics of a wine, such as density and viscosity.

- ▶ **Bouquet**—The scent a wine acquires during fermentation, aging, or any other influence apart from type of grape used.

- ▶ **Chai**—Barrel hall or wine shed.

- ▶ **Cold Fermentation**—Fermenting juice below 55°F to preserve fruity characteristics.

- ▶ **Crush**—Harvest time when grapes are picked.

- ▶ **Free Run Wine**—Wine flows from fermenter using gravity.

- ▶ **Malolactic Fermentation**—a secondary fermentation process converting the primary malic acid into a softer lactic acid.

- ▶ **Microclimate**—weather influencing a very small area, may be as small as a few rows of vines.

- ▶ **Must**—The grape juice, seeds, skins, seeds, and pulp before and during fermentation.

- ▶ **Ph**—A measure of the quantity of acid in wine.

- ▶ **Pressed Wine**—Wine remaining after draining the free-run wine. Often this richer wine is later blended with free-run wine.

- ▶ **Tannin**—Most commonly found in red wines, tannins are naturally occurring polyphenolic compounds. These compounds are usually found in grape skins but are also present in wood, such as the oak used in the barrels storing wine. Tannins help in the aging of red wine and also add flavor and a little bitterness to reds.

- ▶ **Terroir**—A French word that literally means "earth" or "soil." Today it refers to a group of vines or vineyards.

- ▶ **Trellis**—The wooden stakes or posts used to hold up individual vines.

- ▶ **Varietal**—Wine made from primarily a single variety of grape.

- ▶ **Vinification**—The entire process of producing a wine from growing the grapes to bottling the wine.

- ▶ **Viticulture**—The cultivation of grapes. For example, a student would go to college to earn a degree in Viticulture.

Introduction to Napa

Napa County

When California was granted statehood in 1850, Napa County was founded as one of the original 27 counties. Since then, the county has grown and harvested flowers, nuts, various vegetables, and, of course, grapes. In 1976, Napa wines made history, winning a blind taste testing known as the "Judgement of Paris."

Today, the county is 788 square miles with 16 wine appellations. The value of agricultural production in 2012 topped $648 million. Interestingly, Napa County encompasses 485,120 total acres, and just 45,275 acres are planted in vineyards with wine production is only 5% of the total coming out of the state. Another fun fact is that California wineries and vineyards are the second most popular tourist destination in the state after Disneyland, with a total of 14.8 million tourists visiting the state's wine regions each year. The most popular grape grown in Napa County is the Cabernet Sauvignon accounting for 39% of all grapes planted.

Driving around Napa

There are two main roads running north - south. The more popular is the St. Helena Highway /State Route 29 on the west, while Silverado Trail is far more scenic to the east with less traffic. During the summer months and weekends, the St. Helena Highway is clogged with traffic.

Opposite: The Napa Valley Welcome Sign on Highway 29 just south of Calistoga. The Napa Valley Vintners (www.napavintners.com) are the caretakers of the sign.

Classes

If touring endless wineries has become a bore, try classes at one of these two schools:

Napa Valley Wine Academy
8440 St. Helena Highway
Rutherford, CA 94573
Phone: (855) 881-2314
www.napavalleywineacademy.com

Silverado Cooking School
1552 Silverado Trail
Napa, CA 94559
Phone: (707) 927-3591
www.silveradocookingschool.com

Entertainment

Once the sun sets, the entertainment begins at the Uptown Theatre! See their website for current acts.

The Uptown Theatre
1350 Third Street
Napa, CA 94559
Phone: (707) 259-0123
www.uptowntheatrenapa.com

Shopping

There are some fun stores in the town of Napa but most people head to the outlet stores along St. Helena Hwy. See *donapa.com/shopping* for more.

Towns of Napa County

Calistoga
St. Helena
Yountville
Napa
Oakville
Rutherford
American Canyon
Angwin
Lake Berryessa

Napa County Appellations

Atlas Peak AVA
Calistoga AVA
Chiles Valley District AVA
Coombsville AVA
Diamond Mountain District AVA
Howell Mountain AVA
Los Carneros AVA
Mount Veeder AVA
Oak Knoll District of Napa Valley AVA
Oakville AVA
Rutherford AVA
Spring Mountain District AVA
St. Helena AVA
Stags Leap District AVA
Wild Horse Valley AVA
Yountville AVA

Restaurants & Resorts

See page 276 in the appendix.

The Wine Garage

The front page of their website touts "No wine over $25" and "No wine snob attitudes." Sounds great to us. Plus, it was founded in 2003 in an old gas station/tire shop. In 2013, they moved to a new location but retained the name and philosophy. The Wine Garage is located at 713 Washington Street, Suite B, Calistoga, CA 94515. Phone is (707) 942-5332. See *www.winegarage.net* for more information.

Introduction to Sonoma

Sonoma County

Larger and more diverse than its neighbor to the east, Sonoma County is famous for more than its wine. This 1,576-square-mile county borders the Pacific Ocean with 55 miles of coastline to the west and redwood forests to the north.

Grapes were planted in Sonoma County at **Fort Ross** as early as 1812 and was founded in 1850 when California was granted statehood. The town of Sonoma was originally the county seat until that was changed to Santa Rosa in 1854.

Today there are over 370 wineries with over 60,000 planted acres. Chardonnay grapes lead the way with the most planted acres.

Driving around Southern Sonoma

State Route 12 runs from the junction of state route 121 in the south to U.S. 101 in the north by Santa Rosa.

Driving around Northern Sonoma

U.S. 101 is best used to reach most of Northern Sonoma quickly, with California State Route 1 offering unparalleled scenic views of the Pacific Ocean all the way from San Francisco to Eureka.

Downtown Sonoma

Incorporated as a city in 1883, the plaza in downtown Sonoma is a charming mix of historic buildings from Sonoma's Mexican colonial past to modern wine tasting rooms, restaurants, art galleries, and a park.

State Parks & Beaches

Inside Sonoma County there are 11 state parks and 50 regional parks, beaches, and trails that range from the majestic redwood forests of the **Armstrong Redwoods State Reserve** to the equally beautiful Pebble Beach (yes, Sonoma County has its own). See *parks.sonomacounty.ca.gov*.

Entertainment

Performances at the **Green Music Center** at **Sonoma State University** range from bluegrass to the **San Francisco Symphony**. See *gmc.sonoma.edu*.

Shopping

Devoid of the big chain outlet stores that pepper the St. Helena Highway in Napa, downtown Sonoma offers visitors a selection of art galleries, antique stores, and restaurants.

Sonoma Raceway

Located at the southern end of Sonoma County off SR 121, Sonoma Raceway is wine country's world-class racing facility. See page 120 for our story about the raceway.

Sonoma Farmer's Market

Since 1985, local produce, baked goods, and arts and crafts are for sale each Friday from 9:00 AM to 12:00 PM at Arnold Field north of downtown. See the Sonoma Valley Certified Farmer's Market (*www.svcfm.org*)

Opposite: *Sonoma City Hall in the middle of the town plaza in downtown Sonoma.*

Sonoma County Appellations

Alexander Valley
Bennett Valley
Los Carneros
Chalk Hill
Dry Creek Valley
Fort Ross–Seaview
Green Valley
Knights Valley
Northern Sonoma
Pine Mountain–Cloverdale Peak
Rockpile
Russian River Valley
Sonoma Coast
Sonoma Mountain
Sonoma Valley

Restaurants & Resorts

See page 276 in the appendix.

Tip for Families

Wine country does not need to be an adult only experience. Just south of the town of Sonoma on SR 12 is the **Sonoma Traintown Railroad**. The railroad park is open six days a week (closed Thursday). General admission is free and the train costs $5.75 per person. The **Sonoma Traintown Railroad** is located at 20264 Broadway, Sonoma, CA 95476. Their phone is (707) 938-3912. See *www.traintown.com* for more information.

Northern California Wineries & Vineyards

Name	Website	Must-see
1. Adobe Road Winery	www.adoberoadwines.com	See both locations!
2. Andretti Winery	www.andrettiwinery.com	Check ahead if Mario is there
3. Boeschen Vineyards	www.boeschenvineyards.com	The Rose Garden
4. B.R. Cohn Winery	www.brcohn.com	Statues by Patrick Amiot
5. DeRose Vineyards *	www.derosewine.com	The San Andreas Fault
6. Far Niente	www.farniente.com	Wine caves
7. Francis Ford Coppola Winery	www.franciscoppolawinery.com	The Movie Gallery
8. Inglenook	www.inglenook.com	Centennial Museum
9. Lasseter Family Winery	www.lasseterfamilywinery.com	Views from top of the vineyard
10. Palmaz Vineyards	www.palmazvineyards.com	Fermentation tanks
11. Tournesol Vineyards	www.tournesolwine.com	Lake Louise

* = Not inside Napa or Sonoma Counties but in San Benito County north of Monterey.

Adobe Road Winery

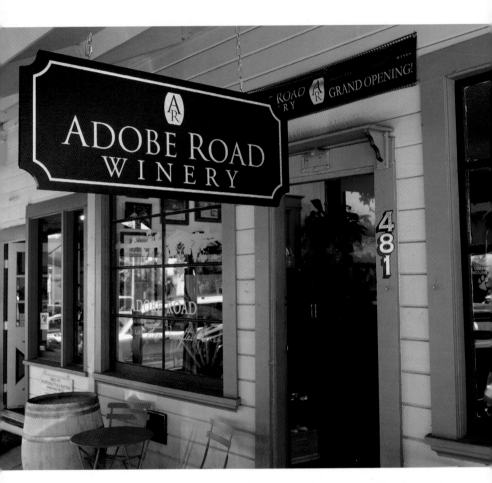

Before there was Adobe Road Winery, there were The Racer's Group and Kevin Buckler. Since 1993, he and his company TRG have provided both professional and club race car drivers the means to win in this very competitive sport. Today, TRG have now taken over as the factory arm for all of Aston Martin Racing in North America. Their determination and commitment to quality have turned to wine making and the Buckler's Adobe Road Winery. Their efforts and success at Adobe Road speak for themselves.

Via Corsa Car Lover's Guide to Northern California

History

Originally started as a "garage wine," Adobe Road Winery opened commercially in 1999 as a boutique winery after some prodding by friends. In 2008, Adobe Road Winery opened their new facility in Petaluma to allow complete control over the entire wine-making process. This new expansion is a state-of-the-art high-tech facility that gives the Adobe Road Winery the very best tools to create the best possible wine.

Today

The winery is still a boutique winery and one that is committed to bringing a variety of quality wines to the public rather than just a single variety. Their current lineup of award-wining wines includes Cabernet Franc, Cabernet Sauvignon, Chardonnay, Grenache, Meritage, Petite Sirah, Pinot Noir, Rosé, Sauvignon Blanc, Syrah, and Zinfandel.

Directions to Adobe Road Winery in Sonoma

From **San Francisco:**

- ▶ Head north on U.S. 101
- ▶ Take exit 460A
- ▶ Right/east on SR 37 towards Napa
- ▶ Left/north on SR 121/Cameros Highway towards Sonoma. Left/North on SR 12/Broadway to Sonoma town center
- ▶ Once in Sonoma, left/west on SR 12/West Napa Street
- ▶ Right/north on 1st Street West
- ▶ Adobe Tasting Room on your left

Opposite: *Adobe Road Winery in Sonoma*
Above Right: *Sonoma Tasting Room*

Quick Facts

- ▶ The Adobe Road Winery is owned by Kevin and Debra Buckler.
- ▶ The wine maker, Michael Scorsone, has an extensive background as a professional chef.
- ▶ Kevin Buckler and TRG won the overall race at the 24 Hours of Daytona in 2003.
- ▶ As of 2008, all wine-making operations are inhouse.

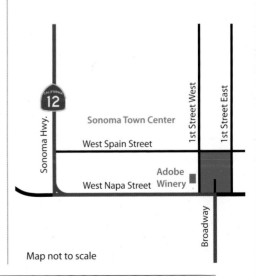

Map not to scale

The Cars

The focus of Buckler's racing passion are obviously endurance racing and Porsche. Their race shop and tasting room in Petaluma are home to a vast display of trophies and race memorabilia covering Buckler's career, including his class win at the Rolex 24 Hours of Daytona in 2002 and his overall win in 2003. Currently TRG is now the factory arm for all of Aston Martin Racing in North America.

The Wine

Adobe Road Winery is a boutique winery that acquires grapes from some very prestigious small-lot vineyards around Napa and Sonoma County.

Awards

Recently, Adobe Road Winery scored well with *Wine Spectator* by receiving 94 points for their 2008 Cabernet Sauvignon, Beckstoffer Georges III Vineyard, 93 points for their 2008 Cabernet Sauvignon, Bavarian Lion Vineyard, and 93 points for their 2009 Syrah, Dry Creek Kemp Vineyard.

Wine Club

Adobe Road's "Inside Track Wine Club" allows members to chose receive 2, 4, 6, or 12 bottles of wine each quarter. Prices range from $18 to $55 per bottle. Please see *www.adoberoadwines.com/wineclub.php* for more information.

Top Left: *Entrance to The Racer's Group*
Above Left: *TRG Petaluma Tasting Room*
Left: *The 2007 Cabernet Sauvignons on the left and 2007 Zinfandels on the right*

Hours - Sonoma Tasting Room

- ▶ Open Monday–Thursday
  10:00 AM to 5:30 PM
- ▶ Open Friday–Sunday
  11:00 AM to 6:30 PM

Contact Information

Adobe Road Winery in Sonoma
481 1st Street West
Sonoma, CA 95476

Phone: (707) 939-9099
Email: *info@adoberoadwines.com*

By appointment only
Adobe Road Winery in Petaluma
1995 S. McDowell Blvd.
Petaluma, CA 94954

Phone: (707) 939-9099
Fax: (707) 935-5889
www.adoberoadwines.com
Email: *info@adoberoadwines.com*
also see *www.theracersgroup.com*

Directions to Adobe Road Winery in Petaluma

From **San Francisco:**
- ▶ Head north on U.S. 101 direction Eureka.
- ▶ Take exit 472B.
- ▶ Left (as you are now facing south)/ east on SR 116/Lakeville Highway towards Sonoma/Napa.
- ▶ Right/south on S. McDowell Blvd.
- ▶ Destination is on your left.
- ▶ Please make sure you call in advance for a reservation.

Top Right: *The TRG-AMR Aston Martin GT4 at Mazda Raceway Laguna Seca*
Above Right: *Kevin Buckler*

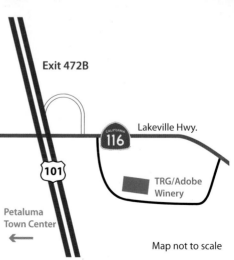

Andretti Winery

When I asked Mario Andretti if he is as passionate about his wine as he was about racing cars, he responded "my heart and my soul are in both." As a favorite destination for wine and car enthusiasts alike, Andretti Winery has become a mecca for those passionate about both. Set back away from the town of Napa in the Oak Knoll District, spending an afternoon here is both relaxing and rejuvenating. Mario frequents Napa and his winery and if you are fortunate to see him, you will be pleasantly surprised that he is approachable, extremely friendly and unpretentious. It is impossible not to like him.

Via Corsa Car Lover's Guide to Northern California

History

In 1996, **Mario Andretti** and his longtime friend **Joe Antonini** founded the Andretti Winery just outside the town of Napa. The winery looks like a Tuscan village, complete with courtyard, fountain, arched windows, tiled corridors and a patio overlooking the 43-acre vineyard. It is a nod to Mario's boyhood home of Montona, Italy (now Croatia) and was built to celebrate the Italian lifestyle. Bob Pepi has been the winemaker since the decision was made to purchase the property. He and Mario share a vision of wine that is well expressed at Andretti Winery. See page 78 for our interview with Mario.

Today

Located in the Oak Knoll District (a sub-appellation) of the Napa Valley, the estate is planted with Pinot Grigio, Chardonnay, Sauvignon Blanc, and Merlot. The Oak Knoll region is lower in elevation and subject to the climate-moderating effects of the San Pablo Bay a few miles to the south.

Directions

From **San Francisco:**

- ▶ Head east on I-80.
- ▶ Take exit 33 to SR 37.
- ▶ West on SR 37 to SR 29.
- ▶ North on SR 29 direction Napa.
- ▶ SR 29 merges with SR 12.
- ▶ Right/east on Trancas Street.
- ▶ Left/north on Big Ranch Road.
- ▶ Winery on east side of road.

Opposite: *Andretti Winery in Napa*
Above Right: *Mario Andretti*

The Andretti Winery reflects the quality one would expect from a winner like Mario Andretti. Like its namesake, who focuses on the present while respecting past achievements, the racing memorabilia displayed is minimal, not showy or ostentatious.

Quick Facts

- ▶ The winery is 42 acres.
- ▶ Located at the heart of the Oak Knoll District of Napa Valley.
- ▶ Mario Andretti is the only person to have won the Indianapolis 500, the Daytona 500, and the FIA Formula One World Championship.

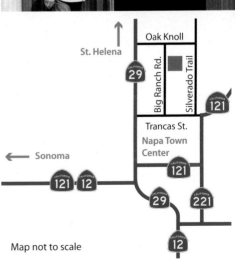

Map not to scale

The Wine

Andretti Winery offers three distinct "portfolios" for the wine enthusiast. The Montona Reserve Series, Napa Valley Series, and the Villa Andretti Series.

The Montona Reserve Series is their ultra-premium wine reaching around $85 per bottle and exclusively created from their estate grown grapes. The wines are Cabernet Sauvignon, Chardonnay, Merlot, and their Super Tuscan (50/50 blend of Cabernet Sauvignon and Sangiovese).

Their Napa Valley Series are premium wines ranging from $33 to $48 with an extensive varietal line up including Cabernet Sauvignon, Pinot Grigio, Sauvignon Blanc, Chardonnay, Sangiovese, Pinot Noir, Syrah, Merlot, and Zinfandel.

Andretti's third portfolio is the Villa Andretti Series. With prices ranging up to $35, these wines are small production runs with grapes sourced from select Napa, Sonoma, and California vineyards.

Wine Club

The Wine Club allows members to enjoy wines sent every March, June, September, and December. There are three levels of club membership; cost varies by club level. Contact Ruth at (877) 386-5070 x225 or email: *wineclub@andrettiwinery.com*

Top Left: *Courtyard at the Andretti Winery*
Above Left: *The award-winning 2007 Andretti Syrah*
Opposite: *A favorite destination for exotic car clubs*

Public Tasting Room Hours

▶ Open Monday–Sunday
   10:00 AM to 5:00 PM

There are a few featured tastings available daily:

Villa Tasting: signature Pinot Grigio, riesling, Dolcetto, and Cabernet Sauvignon $10

Napa Valley Tasting: Sauvignon Blanc, Chardonnay, Zinfandel, Merlot, and Cabernet Sauvignon $15

Delizia Tasting: dessert wine experience, featuring Moscato and Zinfandel Port $5

Private Tastings and Private Tours

Private tastings and private tours are available by appointment. The Founders Tasting is the most lavish experience, which includes a seated tasting in the Tuscan House on the grounds of Andretti Winery and features several reserve wines: Pinot Grigio, Chardonnay, Cabernet Sauvignon, Merlot and Zinfandel port. For reservations, contact Special Events at 888-460-8463 x229 or email: *events@ andrettiwinery.com*

Awards

Andretti Wines have received many accolades over the years, including:

"Best of Class" and 93 points for 2010 Montona Reserve Super Tuscan Blend (*L.A. International Wine Competition*)

"Best of Class" for 2009 Napa Sangiovese (2013 *San Francisco Chronicle* Wine Competition)

"Gold Medal" for 2009 Napa Syrah (2013 *San Francisco Chronicle* Wine Competition)

"Bronze Medal" for 2009 Napa Cabernet Sauvignon (2013 *San Francisco Chronicle* Wine Competition)

Contact Information

Andretti Winery
4162 Big Ranch Road
Napa, CA 94558

Phone: (707) 259-6777
Toll free: (888) 460-8463 or
(877) 386-5070
Tasting Room x227
Wine Club x225
Events x229

Email: *info@andrettiwinery.com*
www.andrettiwinery.com

Mario Andretti Interview

Mario Andretti is quite possibly the best known racer in the world. His name is at or near the top of everybody's list of the greatest drivers of all time. He is the only man who has won the Indianapolis 500, the Daytona 500 and the Formula One World Championship. One of the latest chapters in his storied life is in the lush northern California wine country: the Andretti Winery in Napa Valley. And the perennial favorite of race fans is often found on the back patio of his winery raising a glass of Sangiovese with tourists who visit there.

Via Corsa: You lived in Italy until age 15. Did you experience wine there?.

Mario Andretti: Growing up in Italy, wine was a part of everyday life. I certainly didn't prefer it; I preferred soda pop. But wine was at our table every day. I just had no appreciation for it.

VC: When did you start to really appreciate wine?

MA: In my thirties, not before that. And it was my career in racing that actually led to my love of wine. I was fortunate while racing to travel the world - Asia, Africa, Europe, North America, South America. I raced on every continent. And my travels to exotic places -- combining great dining with fine wine - led to my ultimate appreciation of wine as one of life's pleasures. I remember being in South Africa in the early 1970s. I was somewhat surprised at the extent of the wine list at the restaurant we were at in Johannesburg. It certainly wasn't what I would expect in South Africa. That tells you how limited my knowledge of wines was at that time. All of a sudden, I'm realizing you don't have to have French wines in South Africa. You can have South African wines. And I found the same thing in Argentina. When I raced in Madrid and Barcelona, I found how

good Spanish wines are. After a few more experiences like that -- finding great wines in what I thought were the most unlikely countries -- I made it a point to inquire about local specialties. I would ask and I would try. And I found that wherever I was in the world, if I went with the local specialties -- I was going to like it. And that is what made me more and more curious as I traveled and raced around the world. My interest in wine increased over the years. When I retired at the end of 1994, I turned my attention to wine.

VC: How has wine affected your life?

MA: Wine affected me differently throughout the course of my life. Growing up in Italy, for instance, wine was always at our table. That doesn't mean I preferred it. I had no understanding of it and no interest. When you're a kid, you don't have a palate for wine. Then, during my racing career, I got invited to great restaurants and beautiful homes and I tasted some of the finest wines in the world. That really peaked my interest in wine. Today we produce our own wines at Andretti Winery so I'm affected because I have skin in it - and pride - my name is on the label - and I'm accountable.

VC: What are your favorite wine regions in Italy?

MA: Tuscany because I grew up there and it's the region that gives us great Chiantis and Brunellos. The Piedmont Wine Region because of some of the greatest Barolos.

VC: You have one of the countries most respected winemakers, Bob Pepi. How important is he to the team?

MA: Having Bob Pepi join our team was one of our best moves. He came on board in the first days and was involved in the decision to purchase the property and vineyard. It's like a restaurant hiring a great chef. Bob Pepi has been involved in all the wines made under the Andretti label since the formation of the company. He and I have become good friends and have fun tasting together.

VC: What are you most proud of about Andretti Winery?

MA: I think I'm most proud of our consistency with all of our varietals over the years. We've always been well received. Bob Pepi and I have been true to our styles since the beginning. When he makes his wines, he stays true to my style and his. We talk. We have never deviated. People who enjoy Andretti wines can come back year after year and know the wines are going to be consistently good.

VC: Has the wine line-up changed much at Andretti since it's birth in 1996?

MA: In 1996 we only produced a couple hundred cases of Cabernet and Chardonnay. Today, Andretti Winery produces 16 different wines, including Chardonnays, Merlots and Cabs, a Sauvignon Blanc, Pinot Noir, Pinot Grigio, Sangiovese, Syrah, Riesling, Zinfandel, Dolcetto, Moscato, Port and Barbera. Our wines are in four tiers: the Montona Reserve varietals, our Napa Valley and Villa Andretti varietals and our Andretti Selections series.

VC: You have won every major title in Motorsports. Have any of your wine honors excited you?

MA: Every time our wines are recognized, I get excited. We made the list of "hottest small brands" in *Wine Business Monthly* a few years ago. The list represented small wineries that have achieved success by delivering on quality. The list did not include larger, more established brands and steered clear of new labels from mega-wineries with the capacity and clout to jam vast quantities of wine into the

Right: Mario Andretti at his winery in Napa Valley

distribution system upon product launch. Wine Business Monthly made up a list of brands they think are cool. Wines that people in the trade are excited about. Up-and-coming brands from scrappy wineries that have some momentum. I was pretty excited to be on that list.

VC: What's the most difficult thing for you, when it comes to producing and presenting Andretti wines?

MA: In racing, there is no question who is best - the first one to cross the finish line wins first prize. But with wine, even if you make the best wine in the world, someone isn't going to like it. There is always someone who isn't going to like it because it isn't their style. Judging wine is very subjective. That's difficult. Racing is very black and white

VC: There are two race tracks in this guide book. Do they ring a bell?

MA: Oh yes! Laguna Seca and Sonoma Raceway have brought Northern California international recognition and local pride. Love them both!

Boeschen Vineyards

Not many vineyards can say they were home to a Russian Princess. Nor can many vineyards pull visitors back in time to experience both the elegance and simplicity of Napa around the end of the nineteenth century. Boeschen Vineyard is all that, plus an environmentally friendly and state-of-the-art winery. Today this winery is owned by Dann Boeschen, his wife Susan, and his family. They grow mostly Cabernet Sauvignon on their south-facing hillsides producing very limited and spectacular wines.

History

The estate dates back to 1890 hosting everything from a Russian princess, a prune and walnut orchard, and a Christmas tree farm. The estate house and barn were built in 1890 (for a businessman's mistress) and the greenhouse was built in 1920 (the oldest metal frame greenhouse on the west coast). After the Second World War, the greenhouse was used as a commercial camellia nursery.

Today

The Boeschen Vineyard was founded in 1999 and completed in 2006 as a family-owned-and-run business. The state-of-the-art winery produces six varieties with two-thirds of the vineyard dedicated to Cabernet Sauvignon. Dann and Susan Boeschen run the family vineyard along with their son Doug and Shawn Heffernan.

Directions

From **San Francisco:**

- ▶ Head east on I-80.
- ▶ Take exit 33 to SR 37.
- ▶ West on SR 37 to SR 29.
- ▶ North on SR 29 direction Napa.
- ▶ Follow SR 29 for roughly 30 miles to the town of St. Helena.
- ▶ Take a right/northeast on any of the following streets: Pope Street, Pratt Avenue, Deer Park Road, or Lodi Lane.
- ▶ Follow chosen street to Silverado Trail N. and take a left/northwest.
- ▶ Boeschen Winery is on the right side of the road just past Glass Mountain Road.

Opposite: Mercedes-Benz 300 SL Gullwing sits just inside the barn at Boeschen Vineyards. A Porsche 356 Cabriolet Special is behind the Mercedes-Benz.

Above Right: A bottle of 2006 Cabernet Sauvignon sits in the center of a selection of Boeschen wines inside the underground Boeschen Winery.

Map not to scale

Quick Facts

▶ The estate is seven acres

▶ Best time to see the roses is in March or April

▶ In 2008, became the ninth winery to complete the Napa Countys Green Certified Winery program

The Wine

The majority of the wine from Boeschen Vineyards is their Estate Cabernet Sauvignon. Additional varieties include an Estate Sauvignon Blanc, their Carrera Estate Blend (54% Cabernet Sauvignon, 24% Merlot, and 20% Petit Verdot), and lastly their Katie Rosé (named after a young family member who loves pink).

The Roses

Reminiscent of a 19th-century rose garden, Boeschen Vineyard's formal boxwood-edged rose garden contains over 70 different varieties including white Iceberg roses.

The Cars

As in all wineries featured in our guide, the wine is reason enough to make the trip, and Boeschen Vineyards does not disappoint. But there are some cool cars here too. Dann Boeschen's collection consists of mostly vintage Porsches. The highlight is his 1966 Porsche 906 #906-136, but he also has on display a 1955 Mercedes-Benz 300 SL Gullwing, as well as a 1964 Porsche 356 Cabriolet "Special" and a race-prepared 1956 Porsche 356 Speedster. There are also a lot of memorabilia and engines on display.

Top: A 1956 Porsche 356 Speedster #66 in silver and a 1966 Porsche 906 #60 chassis #906-136 (#36 of 65 built).

Above: A 1955 Mercedes-Benz 300 SL Gullwing in front of a 1964 Porsche 356 Cabriolet "Emory Special".

Boeschen Vineyards Wine Club

Because the wine produced at the Boeschen Winery is so limited, one of the best ways to secure some of their wine is to join their Wine Club. This guarantees an allocation of their annual releases. In the spring, members receive the Estate Cabernet Sauvignon, and in the fall, members receive the Carrera Estate Blend (in a sleek black bottle with the red silhouette of a race car). There are additional benefits and discounts, so contact Boeschen for their latest offerings.

Visiting Boeschen Vineyards

The public is welcome to arrange a visit to Boeschen Vineyards. Tours are led by a member of the family and groups are kept very small. The tour covers the winery, estate gardens and roses, as well as the wine. If you are interested in seeing the car collection as well, this is arranged by special request.

▶ Please call or send an email in advance of your visit. The contact information is listed below.

Contact Information

Boeschen Vineyards
3242 Silverado Trail
St. Helena, CA 94574

Phone: (707) 963-3674
Fax: (707) 676-1684
Email: *info@boeschenvineyards.com*
www.boeschenvineyards.com

Top: *Cabernet Sauvignon grapes as the harvest draws near at the Boeschen Vineyards. Cabernet Sauvignon makes up two-thirds of all grapes.*

Above: *The state-of-the-art underground Boeschen Winery and barrels of aging wine.*

B.R. Cohn Winery

For all the wineries in Sonoma and Napa, there is really just one that personifies the love of the car, the B.R. Cohn Winery. The winery is not just a hot rodder's paradise, but really a must-see for any gearhead. Founded by music manager Bruce Cohn in 1984 as a way to bring quality back in his life, the winery hosts Classic Car Cruise-Ins and an annual Charity Fall Music Festival that draws thousands of spectators while raising millions for charities. If you plan a visit, check out the sculptures at the entrance and try a glass of Olive Hill Estate Cabernet Sauvignon.

History

In 1974 and after several years of managing the rock band **The Doobie Brothers**, Bruce Cohn purchased the Oak Hill Estate Vineyard in Glen Ellen to *"keep some sanity and preserve the quality of life."* Grapes were first sold to local producers including **August Sebastiani**. **Charlie Wagner** of Caymus Vineyards encouraged Bruce to create his own wine after making a batch of Bruce's wine and telling him it was the best Cabernet Sauvignon he'd ever had from Sonoma County. In 1984, Bruce Cohn founded the B.R. Cohn Winery with legendary wine maker **Helen Turley** and began bottling under the B.R. Cohn label. In 1990, the winery began producing gourmet olive oil and vinegars, the first made in Sonoma Valley in almost a century. In 2004, Tom Montgomery joined B.R. Cohn as the wine maker.

Directions

From **San Francisco:**

- ▶ Head north on U.S. 101 direction Eureka.
- ▶ Take exit 460A direction Napa.
- ▶ East on SR 37.
- ▶ Left/north on SR 121 direction Sonoma.
- ▶ Follow SR 121 as it merges with SR 12. Follow SR 12 north through the town of Sonoma.
- ▶ B.R. Cohn Winery is roughly 4 miles north of the town of Sonoma just past Capastaic Road.

Opposite: *A sculpture by Patrick Amiot of a 1946 Ford Woody Wagon sits in the gardens at the entrance to the B.R. Cohn Winery.*

Top Right: *The Panel Wagon Pinot Noir Classic Car Wine.*

Today

The B.R. Cohn winery is still owned and operated by Bruce Cohn and his family. The winery produces a variety of wines, with Cabernet Sauvignon being the predominant grape. The winery is also very active with the community by hosting a number of annual events for the public and raising money for both Sonoma-based and national charities.

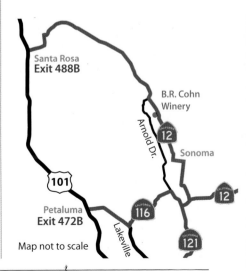

Classic Car Wine

With label art penned by local Sonoma Valley artist **Will Combs** (once a Hollywood art director; see *www.willcombs.com*), the B.R. Cohn Classic Car Wine collection is a tribute to Bruce Cohn's love of cars. There are a total of eight different labels, each one a unique reflection of both a vehicle from Mr. Cohn's collection and Sonoma Valley. Highlights include a 1933 Willys Roadster, 1934 Ford Five Window Coupe, 1941 Willys Panel Wagon, 1946 Ford Woody Wagon, and a 1963 Century Resorter.

Art Sculptures

In the front of the B.R. Cohn tasting room are four sculptures created by local artist **Patrick Amiot** (see *www.patrickamiot.com*). Created out of recycled materials and described by the artist as "junk art," these colorful pieces themed after Bruce Cohn's collection are reminders to us all that the "junk" used to create all these sculptures has both spirit and a history. All four sculptures are located in between the visitor parking lot and the main tasting room and building at the winery.

Quick Facts

- ▶ The estate is 90 acres, with 61 acres planted.
- ▶ Bruce Cohn lives at the winery and still manages the Doobie Bothers.
- ▶ Property had a stagecoach stop for Wells Fargo, where horses on their route from Santa Rosa to Sonoma stopped to be watered.

The Wine

The Cabernet Sauvignon Special Selection and Olive Hill Estate are the flagship wines at B.R. Cohn. The winery also produces a variety of reds and whites covering Merlot, Malbec, Pinot Noir, Zinfandel, Petite Sirah, Cabernet Franc, Sauvignon Blanc, Chardonnay, and Rosé.

Awards

Their Cabernet Sauvignon has received multiple accolades and awards from various trade magazines with ratings up to a 95 by the *Los Angeles International Wine & Spirits Competition*. The B.R. Cohn Winery has also received top accolades for their California extra virgin olive oils, as well as vinegars that include Cabernet, Champagne, Chardonnay, raspberry, pear, and a selection of balsamic vinegars.

The Cars

There is no real collection on display as one would expect in a museum; instead the cars in the Bruce Cohn collection are driven daily by Bruce, so chances are visitors could spot the 1941 Willys Panel Wagon and 1946 Ford Woody Wagon at either the winery or roaring about Sonoma.

Opposite Top: *From the left: 1941 Willys Panel Wagon, 1934 Ford Five Window Coupe, and 1946 Ford Woody Wagon*

Opposite: *Classic Car Wine Collection from the left: Drag Racer Red, Coupe Cuvée, Muscle Car Red, Panel Wagon Pinot, Rider's Red, Woody White, Boaters Barbera, and Roadster Red*

Top: *A sculpture of a 1941 Willys Panel Wagon by Patrick Amiot at the entrance to the B.R. Cohn Winery*

Above: *Vintage Richfield Gas Pump and a winery reminiscent of the 1920s*

B.R. Cohn Wine Club

In addition to discounts on wine as well as complimentary tastings, B.R. Cohn offers a Gourmet Food Club as well. There are five different clubs, and the individual shipments will cost between $40 and $500. Benefits include a 20% discount on most wines, complimentary wine tastings and tours, and preferred invitations to most events. Please contact Darlene McGinnis at *darlene@brcohn.com* or (800) 330-4064 x133.

Visiting B.R. Cohn Winery

The tasting room is open to the public daily as is their patio area. People are encouraged to picnic outside and enjoy all the beauty the estate has to offer. Wine tasting is $10 and is credited towards a wine purchase. Tours of the winery are done by appointment only and may be arranged by calling (800) 330-4064 x124. Contact the winery for the various tour packages and prices.

Weddings & Private Events

The B.R. Cohn Winery is available for weddings, elopements, and other private or corporate events. Contact *vallerie@brcohn.com* for more information.

Hours

- ▶ Open Monday–Sunday 10:00 AM to 5:00 PM
- ▶ Closed Thanksgiving and Christmas Day

Contact Information

B.R. Cohn Winery

15000 Sonoma Highway
Glen Ellen, CA 95442

Phone: (800) 330-4064
Fax: (707) 938-4585
Email: *info@brcohn.com*
www.brcohn.com

Events and Fun

Seasonal Events

"Classic Car Cruise-Ins" are monthly events held from roughly May to October (good weather months). These are typically on a weekend starting at 11:00 AM and lasting until 4:00 PM. Check with the winery as each Cruise-In features a different local car club. To see more, pictures are at *www.flickr.com/photos/brcohn*. Other monthly or seasonal events include olive harvest, private dinners, pourings and tastings, and even a "Paint your own wine glass." Because events may change, visit the winery event page at *www.brcohn.com/events*.

Annual Events

Every year, the winery hosts two must-see events. The biggest is their Charity Fall Music Festival held over four days in late September. Now in its 27th year, the festival draws thousands of visitors to listen to music (like the Doobie Brothers), dine in the vineyard, and play a little golf. More impressive is that the festival has raised over $6 million for charities. Their other popular annual event is the Charity Car Classic held in July. Started in 2009, this car show attracts hot rods, muscle cars, and various classic sports cars.

Opposite: Hot rod on display during a Classic Car Cruise-In

Above: Hot rods and sculptures during a Classic Car Cruise-In

Top Right: Rolls-Royces from the Rolls Royce Owners' Club on display during a Classic Car Cruise-In

DeRose Vineyards

Strange as it may sound, there are at least three types of visitors to DeRose. Wine enthusiasts, classic car enthusiasts, and seismologists. Yes, seismologists—because DeRose sits directly on the San Andreas fault, it has become a case study in tectonic movement. Earthquakes aside, DeRose has also become known for harvesting rare grapes such as their Négrette. But such unusual offerings don't create any wine snobs here. Instead, expect a no-frills and friendly, laid-back approach to wine and tasting at this family-owned and-operated winery.

History

Founded in 1854 in the Cienega Valley, DeRose is today the oldest existing winery in California.

Today

With 10 generations of wine making behind them, the property was bought by the DeRose and Cedolini families in 1988.

Wine

DeRose is best known for a rare, 115-year-old dark-red wine grape called Négrette. This grape was originally from Cypress and is now planted only near Toulouse, France and San Benito County (where DeRose is located).

Nostalgia Vintage Car Museum

The focus of the museum is the Graham-Paiges in honor of Mary DeRose, the family matriarch. Visitors may also see Ford Thunderbirds, a 1925 Flint, and a Lincoln once owned by actress **Doris Day**. The museum is open the first Saturday of the month from 11:00 AM to 3:00 PM or by prior arrangement.

Directions

From **Monterey:**

- Head north on U.S. 101 direction San Jose.
- Take exit 345.
- Right/east on SR 156 direction Hollister for 7.2 miles.
- Right/east on Union Rd. for 3.6 miles
- Right/south on Cienega Road for 7.3 miles (no services available en route)
- Winery and parking on right.

Opposite: *A modified 1940 Graham Hollywood inside DeRose.*

Above: *DeRose Tasting room*

Quick Facts

- ▶ Sits directly on top of the San Andreas fault which cuts a path through the main building
- ▶ Known for their century-old vines and dry-farming technique

Tasting Room Hours

- ▶ Open Saturday–Sunday 11:00 AM to 4:00 PM

Contact Information

DeRose Vineyards
9970 Cienega Road
Hollister, CA 95023

Phone: (831) 636-9143
Fax: (831) 636-1435
Email: *info@derosewine.com*
www.derosewine.com

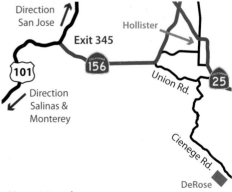

Map not to scale

Far Niente Winery

After sixty years of disrepair, Gil and Beth Nickel rescued the ex-John Benson winery renaming it "Far Niente" (means "without a care" in Italian). In subsequent years, the Nickels purchased additional properties and opened additional wineries. Today, the Nickel family and partners own and operate the Far Niente, Dolce, Nickel & Nickel, and EnRoute wineries maintaining a focus on single-vineyard wines. Far Niente currently produces an estate-bottled Chardonnay and an estate-bottled Cabernet Sauvignon.

History

Founded in 1885 by goldrush pioneer John Benson in western Oakville as a gravity flow winery. During Prohibition, the winery fell into disrepair.

Today

Purchased by Gil Nickel in 1979 followed by a three-year-long restoration of the property.

Wine

First harvest was in 1982 with a Cabernet Sauvignon. Today Far Niente is focused on small-lot, single-vineyard wines.

Visiting Far Niente

Visits are by <u>appointment only</u>. Please call Far Niente for more information.

Contact Information

Far Niente Winery
1350 Acacia Drive
P.O. Box 327
Oakville, CA 95442

Phone: (707) 944-2861
Fax: (707) 944-2312
www.farniente.com

Directions

From **Napa:**

▶ Head north on SR 29 direction Yountville/Calistoga
▶ Travel north for roughly 11 miles
▶ Left/west on Oakville Grade Road
▶ Left/south on Acacia Drive

Opposite: *The farmhouse at Far Niente dates back to 1885.*

Top Right: *Caves at Far Niente maintain a constant 58–60 °F temperature.*

Above Right: *Significant and classic cars on display in the Carriage House.*

Map not to scale

Francis Ford Coppola Winery

Tucked away in the northern end of Sonoma, near Geyserville in the warm Alexander Valley, is the Francis Ford Coppola Winery. Even though this wonderful winery sits just off the bustling Highway 101, it is a quiet exploration into wine, food, and fun. Or, as Francis Ford Coppola calls it, "a wine wonderland." How can anyone dispute this? He is offering the public a glimpse into movie making, his favorite culinary delights, swimming, and of course a wine for every palette. This winery is a bit out of the way but is worth visiting. Plan for at least a full afternoon.

History

Originally built in 1973 and owned by a number of concerns up until 2006 when Mr. Coppola purchased the property from Treasury Wine Estates. When Mr. Coppola purchased the property, he also bought the use permits as well. This was important to him, as the restaurants where visitors may now dine are very difficult to obtain today. In 2010, after extensive renovations, Francis Ford Coppola Winery debuted new tasting rooms, Rustic restaurant, a movie gallery, and a winery park area with swimming pools and a performing arts Pavilion.

Today

The winery is environmentally friendly, and the surrounding land is only 88 acres of which 24 acres are planted. The philosophy behind the design of the winery is to create a family destination with everything available for a day of fun for the whole family at a world-class winery. What defines family fun? How about two pools totaling 3,600 square feet, 28 cabines (changing rooms), a pool cafe, four bocce courts, a full-service restaurant, performing arts Pavilion, a movie museum covering the career of Francis Ford Coppola, and of course, wine tasting.

Quick Facts

▶ The mural in the pavilion by the pool was featured in the 1974 movie *The Godfather: Part II*.

▶ Wine label designed by Oscar-winner Dean Tavoularis.

▶ A pool pass is not needed to dine at the Pool Café

Directions

From **Santa Rosa:**

▶ Head north on U.S. 101 direction Eureka.

▶ Take exit 509.

▶ Left/west on Independence Lane / Via Archimedes.

▶ Winery/parking is on the south side of the road.

▶ Depending on traffic, the driving time is roughly 90 minutes from San Francisco and roughly 30 minutes from Santa Rosa.

Opposite: *Entrance to the Francis Ford Coppola Winery on Via Archimedes*
Above Right: *Entry gate to the winery.*

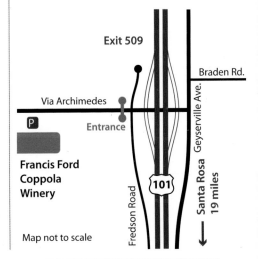

Francis Ford Coppola

Mr. Coppola was born in Detroit, Michigan in 1939 into a family of artists. His mother was an actress and his father a musician and composer of Italian ancestry. As a youngster he was interested in both science and cinema and eventually attended the UCLA Film School. While many may know his name to be associated with many of the greatest films of the 20th and 21st centuries, it is his passion and love of wine that is behind his two remarkable wineries in Napa and Sonoma counties.

This chapter of his life began in 1975 with the purchase of 1,560 acres of land in Napa County that was once the **Inglenook** winery (see page 145) from proceeds earned from the movie *The Godfather*. This was followed with a purchase in 1995 of 94½ more acres in Napa, as well as the 2005 acquisition of this Sonoma County winery. Today the wineries operate independently of one another, but are both owned and operated by the Coppola family.

Above: Francis Ford Coppola.

The Pools

The pool is open daily during summer from May 24 to September 29 and Friday to Sunday from October 4 to October 27. The pool and winery hours are 11:00 AM to 6:00 PM and a day pass costs $20 for adults, $10 for children ages 3–14, and seniors are $10 (ages 65+). Cabines cost $125 per day for the general public and include four pool passes. Call (707) 857-1471 to book either a cabine or pool reservation.

The Restaurants

Visitors have a choice of eating at the Pool Cafe or dining at the full-service restaurant **RUSTIC, Francis's Favorites**. Given the choice, skip the Pool Cafe. RUSTIC and its international/Italian menu features everything from grilled salmon to traditional pizzas cooked in a wood-fired Parrilla. We personally loved the Italian Cream Puff dessert. The restaurant is open 11:00 AM to 9:00 PM. To make a reservation at the restaurant, please call (707) 857-1485.

The Wine

The word here is "tiers." Each of the wines bottled here fits into a range (or tier) of both taste and cost. In contrast to the estate wines created at Inglenook in Napa County, most of the wines bottled here is from grapes not grown on the property, but rather sourced out and purchased from other vineyards in the area. The prices currently range from $12 to $52 for the 2006 Archimedes.

The Reserve Wine Labels

Designed by Dean Tavoularis (who won an Oscar in 1975 for Art Direction-Set Decoration for his work on *The Godfather: Part II*).

Opposite: *wine barrels in the tasting room.*
Above: *2008 Director's Cut Sonoma Coast Pinot Noir.*
Right: *Pools at Francis Ford Coppola*

Awards

In 2011, the Francis Ford Coppola Winery received seven awards for their wines from the 2011 *San Francisco Chronicle* Wine Competition. See *www.winejudging.com*.

Double Gold

- ► 2009 Director's Cut Russian River Valley Chardonnay
- ► 2008 Francis Ford Coppola Reserve Russian River Valley Chardonnay

Gold

- ► 2006 Archimedes
- ► 2009 Diamond Collection Silver Label Pinot Noir

Silver

- ► 2008 Director's Cut Cinema
- ► 2008 Director's Cut Alexander Valley Cabernet Sauvignon

Bronze

- ► 2009 Director's Cut Sonoma Coast Pinot Noir

Tip for Families

The pool is a great summer experience for both young and old! However, please remember to book your visit several weeks in advance. And once the sun has set, be sure to check out with the staff if there is a movie later in the pavilion.

Tasting & Experiences

There is a wealth of information available for even the most discerning wine enthusiast when you take an **Experience** at the Coppola Winery. All Experiences require advance reservations while the wine tasting does not, unless you have a group of 12 or more. To book, call Guest Services at (707) 857-1471.

Experiences

Ready for fun? Try a **Coppola Experience**! There are several available, and reservations are required. Not all Experiences are available all the time. Please see *www.franciscoppolawinery.com* for current information.

▸ **Tasting in the Dark**—Turn off the lights and head on into the Winemaker's Lab for 2 hours of blind taste testing! This is a fascinating way to explore how flavors and aromas are accentuated by simply turning out the lights. $75 per person.

▸ **Wine & Food Paring**—Offered Wednesday to Sunday at 4:00 PM. One hour and includes tasting of four wines paired with food. The food is prepared using seasonal ingredients grown at the estate. $50 per person.

▸ **Bottling Ballet Mechanique**—See the state-of-the-art bottling facility and learn about the estate and vineyard. The Experience is named for the little dance the wine bottles do as the move across the production line. 1 hour & $20 per person.

Wine Tasting

There are currently three different wine tastings, the **Rosso & Bianco Tasting**, the **Family Tasting**, and the **Neighbors Tasting**. The tasting hours are 11:00 AM to 6:00 PM. Reservations are not necessary.

The Movie Gallery

Explore authentic movie memorabilia and the five decades of movie making by Francis Ford Coppola. Highlights include Don Corleone's desk from *The Godfather* and, of course, the Tucker!

Contact Information

Francis Ford Coppola Winery
300 Via Archimedes
Geyserville, CA 95441

Phone: (707) 857-1400
Toll free: (877) 590-3329
Email: *GuestServices@ franciscoppolawinery.com*
www.franciscoppolawinery.com

Tucker: The Man and His Dream

Preston Tucker's dream was to use an old factory in Chicago to build thousands of his revolutionary automobiles. He created a network of ore than 1,800 dealers and distributors and had almost 50,000 shareholders. But in the end, only 51 cars were built.

Safety was a key feature to Tucker, and his ideas were revolutionary for his day. In each Tucker, he installed padded dashboards, a laminated pop-out windshield, a roll bar in the roof, side impact protection, and self-sealing tires. For more information on Tucker, please see *www.tuckerclub. org*. The Tucker 48 #1037 on display at Coppola is painted in the original "Maroon/600" color scheme.

The Movie

In 1988, Francis Ford Coppola teamed up with George Lucas to tell the true story of Preston Tucker in the 1988 biographical movie **Tucker: The Man and His Dream**. The movie follows Tucker (Jeff Bridges) and his partner Abe Karatz (Martin Landau) as they develop their new automobile and then their subsequent failure due to a number of factors. Francis Ford Coppola directed the movie, George Lucas was the executive producer, and Lucasfilms produced the film.

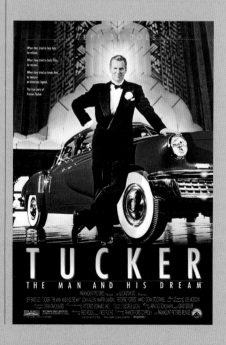

The Automobile

Opposite: *The "Bottling Ballet Mechanique" tours the bottling facility*

Above: *Tucker #1037 inside the Coppola Movie Gallery*

Right: *The movie poster from* **Tucker: The Man and His Dream**

Inglenook

One of the greatest stories ever told about a Napa Valley winery could be the story of the rebirth of Inglenook. Inside the Rutherford appellation (only 6,650 acres), Inglenook may be one of the crowning achievements Napa has ever made. After decades of mass consumerism by a number of corporations, Francis Ford Coppola and his family reunited the last piece to the puzzle in 2011, when he acquired the Inglenook trademark and name. Today, the winery is posed to reclaim the glory of the Niebaum family and their world-class wine.

History

In 1872, **William Watson** bought 78 acres of Napa farmland and started a winery under the name "Inglenook" (a Scottish expression meaning "cozy corner"). In 1880, Finnish sea captain **Gustave Niebaum**, who made his wealth by trading furs from Alaska, buys Inglenook. Under Niebaum, the stone château is built, a gravity-flow system is installed, and 712 additional acres are purchased. Upon his death in 1908, his wife and later **John Daniel, Jr.** managing the Inglenook Winery. It is during this time that Inglenook achieves recognition as a world-class winery with the 1941 Inglenook Cabernet Sauvignon becoming an icon for the very best Napa has to offer to the world.

However, in the 1960s, the property was divided when John Daniel, Jr. sold the front part of the estate to United Vintners. The trade name Inglenook was also sold during this period. The Coppola family bought the back part of the estate in 1975 following the death of Daniel in 1971 when his widow decided to sell the estate.

Directions

From **Napa:**

▶ Head north on SR 29/St. Helena Highway for 14 miles.

▶ Just before SR 128/Rutherford Road visitors will see the entrance to the left/west. Parking on your left.

Opposite: Completed in 1887, the Inglenook Château took 7 years to be built

Above: Inside the front entry to the Inglenook Château

Today

In 1995, Coppola purchased the remaining Inglenook vineyard, and in 2011, acquired the Inglenook trade name, thereby fully restoring all the land, buildings, and name to one of Napa Valley's most prized wineries.

Quick Facts

▶ *Wine Spectator* Magazine awarded the 2009 Inglenook Rubicon with 93 points.

▶ In 2006, the winery was renamed "Rubicon Estate Winery."

▶ The winery was renamed "Inglenook" in 2011 and will forever remain as such.

Map not to scale

The Wine

Roughly three years after founding the Niebaum-Coppola Estate Winery, Coppola harvested the grapes for his flagship wine "Rubicon", which is derived from Julius Caesars crossing of the Rubicon River in Italy and his "point of no return". For the Coppola family, it refers to their venture into the world of fine wine and their commitment to the estate.

The first vintage of the Rubicon was 1978, which was released in 1983. Today, Rubicon, is the flagship wine at Inglenook. It is a blend using primarily organically farmed Cabernet Sauvignon grapes and is known around the world as one of the best Cabernet Sauvignon.

Additional wines in their portfolio include Blancaneaux, a blend of Marsanne, Rousanne, and Viogner; Inglenook Cabernet Sauvignon, Cask, RC Reserve Syrah, and Edizione Pennino Zinfandel.

Above: *Inglenook Vineyards*
Right: *The underground caves*

Awards

▶ 2009 Rubicon get 93 points from *Wine Enthusiast* magazine

▶ 2009 Rubicon gets 92 points from wine critic **Robert Parker**

▶ 2005 Rubicon gets 93 points from *Wine Spectator* magazine

▶ 2004 CASK Cabernet Sauvignon gets four stars from *Decanter* magazine

Heritage Society

There are two available membership levels at Inglenook. The **Rubicon Membership** enjoys a 25% discount on wine and merchandise at the Estate, online, and in club shipments, while the **Excelsior Membership** receives one 12-bottle case of the Cabernet Sauvignon Cask and one 12-bottle case of Rubicon, their flagship Bordeaux-blend. Both enjoy complimentary Heritage Society tastings. Contact *heritagesociety@inglenook.com* or phone (877) 697-8242 for more information.

Visiting Inglenook

Inglenook is open to the public and offers daily tours, seated tastings, and specialty experiences to accommodate your needs. Advanced reservations are recommended and private groups both large and small are welcome.

Sample of Tasting & Experiences

▶ **Inglenook Experience**—Tour of estate and winery followed by tasting. 90 minutes & $50 per person.

▶ **Amuse Tasting**—A culinary sampling with three estate wines. 1 hour & $60 per person.

▶ **Private Tour and Tasting**— Enjoy a tour and tasting especially tailored for your group. 90 minutes and beginning at $75 per person ($300 minimum).

Tasting Room Hours

▶ Open Daily
10:00 AM to 5:00 PM

The Bistro

Enjoy wines by the glass or share a bottle in this comfortable wine bar reminiscent of a European café. The Bistro opens at 10am, an hour earlier than the Chateau.

Contact Information

Inglenook
1991 St. Helena Highway
Rutherford, CA 94573

Toll-free: (800) 782-4266
Phone: (707) 968-1100
www.inglenook.com

Centennial Museum

Opened in 1997, on the second floor inside the Inglenook Château is the Centennial Museum. This walk into the past lets visitors explore the innovation and ingenuity behind various enterprises that have inspired Coppola.

Of particular interest is the collection of 19th-century zoetropes and magic lanterns, which were instrumental to the development of the modern film age. The museum also walks visitors through the early years at Inglenook and the wine-making methods employed by Niebaum—such as the gravity flow system, pasteurization, and record-keeping.

One highlight is certainly the Tucker 48 #1014. This "car of the future" was featured in Coppola's movie *Tucker: A Man and His Dream*. See page 99 for more information. The Centennial Museum also houses artifacts from the original owner, Gustav Niebaum.

Above: *The 1948 Tucker 48 "Tucker Torpedo" #1014 is only one of 51 cars ever produced.*

Lasseter Family Winery

Back in 1992, self-proclaimed car enthusiast John Lasseter (of Pixar Animation Studios) and his wife Nancy moved to Sonoma, only to discover the art of wine making. In 2002, just down the road from their friends at the Smothers Winery, they closed escrow on a vineyard in need of restoration. Today, this small winery reflects their passion for the wine and their love of France. With each bottle named after a fond memory or memorable experience, their wine has become a work of old-world art.

Via Corsa Car Lover's Guide to Northern California

History

After moving to Sonoma in 1992 and discovering the art of winemaking, John and Nancy Lasseter purchased a vineyard in need of restoration in Sonoma County in 2002.

Today

The Lasseters and wine maker **Julia Iantosca** are dedicated to producing organic and environmentally friendly wines reminiscent of old-world blends from their vineyards.

The Wine

The Lasseter Family offers a small selection of wines, with each reflecting their love of France. The *Enjoué* is a Rosé blend reminiscent of dining at a café in the south of France. The *Chemin de Fer* is a Rhône-style blend of reds, and the *Paysage* is an estate grown Bordeaux style. The last is the *Amoureux* (French for "lovers") and a Malbec blend. The label on each bottle is a painting by local artist **Dennis Ziemienski** (see *www.ziemienski.com*) and a snapshot of the vineyard or their travels in France.

Directions

From **Sonoma:**

- ▶ Head north on SR 12 direction Santa Rosa.
- ▶ After roughly 6 miles, left/west on Arnold Drive.
- ▶ Immediate right/north on Dunbar Road.
- ▶ Left/west on Henno Ranch Road.
- ▶ Immediate left/south on Vintage Ln.

Opposite: *Lasseter Family Winery*
Top Right: *Lasseter Wine Room*

Visiting Lasseter

Visitors are welcome, but advance reservations are required. There is a cost of $25 per person.

Contact Information

Lasseter Family Winery
1 Vintage Lane
Glen Ellen, CA 95442
Phone: (707) 933-2800
www.lasseterfamilywinery.com
Email: *info@lasseterfamilywinery.com*

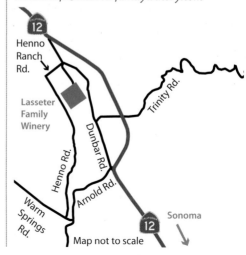

Palmaz Vineyards

People visiting Palmaz already know the wine is spectacular, in particular their Cabernet Sauvignon. What a visitor may not expect is the sheer scope of the winery and their gravity-flow system. This technological marvel is where the old world meets the new world. Originally founded by Henry Hagen in 1881 as one of the founding wine pioneers of Napa and now owned by the Palmaz family, the winery's amazing technological prowess has really one goal (other than to amaze visitors). And that is to gently craft some of the best wines possible.

History

Henry Hagen founded the Cedar Knoll Winery in 1881 and became one of Napa's pioneer wine makers. After the prohibition of the 1930s shut him down, the winery fell into disrepair, until Amalia and Julio Palmaz (famous for inventing the heart stent in 1985) resurrected the vineyard in 1997.

Today

The winery is still owed by the Palmaz family, which now include daughter Florencia Palmaz and son Christian Palmaz, as well as their grandchildren. When not attending to the business at the winery, family members might be spotted at select automotive events.

Quick Facts

- ▶ 610 acres with only 55 planted
- ▶ Their yield is only 1.5 to 2.0 tons per acre.
- ▶ The underground cave is as tall as an 18-story building.

Directions

From **Napa:**
- ▶ Head north SR 29.
- ▶ Exit 18B East.
- ▶ East on Lincoln Avenue.
- ▶ Left/north on Silverado Trail.
- ▶ Right/east on Hagen Road.
- ▶ Follow Hagen Road for 2 miles until it ends at Palmaz Vineyards.

Opposite: *Inside the Palmaz winery gravity-flow system and the 24 rotating fermentation tanks*
Top Right: *Old world grape press*

The Wine

The Palmaz Estate Cabernet Sauvignon is the heart and soul of the winery. With Cabernet grapes grown at all elevation points, the wine is the realization of a lifelong dream of Julio and Amalia Palmaz. The winery also produces a Chardonnay, a Muscat, and a Johannisberg Riesling. Their Gaston Cabernet Sauvignon is not made annually and is released only when warranted.

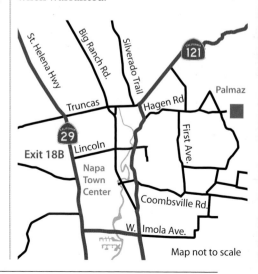

Map not to scale

Brasas Society Wine Club

There are three levels of membership available to the public with each club level able to be customized to focus on personal taste. All members may receive releases two weeks prior to the public release as well as invitations to winery events and discounts on wine purchases.

Visiting Palmaz

There is a charge of $60 per person for small groups and a charge of $80 person for groups of 12 or more. All tours must be arranged in advance (see information below)and are usually given by a Palmaz family member. While the tasting may depend on availability, guests will enjoy the Palmaz Vineyards Riesling "Louise," Palmaz Vineyards Chardonnay "Amalia," Palmaz Vineyards Muscat Canelli "Florencia," and two of the Palmaz Vineyards Cabernet Sauvignons.

Contact Information
Palmaz Vineyards
4029 Hagen Road
Napa, CA 94558

Retail Sales: (800) 592-2306
Phone: (707) 226-5587
Fax: (707) 251-0873
www.palmazvineyards.com
Email: *contactus@palmazvineyards.com*

Top Left: *The Palmaz property spans nearly 1,500 feet in elevation changes.*

Middle Left: *Amalia Chardonnay sits in front of the Cabernet Sauvignon and the Muscat Canelli Florencia in the back.*

Bottom Left: *Pairing wine with hors d'oeuvres at a Palmaz wine tasting.*

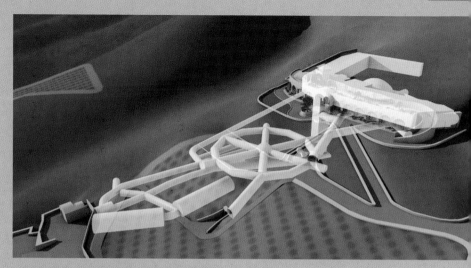

Gravity Flow System

At first glance, the unassuming Palmaz winery resting on the side of Mount George doesn't reveal any of the secrets hidden inside. An engineering feat worthy of a Hollywood super-villain, the Palmaz winery is really an underground 100,000 sq ft complex consisting of four connecting caves with a maze of tunnels and domes all built to be a true gravity-flow winery. The top level is the fermentation dome, where the grapes are de-stemmed and dropped directly into the 24 fermentation tanks set on a rotating carousel. From there, the free-run and pressed wine flow down to their respective settling tanks. The last major step is letting the wine gently flow from the tanks down another level to the barrels for aging. The last level of the cave consists of a water-treatment plant.

Top: The underground caves of Palmaz.
Above Left: *Top level with grape sorting.*
Middle Left: *Two of 24 fermentation tanks.*
Left: *Cabernet is stored for two years.*

Tournesol Vineyards

Guests who wish to stay at Tournesol Vineyards will see a small, family owned estate that is the result of a passion formed more than 30 years ago. The proprietors, Bob and Anne Arns, planned it that way from the start. Founded in 1998 with the help of noted viticulturist Mary Hall, Tournesol Vineyards is a certified organic winery that specializes in creating "a mosaic of several Bordeaux red varieties." The public is invited to stay at the vineyard in one of their guest houses or villas, the largest being a four-bedroom home overlooking Lake Louise.

History

Inspired by the blind tasting in Paris in May 1976, a competition that ended with California wines winning against French wines, Bob and Anne Arns started to dream of one day crafting their own Bordeaux varietals. This dream was realized in 1998 when they purchased a small property in the southeastern part of Napa Valley just to the east of the town of Napa.

Today

Set in the Coombsville sub-appellations of the Napa Valley AVA, Tournesol Vineyards lies between Lake Louise to the north and Murphy Creek to the south. Visitors are welcome to stay at Tournesol Vineyards. All bookings must be for a minimum stay of 30 days, per Napa County law.

Quick Facts
▶ "Tournesol" is the French word for "sunflower," and it literally means "turn to the sun."

Contact Information

Tournesol Vineyards
4297 East Third Avenue
Napa, CA 94558

Phone: (707) 224-3960
Fax: (707) 927-5052
www.tournesolwine.com
www.tournesolestate.com
Email: *info@tournesolwine.com*

Directions

From **Napa:**
▶ Head north on SR 29 to Exit 16.
▶ Take Exit 16 and head right/east on West Imola Avenue.
▶ Left/north on Soscal Ave/SR 121.
▶ Merge right and continue north onto Silverado Trail/SR 121.
▶ Right/east on Coombsville Road
▶ Left/north on Third Avenue
▶ Right/east on East Third Avenue
▶ Right on Kirkland Road followed by quick left back onto East Third Ave.

Opposite: *Tournesol "Stream Vineyard"*
Top Right: *Bob Arn's car collection*

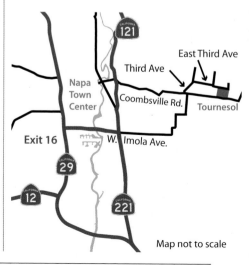

Map not to scale

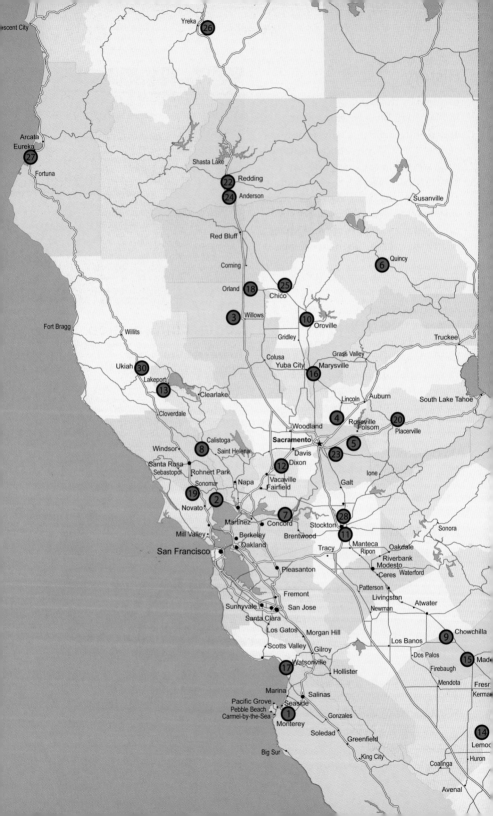

Race Tracks

Northern California Road Courses

1–Mazda Raceway Laguna Seca
2–Sonoma Raceway
3–Thunderhill Raceway

Northern California Ovals, Dirt Tracks, and Drag Strips ∗

4–All American Speedway
5–American Quarter Midget Association
6–American Valley Speedway
7–Antioch Speedway
8–Calistoga Speedway
9–Chowchilla Speedway
10–Cycleland Speedway
11- Delta Speedway
12–Dixon Speedway
13–Lakeport Speedway
14–Lemoore Raceway

15–Madera Speedway
16–Marysville Raceway Park
17–Ocean Speedway
18–Orland Speedway
19–Petaluma Speedway
20–Placerville Speedway
21–Plaza Park Raceway
22–Redding Drag Strip
23–Sacramento Raceway Park
24–Shasta Speedway
25–Silver Dollar Speedway
26–Siskiyou Motor Speedway
27–Samoa Drag Strip
28–Stockton Speedway
29–Thunderbowl Raceway
30–Ukiah Speedway

∗ = See page 272 in the appendix for a full listing of addresses & websites

Mazda Raceway Laguna Seca

Yου know a group of racers have been around for a while when they refer to this race track as just "Laguna Seca." However, these days when you say "Laguna Seca," you are referring to just the recreational area around the track. A big difference. But no matter what you call it, this is a track of legend. Car enthusiasts around the world know all about "The Carousel" at the Nordschleife and "The Kink" at Road America. But here, there is something even *more famous*. . ."The Corkscrew." Welcome to **Mazda Raceway Laguna Seca**!

History

The racetrack once known as Laguna Seca Raceway started life in 1957 as one of the premier paved road courses in North America. The building of the race track was in part due to the dangers associated with the racing at Pebble Beach and the Del Monte Trophy from 1950 through 1956.

1956–After the tragic death of **Ernie McAfee**, citizens and local government work to find a new permanent racing venue. A site is found and called **Laguna Seca** ("dry lagoon" in Spanish).

1957–**Pete Lovely** wins the first race in his Ferrari Testa Rossa.

1965–**Jackie Stewart** makes his U.S. debut driving a Lotus Cortina

1966–First Can-Am race features **Phil Hill**, **Dan Gurney**, and **Mark Donahue**.

1973–NASCAR comes to Laguna Seca with the Grand National West Tour.

Directions

From **Monterey by car:**

- ▶ Take California Highway 1/Cabrillo Highway north from Carmel or south from Seaside.
- ▶ Exit 401B onto SR 68/Salinas Highway east towards Salinas
- ▶ Drive 7 miles on SR 68
- ▶ Turn left/north on B Road and into the Laguna Seca Recreational area.
- ▶ Traffic during major events may be re-routed.

Opposite: *A 1965 Merlyn MK-6 follows a 1964 Brabham BT8 out of turn 3 during the Rolex Monterey Motorsports Reunion*

1983–First CART Indy Car race is held.

1996–**Alex Zanardi** passes **Bryan Herta** in The Corkscrew on the last lap of the CART race.

2001–The legal name of the race track becomes Mazda Raceway Laguna Seca.

Today

Set against the backdrop of the Monterey Peninsula, Mazda Raceway continues to host world class race events through out the calendar year.

Quick Facts

- ▶ 2.238 miles & 11 turns
- ▶ 4 right turns, 6 left turns, 1 ess (**The Corkscrew**)
- ▶ There is an elevation change of 109 feet (equal to a 10-story building) between turns 8 and 9
- ▶ 542 acres
- ▶ Lap record is 1:06.039 set by **Ricardo Zonta** in 2006

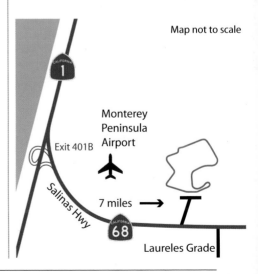

Map not to scale

Monterey Peninsula Airport

Exit 401B

Salinas Hwy

7 miles →

68

Laureles Grade

series, Grand-Am also runs proto-types and GT. 2014 will see a merger of both the ALMS and Grand-Am under IMSA. See *www.grand-am.com* for more.

Red Bull U.S. Grand Prix

When the **MotoGP** comes to Monterey, expect to see crowds in excess of 100,000. The MotoGP has been called the motorcycle version of **Formula One** and is now in its ninth year. See *www.motogp.com* for more.

Rolex Monterey Motorsports Reunion

Every August, as part of the larger Monterey Car Week, classic and vintage cars come to race. See <u>page 147</u> for more.

FIM Superbike World Championship

This FIM (**Fédération Internationale de Motocyclisme**) sanctioned event is the only North American running and one of 15 rounds held around the world. See *www.worldsbk. com* for more.

Other Events

There is a host of other events that run periodically, such as the Ferrari Challenge and the Porsche Rennsport Reunion. Check out *www.mazdaraceway.com/events* for more.

Major Events

American Le Mans Series

The **ALMS** series comes to Monterey in May each year as part of its 10-race championship. Spectators will see everything from P1 prototypes to production-based GT cars such as the Aston Martin Vantage, BMW M3, Corvette C6, Ferrari 458, and the Porsche 911 GT3. See *www.alms.com* for more.

Continental Tire Sports Car Fest

Grand-Am headlines this September race weekend. Similar to the ALMS

Top Left: *A 1969 Porsche 917K exits out of the famed Corkscrew ahead of a 1968 Porsche 908 during the Monterey Motorsports Reunion.*

Above Left: *Rolex is a major sponsor at the Monterey Motorsports Reunion every August.*

Opposite: *The new pit with garages and premier pit row seats above*

Parking

During major events, there are three main entry points to the facility. The main gate is on SR 68 with another entrance on the west side via South Boundary Road/Barloy Canyon Road. This entrance has access to the "Purple Parking" lots to the north of the track. The entrance to the east is accessible by heading north on Reservation Road off of SR 68 between Salinas and Laguna Seca. Please check for entry restrictions at their website.

Camping

The Laguna Seca Recreation Area is available for both RV and tent camping for a cost of $35 & $30 per night. Also new to the park is the new Trackview Pavilion (Red Bull Energy Center) and available for rent. The recreational area is part of the Monterey County Park System. See *www.co.monterey.ca.us/parks/lagunas-eca_camp.html* for more.

SCRAMP

The **Sports Car Racing Association of the Monterey Peninsula** started operating in 1956. Today, as a not-for-profit 501(c)4 organization, it operates and maintains the track for the Monterey County Parks Department.

Ticket Information

Tickets may be bought in advance at *www.mazdaraceway.com/buy-tickets*. Will Call is located at the Embassy Suites Hotel at 1441 Canyon Del Rey, Seaside, CA 93955.

Contact Information

Mazda Raceway Laguna Seca
1021 Monterey-Salinas Highway
Salinas, CA 93908

Tickets: (800) 327-7322
Office: (831) 242-8201
www.mazdaraceway.com
Tickets: *Tickets@MazdaRaceway.com*

A Lap of Mazda Raceway Laguna Seca with Justin Bell

Justin Bell is the son of legendary race car driver **Derek Bell** and won the GT2 Class of the 1997 **FIA GT Championship** and the 2001 **Trans Am Series** race at Mazda Raceway Laguna Seca. Today, fans may follow his antics at *www.justinbell. com.* Thanks to Justin for talking us through a lap of this great track!

I have to say one of my favorite tracks. I won the World Championship there. I know it well!

Straightaway

You know what? Just sitting there watching in the stands, you don't know how difficult the brow is under the bridge on the main straight. In a prototype, the car is nice and low to the ground. In a GT car, you are trying to keep it full-throttle, but the car moves a ton, as you come up past the pit lane up over the brow.

Turn 2

It is one of the best overtaking areas on the track and a very difficult corner to defend, as there are so many lines going into turn 2. The key to turn 2 is roll good speed through the apex as it is all about the exit. So in a defending situation, you can still overtake a guy or block him and make the corner. For me it is a single apex. I have a strange mid-track approach, then I cut down tight on the apex.

Turn 3

Turns 3 & 4 are two of the most innocuous-looking corners on the American race scene. There is nothing happening there other than these flat corners. They are almost stereotypical: turn in right, apex, and let the car track out. But every time you go through there, you think, "I should have been quicker" and the moment you try and go quicker, you get wide on the rumble strips.

Right: *Justin Bell*

Turn 4

I think turn 4 is where if your car is set, you've got a lovely rolling speed and can pick up a lot of time going into the turn because the exit is so wide. But don't turn in early. If you turn in early, you will have to back off on the exit or you will hit the rumble strips too hard. Very smooth hands and roll the car in there.

Turn 5

The run-down to turn 5 is for me like the calm before the storm. The entry to 5 is a great overtaking spot if you made a good exit on 4. I took the lead in Trans Am there once. I was in sixth place and they all hit each other, and I went down on the inside and took the lead, and never lost it. You have got to carry momentum. The exit to turn 5 is uphill, so use that camber, and I turn in a lot more aggressively than the corner actually looks.

Turn 6

Six is a corner that gives you a bit of a fairground ride. It goes down a little at the entrance and you get some compression at the apex. Roll in there and get a stable platform to your car and then really use the throttle to drive out using the compression. If you go into fast, you will lose the advantage of the compression and use all of the curb at the exit.

The Corkscrew

It is important to be very consistent with your brake point, so set your brake point and live by it. I am probably in the middle of the road as I approach it. Just be nice and disciplined. I have to be honest, I know the tree and I never look at it. If you are always "all over the shop" as you approach it, you will need to look at the tree as you exit.

Turn 9

The hardest corner on the race track. It is downhill, you are carrying a lot of speed. A lot of time is made up here. I am a "in the middle to three quarters of the road" guy, and then roll in. If you are going to short-shift, shift before you turn in. You need to use the car's momentum rather than high revs. If you are good at it, you will gain more time here than anywhere else.

Chute to 10

By now, you can't screw this lap up if you have done it right, because 10 is a lovely momentum corner to the right. It is faster than it looks, and I am all the way to the left. Nicely balanced and sometimes have to go down a gear. It's got nice camber and use the inside curb, as it is a flat curb and enjoy the car tracking out. Track all the way out to the pit lane entrance. And get yourself set for 11.

Turn 11

If you are in an overtaking situation, 10 is critical, and if you are down inside of someone, you just got him into the corner. If he defends, you need to do the old switch-a-roo and stay out wide and get him on the inside as you exit. Never brake too late here. It is all about corner exit and not entrance.

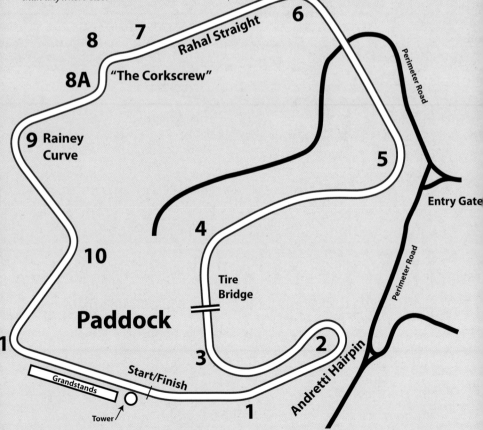

Sonoma Raceway

Undoubtedly one of the most challenging tracks, Sonoma Raceway (first named Sears Point and then Infineon Raceway) is a track made for the driver. While lacking that singular point of panic like the Corkscrew of Mazda Raceway, Sonoma Raceway instead offers 2.52 miles of edginess—faint of heart need not apply. For the spectator, Sonoma Raceway offers grandstands and hills to watch the wildest ride anywhere. Elevation changes coupled with ess turns mean that there is no wrong place to watch some of the best road racing anywhere.

History

1968–Opens as Sears Point Raceway (named after an early 1900s farm once on the site).

1970–**Dan Gurney** wins the USAC IndyCar® race, beating **Mario Andretti**, **Mark Donohue**, and **Al Unser**.

1973–**Bob Bondurant** moves his high-performance driving school from Ontario, CA to Sonoma Raceway.

1988–The **NHRA** holds its first sanctioned drag race on the facilitys ¼ mile drag strip.

1991–The Skip Barber Racing School replaces the Bob Bondurant School of High Performance Driving (Bondurant moved to Phoenix, AZ).

1998–The "Chute" is added. This high speed straightaway connects turn 4 and turn 7 to create a faster and shorter track (1.949 mile).

2005–The IndyCar®Series returns to Sonoma for the first time in 35 years with **Tony Kanaan** taking the win.

Directions

From **San Francisco by car:**

▶ Take US-101 north to SR 37
▶ Exit 460B and head east on SR 37
▶ Left/north on SR 121
▶ Turn left/west at the main gate (roughly 1/2 mile north of the intersection of SR 37 & SR 121)
▶ Use gate 7 and 9 during major events

Opposite: *The Ferrari 458 Challenge race cars take the green flag at the Ferrari Challenge Race Series.*
Above Right: *Gate 1 at Sonoma Raceway*

Today

Recently known as Infineon Raceway, the facility changed its name to Sonoma Raceway in 2012. Today, the track still retains the original 2.52-mile road course and drag strip. Both are used for a number of major events, driving schools, and private or corporate functions.

Quick Facts

▶ 2.52 miles & 12 turns
▶ 160 feet of elevation change
▶ Full-course lap record is 1:20.683 set by **Allan McNish**
▶ 1,600 acres
▶ Permanent seating for 47,000

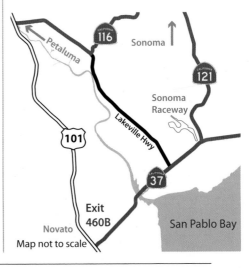

Map not to scale

Major Events

Sonoma Historic Motorsports Festival

For the last 27 years, vintage and historic cars have come every May to Sonoma. Each year, 400 cars battle it out in 15 different groups ranging from production cars to Grand National to IMSA GT. See *www.generalracing.com* for more. In addition to the racing, there is also the **Marin Sonoma Concours d'Elegance**. See *www.marinsonomaconcours.org*.

NASCAR Sprint Cup Series

In June, Sonoma hosts the **NASCAR Sprint Cup Series** on the shorter 1.99-mile 10-turn course. Currently billed as the **Toyota/Save Mart 350**, expect crowds to hit 100,000 for this 110-lap race. See *www.nascar.com*.

NHRA Division 7

The **NHRA** runs two race weekends at Sonoma for their Division 7 and National Championships back to back in July. Spectators will see Top

Alcohol Dragsters and Funny Cars as well as Pro Modifieds. See *www.nhradiv7.com* and *www.nhra.com/events*.

IZOD IndyCar® Series

Known as the **GoPro Grand Prix of Sonoma**, this August event ran at the raceway in 1970 and returned to the track after a 35-year hiatus in 2005. Unlike NASCAR, these open-wheel race cars use the interior carousel, but leave out turn 11, making it a 2.2-mile lap. See *www.indycar.com/schedule*.

FIA WTCC

The latest series to come to Sonoma is the **FIA World Touring Car Championship**. This September event showcases production-based four-door saloons in a series normally run only in Europe. See *www.fiawtcc.com*.

Best Seats

The best seats are going to be in the main grandstands overlooking the start/finish line. The turn 9 terrace general admission seating is a good alternative to the main grandstand. Many people prefer to sit on the grass between turn 2 and the exit of turn 3a.

Parking

Gate 1 is restricted to permit parking during the NASCAR, NHRA, and IndyCar® races. Gate 7 and 9 are used for general parking (north of gate 1). Expect heavy traffic along SR 37 and SR 121 during major events.

Ticket Information

Tickets may be bought in advance at *www.racesonoma.com/tickets*. Will Call is located at the Guest Services building at gate 1. Premium seating arrangements may be arranged through Brad Lawrence at (707) 933-3939 or by emailing *blawrence@ racesonoma.com*.

Motor Sports Park

Tucked away up and to the south of the track is a small business park and Go Kart track. The more than 70 different businesses there cover everything from race preparation to storage of vintage cars. To reach the park, take an immediate left past gate 1. To see a full directory of businesses, see *www.racesonoma.com/raceway/ industrial*.

Opposite: *Go Kart on track at the Simraceway Performance Karting Center.*
Above: *A 2001 Ferrari, ex-Michael Schumacher Formula 1 car exits turn 2 during the Ferrari Challenge weekend.*

Go Kart Track

For information on **Simraceway Performance Karting Center** and their karting school, see *www.simraceway. com/pdc*. Also see **Infinity Karting** for storage and race preparations at *www.infinitykartingllc.com*.

Contact Information

Sonoma Raceway
29355 Arnold Drive
Sonoma, California 95476

Phone: (800) 870-7223
www.racesonoma.com
Email address:
Tickets: *ticketing@racesonoma.com*
Info: *trackinfo@racesonoma.com*

Wine Country Motorsports

Forget your helmet on the way to an open-track day at Sonoma Raceway? Fear not, Wine Country Motorsports is there for you. Opened in 1992 near turn 11 at the entrance to the paddock area, Wine Country Motorsports offers race suits, shoes, and helmets for the racer and everything from camera accessories to diecast model cars for spectators. Phone is (800) 708-7223 or see *www.winecountry-motorsports.com* for more.

A Lap of Sonoma Raceway with Tommy Kendall

Tommy Kendall is a longtime and well-known driver who has raced in the **NASCAR Sprint Cup Series** and **IROC**. Today Tommy is racing the **American Le Mans Series**. Thank you, Tommy, for taking us on a lap of the track!

About Sonoma Raceway

Well, it is one of the most challenging and has a little bit of everything. One of the predominant features is how much elevation change it has, which makes for a lot of blind corners, blind entries, blind exits. It is widely regarded as one of the most difficult courses in the U.S.

Turn 1

It is a left bend, and you start heading up the hill, and it is this big sweeping left hander all the while the road climbing pretty dramatically. It is a very fast section of the track and you don't want to turn in too late, if anything you want to turn in a hair early. Because the road is climbing to meet you, it really gives you a lot of grip. You don't brake that hard as it is pretty steep uphill.

Turn 2

Then as you turn into Turn 2, you can't see anything, you can't even see the apex. You are not slowing down, not accelerating as you go up and over. Whatever you are doing is going to be exaggerated, so I try to keep the car neutral and as flat as possible.

Turn 3

Power in using all the road and work your way back to the right as quickly as possible for the 3 and 3A combination. There is a dip entering 3 that really compresses the car. You want to hold the car as tight in that left hand curve as you can to give yourself as much radius speed up to the top of 3A. 3A is another blind exit, but after enough laps you will eventually get the feel for where you turn and at what speed and where you are going to land at the exit. Up and over 3A and crest the hill, and use every inch of the road.

Turn 4

Brake in a straight line for turn 4. Because you are going downhill the car really doesn't heavy braking. You've already got the weight on the nose because of the hill, and if you try to charge that corner, the car just won't turn. Be easing off the brakes as you are turning, as it is a tight corner and you have to let the weight transition.

Turn 5

Flatout or pretty close to flat-out, depending on the car. You want to accelerate out through there. In some of the sedans, it will put you all the way to the left for turn 6. I find it usually a little better to maybe give it a little bit of a breather on the throttle in turn 5 to let you stay a little closer to the right as a set-up for turn 6.

Left: *Tommy Kendall*

Turn 6–Carousel

There's kind of a jump as you enter turn 6, another elevation change (Tommy laughs) I've seen pictures of cars with daylight under the tires. The exact spot you want to brake is when the car is light, and I find it better to run relatively tight. When you finally get to the far end of the corner, you will be turning the car a little bit more, but I find what you give up in exit speed you get back by getting there faster.

Turn 7

You don't slow the car down as much as you think—it's natural to overslow the car and by the time you move your eyes to look around the corner, you've slowed it down too much. You have to force yourself to keep your eyes up and roll with a bit of speed between the two apexes.

Turn 8 & 8A

They are really a momentum series of corners. You need to carry as much speed through there as you can. As you start to get into 8, give a dab of the brakes to take a little speed off and put some weight on the nose to turn in. To really get the most through there, you really want to be set up hard on the left side of the track coming out of 8.

Turn 9

You can get seduced into trying to carry as much throttle through 9 and 9A, and that will put you on the right side of the road. Because it is so fast, you don't want to be jabbing the brakes.

Turn 10

Keep the car as flat and stable, as there is no banking to help as it is a pretty fast corner and there is not a lot of run-off.

Turn 11

Hard braking into the final horseshoe. Turn 11 literally changes based on where they have the stack of tires. There is red and white FIA curbing painted on the surface, but don't pay too much attention, pay attention to where the stacks of tires are, and if they are on the inside of the curbing, you should apex off the tires.

Turn 12

Flat out in every car I've ever driven and you have to be careful of passing someone here.

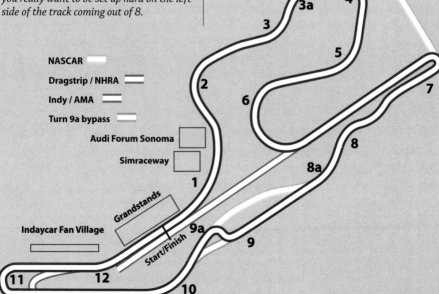

NASCAR

Dragstrip / NHRA

Indy / AMA

Turn 9a bypass

Audi Forum Sonoma

Simraceway

Indaycar Fan Village

Grandstands

Start/Finish

Thunderhill Raceway Park

Longer than either Sonoma Raceway or Mazda Raceway Laguna Seca, Thunderhill is a club racer's paradise. Formed by the San Francisco Region of the SCCA as an alternative to the other Northern California road course racetracks, this 2.86 mile road course pulls drivers up "The Cyclone" and back down again in what is just the beginning of 250 feet of elevation change per lap. The best thing about having a track like this around is that it is available to everyone, even for small groups or private functions.

History

1980s–Several member of the **San Francisco Region of the Sports Car Club of America** (SFR/SCCA) were dissatisfied with the other race tracks serving the area and chose to build their own.

1993–After several years of trying to find a suitable location, land is found near Willows and the racetrack starts construction in January. In September, a 1.9-mile track is finished. Opening weekend was on Halloween.

1990s–As funds permit, electricity, landscaping, curbing, and a paved paddock are added.

2008–Original asphalt laid in 1993 is finally replaced.

Today

The track is still owned and operated by the San Francisco Region of the SCCA and is home to NASA's **25 Hours of Thunderhill**, one of the longest road-course races in the U.S.

Directions

From **San Francisco by car:**

▶ Take I-80 east to I-505 to I-5 north.
▶ Take I-5 for 50 miles to Willows.
▶ Exit 603 to Biggs-Willows Road.
▶ West on Biggs-Willow/SR 152 for roughly 7 miles.
▶ Entrance to raceway is on the right/north.

Opposite: *Open track day at the start/finish line.*

Above Right: *Starter's stand and turn 5 in the background.*

Quick Facts

▶ There are three configurations: 2.866 miles & 15 turns, 1.814 & 9 turns, and 1.796 & 7 turns
▶ Full-course lap record in an SCCA event is 1:35.882 in the DSR Class using a Stohr WF1
▶ Unique to Thunderhill, the finish line does not line up with the starter's stand
▶ 250 feet of elevation change in a single lap

Thunderhill Raceway

Exit 603

Willows

6.6 miles

Sacramento (92 miles)

Map not to scale

Club Racing Highlights

SCCA–San Francisco Region

Founded 60 years ago, the SFR/SCCA is the first, and by all accounts, best competition sports car organization in Northern California. Based in Willow, CA, the region organizes amateur, professional, and vintage road racing, Solo/Autocross, and Concours d'Elegance. For more see *www.sfrscca.org*.

NASA

Since 2001, the **North Auto Sports Association** (NASA) has held one of the longest car races in North America. Their 25-hour race is held in December and open to six different race classes. For more, see *www. nasa25hour.com*.

In addition to the annual 25-hour race, NASA holds open track days and driving schools for all levels from the novice up to the professional driver. For more, see *www.nasanorcal.com*.

AFM

The **American Federation of Motorcyclists** was formed in 1954 as a non-profit corporation dedicated solely to motorcycle road racing. This Northern California-based organization holds events at Sonoma Raceway, Buttonwillow, and of course, Thunderhill. For more, see *www.afmracing. org*.

Above Top: *Open track day*
Above Middle: *The California Mille at Thunderhill Raceway Park*
Left: *Thunderhill Pro Shop*

Amenities

The two main facilities open at Thunderhill are the Pro Shop (see *proshop.thunderhill.com*) and the Thunderhill AIM Tire Center (see *www.thunderhillaimtire.com*). There is also Sunoco fuel available on site.

Rental

The track and various facilities are available for rental. This includes the road course, skid pad, and track facilities. Contact Shannon Ell at: (530) 934-5588 x103 or at *shannon@ thunderhill.com*

Contact Information

Thunderhill Raceway Park
5250 Highway 162
Willows, CA 95988

Phone: (530) 934-5588
www.thunderhill.com
www.nasacarcontrol.org
Email: *office@thunderhill.com*

Pro-Shop (530) 934-5588 x108
AIM Tire (530) 934 5588 x118
Banquet Facilities—Jim Thompson
(530) 934-5588 x107

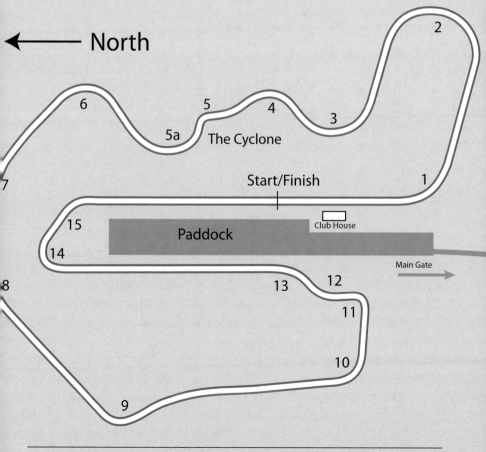

Driving Experiences & Schools

As they say, you can never stop learning. Usually when people hear this, they are referring to job, business, school, or marriage. But here let's talk about driving a car. It would be impossible to say that after one or two classes/courses/experiences that you are now a great driver. Better, yes but great, no. Northern California offers the very best opportunities for everything from learning the basics of high-performance driving to buying a seat in a full-out race series ■

Driving Experiences & Schools		
Audi sportscar experience	**Simraceway**	**Skip Barber Race school**
Sonoma Raceway	Sonoma Raceway	Mazda Raceway Laguna Seca
Major Sponsor—Audi	Major Sponsor—Mitsubishi	Major Sponsor—Mazda
Audi R8	Mitsubishi Lancer	Mazda MX-5 Cup
No open wheel cars	Open-wheel: SRW-F3 Formula 3	Open-wheel: Formula Skip Barber
One location in U.S.	One location in U.S.	U.S. locations include Lime Rock Park & more
Worldwide locations in Europe, India, & Dubai	Additional location at Mont Tremblant, Canada	Schools and courses at tracks across all of the United States
21 years of age	14 years of age	18 years of age with exceptions
On-track programs Audi R8 programs Off-track excursions	Stock Car stages Racing stages Performance stages Lancer Evo Experience Go Kart Center	Formula racing schools Formula race series High Performance Driving School Mazda driving school *MAZDASPEED*
$295 to $2,995	$295 to $7495	$1,000 to $10,500
Founded in 1983	Founded in 1957	Founded in 1975
audidrivingexperience.com	*www.simraceway.com/pdc*	*www.skipbarber.com*

Opposite: *A Simraceway instructor in a Mitsubishi Lancer Evo leads a student in the SRW-F3/FJR-50 open-wheel race car into turn 3 at Sonoma Raceway.*

Audi sportscar experience

The Audi sportscar experience offers you the opportunity to test the performance envelope of Audi's technologically advanced R, RS, and S Model vehicles on America's most challenging racing circuits, Sonoma Raceway, and the surrounding areas. Whether you choose from a pure racetrack experience or a spirited lifestyle drive through Northern California's Wine Country, professional drivers will guide and coach you, boosting your knowledge of vehicle dynamics, and car-control.

History

Started in 1983 in Germany as the **Audi Driving Experience**, participants learned how to improve their driving skills by introducing them to the unique features of an Audi automobile. This relatively easygoing experience was supplemented in North America by the creation of the **Audi sportscar experience**. Founded in 2007 and held at the Audi Forum Sonoma at the Sonoma Raceway, participants have several different programs from which to chose.

Today

Today, the **Audi sportscar experience** is based at the **Sonoma Raceway** at the Audi Forum Sonoma. The Audi sportscar experience offers a skill set, once understood and practiced, will not only help you excel in their environment, but it will open your eyes and help you approach everyday driving with a new sense of confidence.

Directions to Sonoma Raceway

From **San Francisco by car:**

- Take US-101 north to SR 37
- Exit 460B and head east on SR 37
- Left/north on SR 121
- Turn left/west at the main gate (roughly 1/2 mile north of the intersection of SR 37 & SR 121)
- See map on page 121

Opposite: *The Audi Forum Sonoma over looks Turn 1 of Sonoma Raceway*

Above Right: *Audi R8s await action at the Audi sportscar experience*

While this is the only U.S.-based Audi sportscar experience, there are Audi experiences operating around the world at such famous tracks as the Nürburgring in Germany, Silverstone in the United Kingdom, and even ice fields in Finland and the Dubai Autodrome.

Quick Facts

- There are On Track Programs, R8 Exclusive Programs, Off Track Programs, and Private & Corporate Experiences
- Prices range from $295 to $2,995.
- Audi Forum Sonoma is a multi-million dollar facility that houses a café, lounge, and conference center.
- The Audi sportscar experience and the Simraceway Performance Driving Center are both located at Sonoma Raceway.

The Programs

On Track Programs

Progressive sessions both on and off the track to experience the full potential of the Audi brand. For a full description of each program, see *www.audisportscarexperience.com*

Audi Autocross Challenge
Audi R8, S4, S5, TTS
Price: $495

Audi Sport
Audi RS 5, S4, S5, TTS
Price: $1,195

Audi R8—Introduction
Audi R8, RS 5
Price: $1,895

Audi R8—Progression
Audi R8, Optional: TTRS, RS 5
Price: $1,995

Audi R8—Advanced
Audi R8, Optional: TTRS, RS 5
Price: $2,995

Off Track Program

Experience the best wine country has to offer in these relaxed drives.

Audi R8—Roads of Sonoma
Audi R8
Price: $995 shared, $1,495 private

The Cars

Audi R8—V8 with 430 hp

Audi TTS—2.0 liter TFSI® 4 cylinder with 265 hp

Audi RS 5—4.2 liter FSI® V8 with 450 hp

Audi S5—3.0 liter TFSI® V6 with 333 hp

Audi S4—3.0 liter TFSI® V6 with 333 hp

Below: Audi R8 at Sonoma Raceway
Opposite: An Audi R8 tackles turn 6 at Sonoma Raceway

Schedule

The day begins with a briefing inside the Audi Forum, followed by a series of exercises in the paddock. Track time is on the Sonoma Raceway with each session at progressively higher speeds. A light snack and gourmet lunch are served at all but the Challenge programs.

Requirements

Participants must be 21 years or older with a valid drivers license. Knowledge of a manual transmission is not required.

What to wear

Please wear comfortable, closed flat shoes with a thin sole. A warm jacket is recommended, and the programs will run rain or shine. Helmets are provided.

Insurance

Participants are not liable for vehicle damage.

Instructors Background

Instructors are professional race car drivers and will adjust the program curriculum to the different participants' abilities.

Groups

Open to both private and corporate events, the 7,000 sq ft Audi Forum Sonoma is the perfect place to entertain. The use of the track is also available.

Contact Information

Audi sportscar experience

c/o Audi Forum Sonoma
Turn 1, Sonoma Raceway
29359 Arnold Drive
Sonoma, CA 95476

Phone: (800) 466-5792
or (707) 939-4600
www.audisportscarexperience.com
Email: *info@audidrivingexperience.com*

Simraceway Performance Driving Center

Ever played a video game and thought, "sure it's cool, but it isn't real life?" Well, for the first time, an online gaming company and a race car school have partnered to create the first fully integrated program that bridges the online world and the offline (real) world. Enthusiasts can go online to Simraceway.com and partake in buying a racecar, prepping it, and then racing it against other users around the world. Then, they can sign up here at the Simraceway Driving Center to drive that exact same car on the exact same track. Sounds pretty neat to us. . .

History

Jim Russell was born in 1920 in Norfolk, England, and began racing at the age of 32 with a Cooper Mk Vi. During his career, he won 64 Formula 3, 11 Formula 2, and 6 sports car races. He also took home three Formula 3 championships in a row. 1957, Jim Russell founded his racing school at the **Snetterton Circuit** in England (*www.snetterton.co.uk*). This was the first racing school founded in the United Kingdom. In 1966, he famously helped **John Frankenheimer** for his film *Grand Prix*.

When the Jim Russell school came to the United States in 1966, he used **Willow Springs Raceway** and ran Lotus Formula Fords. The cost? Fifty dollars. In 1996, Jim Russell moved to Sonoma Raceway, replacing the Skip Barber Racing School that has since relocated to Mazda Raceway Laguna Seca. Before the Lola F3s used today, the Russell school ran open-wheel Formula Mazdas.

Directions to Sonoma Raceway

From **San Francisco by car:**

▶ Take US-101 north to SR 37.
▶ Exit 460B and head east on SR 37
▶ Left/north on SR 121.
▶ Turn left/west at the main gate (roughly 1/2 mile north of the intersection of SR 37 & SR 121).
▶ See map on page 121

Opposite: *Entering turn 4 at the Sonoma Raceway with the SRW-F3/FJR-50 race car*
Right: *Jim Russell's Lotus Formula Ford #57*

Today

Today, the school sits next to turn 1 of the Sonoma Raceway and operates out of a 16,000 sq ft facility that includes a lounge, café, meeting center, multimedia rooms, and a state-of-the-art garage. By 2007, more than 25,000 students has graduated from a Jim Russell course and in 2011, the Jim Russell school partnered with the online gaming company **Ignite Game Technologies** (*www.simraceway.com*).

Quick Facts

▶ The SRW-F3 open-wheel race car is built by Lola Cars of England
▶ Ignite Game Technologies, an online gaming company, partnered with Jim Russell in 2011 to create the first integrated offline/online experience
▶ Children as young as 14 may drive in the race school
▶ 70 race cars and running more than 120 track days a year

The Programs

Racing Schools

Progressive set of programs using the open wheel SRW-F3.

▶ Stage 1: 2 day introduction starting with the Evos and progressing to lapping in open wheel

▶ Stage 2: 2 day course using the skid pad, corner entry, and threshold braking

▶ Stage 3: course focuses on corner speed, load transfer, slip angle, and downforce

▶ Stage 4: 2 day course focuses on passing, drafting, and qualifying

Mitsubishi Driving Schools

Driver's aids are switched off so students can take control of this flagship Mitsubishi. One course available.

Defensive Driving

One half-day and one full-day course focusing on highway survival.

Drive Your Own Car

Three stages available for those wishing to learn to drive their own sportscar.

Sprint Karting

Held at the karting track to the south of the track, there is everything from an "Arrive & Drive" race series lasting 9 weekends to courses geared towards youngsters. Lots of options for all skill levels.

Top Left: *Exposed carbon/kevlar monocoque of the SRW-F3 chassis*
Left: *The SRW-F3 open wheel race car*
Opposite: *Simraceway paddock area*

The Cars

- **SRW-F3**: Based on the Lola B06/30 Formula 3, this open-wheel race car was designed and built by **Lola Cars** (*www.lolacars.com*) in England. Using a Mitsubishi 2.0-liter turbocharged engine, it produces 220 hp for the school and 300 hp in race trim. The SRW-F3 chassis is a carbon/kevlar composite monocoque with a steel roll bar. The entire car weighs in at 1,023 lb. In other words, this is a modern purpose-built race car.
- **Mitsubishi Lancer Evo X**: This tenth generation version came out in 2007 with 291 hp and a top speed of 155 mph.
- **Karts**: The Sprint Kart uses a 125cc single cylinder producing 28 hp and the Grand Prix Kart uses a 85cc engine producing 15 hp.

Requirements

Participants as young as 14 years may participate in the racing school. Children as young as age 8 may drive in the karting school.

What to wear

If you own a Snell-approved helmet and two layer Nomex suit, you are welcome to use it. Otherwise, the school provides everything you need including racing shoes.

Insurance

There are deductibles for damage, please contact Simraceway for more.

Corporate Events

All vehicles and amenities are available to corporations and private groups for a number of events, starting with a two-hour autocross up to multi-day product launches.

Contact Information

Simraceway Performance Driving Center Campus
Sonoma Raceway–Turn 1
29359 Arnold Drive
Sonoma, California 95476 USA

Phone: (800) 733-0345
or (707) 939-7600
www.simraceway.com/pdc
Email: *pdc_info@simraceway.com*

Skip Barber Racing School

To many people, the idea of starting from zero to piloting a race car over 100 mph in a real automobile race would seem a near impossible dream. Perhaps you may not know where to go or how to begin or perhaps you may question your driving skills. Fear not, as all anyone with such aspirations needs to do is make a phone call. The Skip Barber Racing School is there to coach a novice from the basics and bring them up all the way onto the starting grid of a racetrack. If this sounds appealing, the school at Mazda Raceway is there for you.

Via Corsa Car Lover's Guide to Northern California

History

In 1975, after his underfunded racing career came to an end, John "Skip" Barber III started his **Skip Barber School of High Performance Driving** with two Lola Formula Fords, believing that driving a race car is a teachable skill. Renamed in 1976 as **Skip Barber Racing School**, this fully integrated system grew to include the racing school, several "arrive and drive" spec racing series, and corporate events.

The Barber Pro Series was founded in 1986, using Saab engines as a series enabling young professional drivers to showcase their talent to the world in this spec open-wheel series. In 1995, the engine supplier was switched to Dodge, and in 2004 the series was not renewed in an effort to focus on the regional and national open-wheel Skip Barber Formula series. Graduates of Skip Barber include **A.J. Allmendinger**, **Marco Andretti**, **Ryan Hunter-Reay**, **Danica Patrick**, **Jeff Gordon**, and many more.

Directions to Mazda Raceway Laguna Seca

From **Monterey by car:**

▶ For directions to Mazda Raceway Laguna Seca and a map, see "Directions" on page 115.

▶ Once inside Mazda Raceway, look for the Skip Barber racing School building in the paddock area.

Opposite: *The hot pit is full of Formula Skip Barber open-wheel race cars*

Above Right: *Mazda MX-5 race cars at Mazda Raceway Laguna Seca*

Today

The Skip Barber Racing School owns 150 race cars, 60 street cars, 30 transport and support vehicles with a staff of more than 200. All programs and races are run in an "Arrive & Drive" format. In other words, Skip Barber provides just about everything a driver may need.

John "Skip" Barber III

Born in 1936, Skip Barber started racing in 1959 and won three SCCA National Championships in a row in the mid 1960s. In 1969 & 1970 he won back-to-back Formula Ford National Championships. 1971 saw Skip Barber enter seven grand prix, but sadly, the underfunded driver saw six car failures. In 1975, after a ride fell through, Skip Barber founded what is today called the Skip Barber Racing School.

The Cars

In addition to the cars listed below, Skip Barber runs select models by Porsche and the Lexus IS F.

Formula Skip Barber

5-speed sequential transmission and a front and rear wing
Engine: 2.0-liter SOHC 4-cylinder with 132 hp @ 6,000 rpm
Performance: 0–60 mph in 4.5 seconds with a top speed of 135 mph

Mazda MX-5 Cup

Open cockpit with a full roll cage and two seats
Engine: 2.0-liter DOHC 4-cylinder with 167 hp @ 7,000 rpm
Performance: 0–60 mph in 6.8 seconds with a top speed of 130 mph

Mazda 3 Sedan

4-door hatchback with fwd
Engine: 2.3-liter DOHC 4 cylinder with 148 hp @ 4,500 rpm
Performance: 0–60 mph in 6.1 seconds with a top speed of 155 mph

Mazda RX-8

Rotary (Wankel) engine and successor to the RX-7.
Engine: 1.3-liter 2-rotor with 232 hp @ 8,500 Rpm
Performance: 0–60 mph in 6.6 seconds with a top speed of 145 mph

Top Left: *Mazda MX-5 takes on the Corkscrew.*

Middle Left: *Open-wheel Formula Skip Barber race cars.*

Middle Lower: *Detachable steering wheel sits on top of a Mazda MX-5.*

Bottom Left: *Mazda MX-5 Cup cars.*

The Programs

Mazda Driving Schools

The driving school is offered at the infield facilities at Mazda Raceway Laguna Seca. Drivers under the age of 18 allowed for some programs.

- ▶ 1-Day Mazda Driving School
- ▶ 2-Day Mazda Driving School
- ▶ Teen Safety & Survival School
- ▶ Advanced Car Control *

High-Performance Driving Schools

Experience a wide range of sports cars during a very short period of time. Possible models by such manufacturers as Lexus, Mazda, and Porsche. School held both on and off the racetrack.

- ▶ 1-Day High Performance Driving School
- ▶ 2-Day High Performance Driving School
- ▶ Advanced Car Control *

MAZDASPEED Racing Schools

Learn to drive and race the same cars used in the SCCA Pro MX-5 Cup series. No experience necessary to begin.

- ▶ Introduction to Racing
- ▶ 1-Day Racing School
- ▶ 3-Day Racing School
- ▶ Advanced 2-Day Racing School *
- ▶ Advanced Car Control *
- ▶ Lapping *

Formula Car Racing Schools

If you ever wanted to learn to race an open-wheel race car, this system of programs cannot be beat. Graduates of the 3-day school may be eligible for a Regional SCCA Competition License.

- ▶ Introduction to Racing
- ▶ 1-Day Racing School
- ▶ 3-Day Racing School
- ▶ Lapping *
- ▶ Advanced Car Control *
- ▶ 2-Day Advanced Racing School *

Race Series

So you have mastered all the above classes and want more? Perhaps a career or just a thrilling hobby? Skip Barber Race Series offers a select number of spec (meaning equally prepared cars) competition race series.

Formula Race Series—A full season is eight race weekends at various tracks around the country.

MAZDASPEED Challenge Series—seven race weekend at the same tracks as the Formula Race Series.

MAZDASPEED Pro Challenge—twelve races at seven tracks across the country. Schedule follows the IZOD IndyCar® Series.

* Prior Skip Barber Racing School classes or experience required. Please contact Skip Barber Racing School at (800) 221-1131 prior to enrolling.

"Skippy Racing"

My first raceweek at Skip Barber at Laguna Seca was actually almost an entire week of driving. I had booked a full four day race week preceded by two lapping days. Probably overkill. The first day began with just four of us casually lapping the track in a thick, wet fog. By Saturday, there were four race groups each with at least a dozen participants. There were teenagers fresh from graduating Karting to "Seniors," all there to race. I don't remember how I placed that day, but I had more fun not winning a race than any of the spectators watching us.

   ∾   *Ron Adams*

Quick Facts

▸ Famous graduates include Paul Newman, Kyle Petty, Scott Speed, and Juan Pablo Montoya.

▸ Has over 150 race cars

▸ Operates events at 15 race tracks around the country.

Partners

Various sponsors though the years have been BMW, Dodge, and now Mazda. Mazda is the official supplier of vehicles, supplying RX-8s, MX-5s, and Mazda 3s, and BF Goodrich is the tire supplier.

Groups

Please call Skip Barber Racing School for any group rate discounts for scheduled events. A **Teen Safety and Survival** group class is offered and may accommodate up to 50 individuals. For private events, see below.

Corporate Events

Private or corporate events are available at a number of race tracks around the country and may be booked for one or two days. Each event is unique and may be tailored to specific needs. It doesn't matter if you are entertaining clients, rewarding employees, or just have a lot of friends, there is a program. Contact *corporatesales@ skipbarber.com*.

Top Left: *Racing a "Skippy" car in 1998. In the late 1990s, Skip Barber used 4-cylinder Dodge engines to power the Skip Barber Formula race car.*

Bottom Left: *A Skip Barber instructor coaches a student after a session in the Mazda MX-5 race car*

Costs

Retail price for a race weekend is $3,500, a practice session is $1,500, and a lapping session is $1,350. Please contact Skip Barber Racing School for current costs of all their programs. Some discounts may apply for booking early.

Instructors Background

Instructors are professional race car drivers, with many having competed in major race series around the world including 24 Hours of Le Mans, 24 Hours of Daytona, 12 Hours of Sebring, GrandAm, and IndyCar®.

Requirements

Participants must be 18 years old with a valid driver's license (exemptions allowed for karting and competition experience). Knowledge of a manual transmission is required for Mazda MX-5 and Formula cars. Certain height and weight restrictions also apply to Formula cars.

What to Wear

Skip Barber provides suits and helmets for use by all participants. Good driving shoes are recommend and people may bring their own approved helmet. Participants in the race series bring their own Nomex driving suits and shoes as well as helmet.

Crash Damage

Participants are liable for damage to their car, unless they buy a damage liability cap from Skip Barber Racing School for an extra fee.

Contact Information

Skip Barber Racing School LLC
5290 Winder Highway
Braselton, GA 30517

Phone: (866) 932-1949
Retail Sales: (800) 221-1131
www.skipbarber.com
Email: *speed@skipbarber.com*

Monterey

F or those car enthusiasts who might just be joining the hobby, there's this little gathering in Monterey every year. Old news to the rest of us. But even after decades of attending Monterey, there is ALWAYS something new to learn, see, or explore. Of all the car events in the world, this is the biggest, the best, and the granddaddy of them all ■

Introduction

For as many pages as we wanted to dedicate to the best single week of automotive indulgence in the world, there will always be more to say. Having said that, we have attended Monterey since 1991 and watched it go through various stages of growth —for better or worse—and we think we have a pretty good handle on how to have a good time there.

First off, what is this thing most people simply call "**Monterey**?" It is roughly a full week of events. Often car clubs will tie in their annual meets to the car week by adding a couple of days before or after the week. What is the proper name of "Monterey"? There isn't really one. This is because the term "Monterey" usually refers collectively to all the named events during this week in August. We will simply call this series of events the "**Monterey Car Week.**"

Opposite: Cypress Tree along 17-Mile Drive at Pebble Beach

The events in Monterey can roughly be categorized as follows.

Collector Car Auctions

Spectators at one of the five auctions held have the chance to see cars that are among the best and most expensive cars on the planet. Records are made in Monterey.

Car Shows & Other Events

These days, a car show in Monterey can mean just about anything. Some shows literally show junk, while the Pebble Beach Concours d'Elegance highlights the best in the world.

Rolex Monterey Motorsports Reunion

There is only once place to see vintage cars race: Mazda Raceway Laguna Seca.

Pebble Beach Events

Everything centers around this one-day concours (although there is the Pebble Beach Tour d'Elegance Presended by Rolex on Thursday).

History

So what is the Monterey Car Week all about, and how did it begin? Back in 1950, the first **Pebble Beach Concours d'Elegance** was held in conjunction with the first running of the **Pebble Beach Road Races**. While the Concours thrives today at the same location, the races met with tragedy in 1956 with the death of Ernie McAfee. As a result, the Laguna Seca race track was built. From there, various individuals, companies, and organizations have begun to host their own automotive-themed events.

F.A.Q.

How soon should I plan my trip?

At least a year in advance. Focus first on a hotel room and then on the hard to obtain tickets like Quail Lodge. Restaurant reservations should be made a few months in advance, although many find little time for a leisurely meal.

Are children allowed?

Yes, except for certain parts of Mazda Raceway Laguna Seca. Bringing children to evening events is not advised.

When is Monterey?

It is scheduled to run the third weekend of August each year. See opposite page for the five-year schedule.

How many people attend Monterey?

According to the **Monterey Visitors Bureau** (*www.seemonterey.com*), over 400,000 people come to the peninsula over the span of that week.

How long is the Monterey Car Week?

The entire series of events usually lasts six days. It kicks off on Tuesday kicks off with Automobilia and ends Sunday with the Pebble Beach Concours d'Elegance.

Is there a "must-attend" event?

Maybe. Most will say Pebble Beach, but honestly, that depends on your taste.

Is traffic a problem?

Yes. In fact, if you drive a classic car that is prone to overheating, you might plan to avoid Highway 1 during peak hours.

Planning your Trip

Most people try to do too much and end up seeing too little. We recommend attending one major event per day and perhaps something in the evening. But even that might be too much for the first-timer.

Weather

December through February are the peak rainy months, so a rain jacket may be left at home. But those not used to the morning or evening fog in Carmel may still want to bring a warm jacket.

What to Wear

If you plan to attend an evening auction, business casual is standard. The Pebble Beach Concours d'Elegance is a classy affair and spectators will wear just about anything from a suit and tie to period clothing. Shorts and t-shirts are not recommended.

Getting There

By Air

The Monterey Regional Airport (*www.montereyairport.com*) regularly serves San Francisco, Los Angeles, Las Vegas, and Phoenix with American, Alaska, United, and U.S. Airways.

By Car

From San Francisco and the Northeast, head south on US-101 until Salinas. West on SR 68 to Monterey. Of course, SR 1 is prettier and runs along the coast into Monterey.

From Southern California and the Southwest, take I-5 north. Most people cross over to US 101 on SR-46 (where the actor James Dean died in his Porsche 550). North on US-101 to SR-68, and head west to Monterey.

Families

Young children are welcome at most all events, but of course, some discretion is needed. Many of the cars sport "do not touch" signs, while many corporate displays allow youngsters to crawl in their automobiles. A number of events are outdoors and last all day (not much is worse for a child than being both tired and sunburnt). Try eating at off hours with children, as many restaurants (especially in Carmel) have long wait times for parties with no reservations. There are a good number of alternative sights for children (see sidebar), as well as some fun stores like Woodies of Carmel (*www.woodiesofcarmel.com*).

Right: Young car enthusiasts enjoying the sites at the Monterey Bay Aquarium.

Future Schedule

The Pebble Beach Concours d'Elegance has been scheduled for the next five years.

- ▶ 2013 – Sunday, August 18
- ▶ 2014 – Sunday, August 17
- ▶ 2015 – Sunday, August 16
- ▶ 2016 – Sunday, August 21
- ▶ 2017 – Sunday, August 20

Please see page 278 in the appendix for a listing of popular hotels and restaurants in the Monterey Peninsula.

Family Fun

Attending the Monterey Car Week with children poses a few problems, but nothing insurmountable. Children may be seen at a number of events, and are even welcome, while others are more adult-oriented. Fear not, as the Monterey Peninsula offers a number of sites geared for children of all ages. The rather pricey **Monterey Bay Aquarium** (*www.montereybayaquarium.org*) and the **Museum of Monterey** (*www.museumofmonterey.org*) next to Fisherman's Wharf are geared towards younger children, while older children may enjoy sea kayaking. Whale watching appeals to all family members. Try *www.montereybaywhalewatch.com* or *www.montereywhalewatching.com*.

Saturday & Sunday

Race Track
▶ Rolex Monterey Motorsports Pre-Reunion

Monday

Rally
▶ The Quail Rally

Tuesday

Events
▶ Automobilia Monterey

Rally
▶ The Quail Rally

Shows & Concours
▶ Carmel-by-the-Sea Concours on the Avenue

Wednesday

Auctions
▶ Bonhams
▶ Gooding & Company
▶ RM Auctions
▶ Russo and Steele

Events & Dinners
▶ Automobilia Monterey
▶ Motorworks Revival
▶ Dine in DiVine at Chateau Julien

Rally
▶ Pebble Beach Motoring Classic
▶ The Quail Rally

Shows & Concours
▶ The Little Car Show
▶ Carmel Mission Concours **

Thursday

Auctions
▶ Bonhams
▶ Gooding & Company
▶ Mecum Auctions
▶ RM Auctions
▶ Russo and Steele

Events & Dinners
▶ Dine in DiVine at Chateau Julien

Race Track
▶ Rolex Monterey Motorsports Reunion

Rally
▶ Pebble Beach Tour d'Elegance

Friday

Auctions
▶ Gooding & Company
▶ Mecum Auctions
▶ MidAmerica Motorcycle Auction *
▶ RM Auctions
▶ Russo and Steele

Race Track
▶ Rolex Monterey Motorsports Reunion

Shows & Concours
▶ Pebble Beach RetroAuto™
▶ Concorso Italiano
▶ Legends of the Autobahn
▶ Pacific Grove Concours Auto Rally
▶ The Quail, A Motorsport Gathering

Saturday

Auctions

▶ Gooding & Company

▶ Mecum Auctions

▶ MidAmerica Motorcycle Auction *

▶ RM Auctions

▶ Russo and Steele

Events

▶ SCM Insider's Seminar at Gooding & Company

Race Track

▶ Rolex Monterey Motorsports Reunion

Shows & Concours

▶ Barnyard

▶ Pebble Beach RetroAuto™

▶ Concours d'LeMons

Sunday

Auctions

▶ Gooding & Company

▶ MidAmerica Motorcycle Auction *

Race Track

▶ Rolex Monterey Motorsports Reunion

Shows & Concours

▶ Pebble Beach RetroAuto™

▶ Pebble Beach Concours d'Elegance

* For information on the MidAmerica Motorcycle Auction, see *www.midamericaauctions.com*

Monday

Open House

These open house events are not in the Monterey Peninsula. Both are covered elsewhere in this guide.

▶ Blackhawk Museum Open House (see page 29)

▶ Canepa Open House (see page 236)

** New event for 2013

Carmel Mission Concours
Carmel Mission Basilica
3080 Rio Road
Carmel, CA 93923
Phone: (831) 624-1271
www.carmelmission.org
Spectator Fee is $25
Wednesday 12:00 PM–5:00 PM

Woodies of Carmel

Opened in August 2006 by Becky and Chris Sollecito, Woodies of Carmel is paradise for the car buff. The shop is stocked with toys, shirts, auto collectibles, and even a man cave with pit stop furniture. Becky and Chris are there most days with their two dogs, Pepper and Peanuts.

114 The Crossroads
Carmel, CA 93923
Phone: (831) 626-9064
www.woodiesofcarmel.com
Email: *woodiesofcarmel@gmail.com*

Popular Itineraries

Budget & Off Beat

There is no question about it, going to Monterey can be pricey. There are some nice cheap alternatives.

Tuesday

▶ **Carmel-by-the-Sea Concours on the Avenue**—entry is free and crowds are manageable.

Wednesday

▶ **Automobilia Monterey**—entry is $15.

Thursday

▶ **Pebble Beach Tour d'Elegance**—drive out of Carmel to see the approaching cars as they head to lunch.

▶ **Mecum Auctions**—entry is free.

Friday

▶ **Little Car Show**—entry is free and best to do this one early in the morning.

▶ **Legends of the Autobahn**—Entry is free and expect heavy traffic on Highway 1 when leaving.

Saturday

▶ **Concours d'LeMons**—Entry is free.

▶ **Barnyard at Carmel**—Entry is $32 in advance and $40 day of.

▶ **Portola Hotel/RM Auctions**—Lobby is open and free to visitors.

Sunday

▶ **Pebble Beach Concours d'Elegance**—There is no charge to visit Pebble Beach RetroAuto™

Typical Weekend

If you want traffic and delays, do this! Here is the typical route most people take—and don't say we didn't warn you!

Thursday

▶ **Pebble Beach Rally**—Instead of looking for cars on the road, head to Carmel around noon. Standing room only and difficult parking.

▶ **RM Auctions/Russo and Steele** preview nights are a popular place to hang out.

Friday

▶ **Concorso Italiano**—Highway 68 from Monterey will be stop and go traffic. Leave as early as possible.

▶ **Quail Lodge/Legends of the Autobahn**—It is nearly impossible to do two or all three events. Pick the best-suited.

▶ **RM Auctions/Russo and Steele** The real action is once the auctions are underway.

Saturday

▶ **Mazda Raceway Laguna Seca** - spend the whole day at the track.

▶ **RM Auctions/Russo and Steele** or **Gooding & Company** in the evening.

Sunday

▶ **Pebble Beach Concours d'Elegance**—arrive around 9:00 AM or 10:00 AM if you want to see large crowds.

Expensive

Forget that budget and have fun! Remember to reserve your spots early as many events sell out quickly.

Tuesday

▶ **Carmel-by-the-Sea Concours on the Avenue**—held in downtown Carmel, entry is free and crowds are manageable.

Wednesday

▶ **Motorworks Revival** at the Monterey Jet Center, tickets are $325.

Thursday

▶ **Pebble Beach Tour d'Elegance** in Carmel. Watch the tour arrive and park along Ocean Avenue.
▶ **Gooding & Company**
▶ **St. Julien Winery**—dinner in the vineyard.

Friday

▶ **Quail Lodge, A Motorsports Gathering**—Cost is $550
▶ **Bonhams Auction**—Included with the price of the Quail Lodge event.

Saturday

▶ **Mazda Raceway Laguna Seca**
▶ **RM Auctions/Russo and Steele** the place to be on Saturday night is the Portola Hotel and these two auctions. Must be a registered bidder to view the actual auction. Cost is $200.

Sunday

▶ **Pebble Beach Concours d'Elegance**—Pebble Beach Club d'Elegance tickets are $600 (Regular tickets are $225 in advance and $275 the day of)

Photography

Photography is hard enough without hundreds of people walking in front of your camera. Here are some tips for the bigger events.

Tuesday

▶ **Carmel-by-the-Sea Concours**—held in downtown Carmel as early as possible.

Thursday

▶ **Pebble Beach Tour d'Elegance**—Forget the town of Carmel, head to SR 1. Be careful of traffic and where you park.
▶ **Auction Preview Day**—When an auction company has a preview day, go as soon as they open.

Friday

▶ **Little Car Show**—if photographing cute little cars against the backdrop of Pacific Grove is of interest, try this show. As usual, arrive early.
▶ **Portola Hotel/RM Auctions** A good, high-ISO camera will help create spectacular outdoor pictures. Try visiting the Portola lobby at 2:00 AM and have fun! (RM Auctions takes down their display late Saturday night.)

Saturday

▶ **Pebble Beach**—After going to Gooding & Company, walk down to the Pebble Beach clubhouse. No crowds and a few surprises await!

Sunday

▶ **Pebble Beach Concours d'Elegance**—If you have the proper credentials, arrive early.

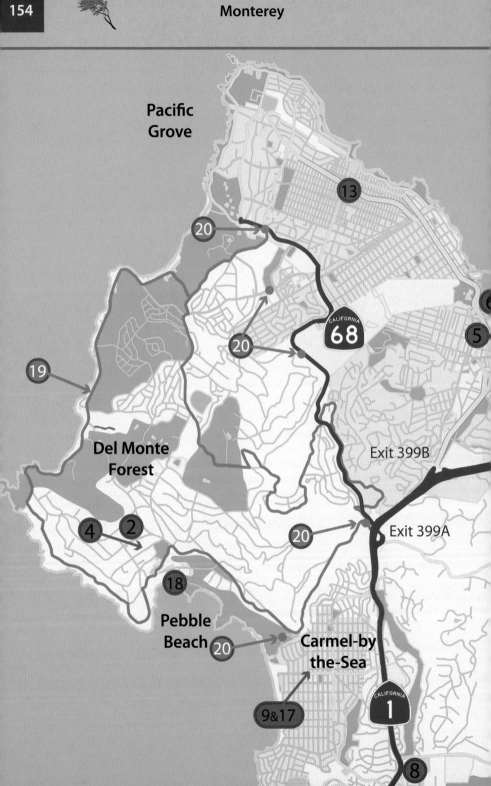

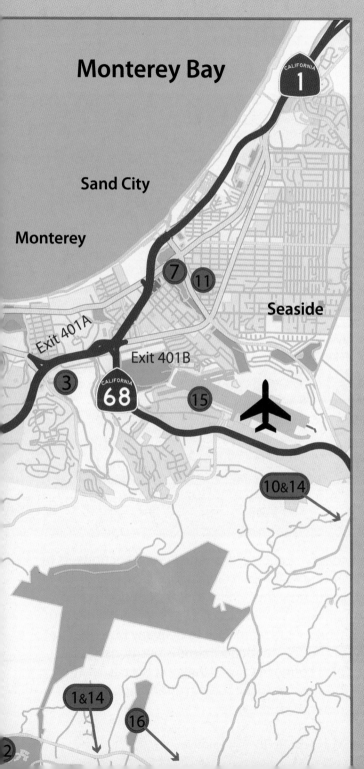

Auctions

1 - Bonhams

2 - Gooding & Co.

3 - Mecum

4 - MidAmerica Motorcycle Auction

5 - RM Auctions

6 - Russo and Steele

Events

7 - Automobilia Monterey

8 - Barnyard

9 - Carmel Concours

10 - Concorso Italiano

11 - Concours d'LeMons

12 - Legends of the Autobahn

13 - The Little Car Show & Pacific Grove Show & Rally

14 - Quail Lodge

15 - Motorworks Revival

16 - Château Julien Winery

Pebble Beach

17 - Pebble Beach Tour d'Elegance Lunch Stop

18 - Pebble Beach Concours d'Elegance

19 - Pebble Beach 17-Mile Drive

20 - Entry gates to Pebble Beach and 17-Mile Drive

Bonhams

Bonhams may be the world's oldest and largest auctioneers of fine arts and antiques. But don't let their diversity lead you to believe they don't know their collector cars. London-based Bonhams has an office in San Francisco with specialists in motor cars, as well as a world-wide team able to help any potential buyer or seller. For the spectator, Bonhams is positioned just to the west of the Quail Lodge in Carmel Valley. It is a casual affair without a lot of the stress associated with attending the larger auctions in downtown Monterey.

History

Founded in 1793, Bonhams is without a doubt the oldest of all the auction houses in Monterey. Their first auction on the Monterey Peninsula was in 1998 under the name Brooks, and in 2002, Bonhams acquired the auction house Butterfields. The Monterey auction functioned under the name "Bonhams & Butterfields" until 2011.

Today

Through out the year, Bonhams holds collector car auctions in both Europe and the United States. In addition to this Monterey auction, Bonhams has an annual presence at the Goodwood Festival of Speed in West Sussex, England and the January auction in Scottsdale, Arizona. In 2012, Bonhams moves their auction location a few hundred yards from the Quail Lodge to an open field to the west. This has given more room to host the auction and for patrons to park and view the automobiles.

Quick Stats

▶ The auction is held in conjunction with The Quail, A Motorsports Gathering

▶ The longest-running continuous auction during the Monterey Car Week.

Directions

From **Monterey by car:**

▶ South on SR 1 (Highway 1)
▶ Left/east on Carmel Valley Road.
▶ Travel two miles to the east.
▶ Right/south on Rancho San Carlos Road.
▶ Drive ¼ mile down the road to 7000 Valley Greens Drive, Carmel, CA 93923

Opposite: *1997 McLaren F1 GTR Longtail Ex-GTC Gulf Team Davidoff.*

Above: *A 1937 Crocker V-Twin sits outside the main entrance to the Bonhams Auction.*

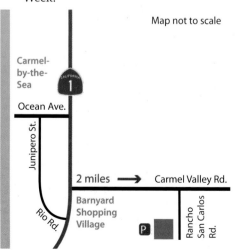

Map not to scale

Carmel-by-the-Sea

Ocean Ave.

Junipero St.

2 miles ➡ Carmel Valley Rd.

Rio Rd.

Barnyard Shopping Village

Rancho San Carlos Rd.

The Auction Setting

The auction location is casual and quiet. Surrounded by fields, the auction tents and consigned cars create a laid-back feel. The location is two miles inland, so expect warm, sunny days and cool evenings.

Highlights

Bonhams has set a number of worldwide records in Monterey around the world. Most recently, Bonhams has made history with the sale of the 1954 Mercedes-Benz W196R Formula 1 Racing Single-Seater for £19,601,500 in the United Kingdom.

Photo Tips

Photographers who arrive early to the auction will not only beat the crowds, but also have a chance to see a little morning fog or cloud cover. Because Bonhams is a few miles inland, don't expect the cover to last as long at the sites by the ocean. The cars inside the tents are fun to photograph during the day (see opposite page), but the evenings are a little dark.

More than Motorcars

In addition to motorcycles, Bonhams in Monterey sells a wide range of automobila ranging from yearbooks and manuals to hood ornaments and glass crystal mascots.

Tips for Attendees

The dress is casual for the most part, but during the auction, business casual is more the norm. If you also attend "The Quail, A Motorsports Gathering" at the Quail Lodge, their ticket gains entry into Bonhams. However, a Bonhams catalog does not permit entry into Quail Lodge.

Best Time to See Cars

Wednesday morning is the best time to see the cars. But if that is too early in the week, wait until Thursday morning as not everything (like vendors) is set up and manned.

Best time to see action

The car auction starts and continues all day to roughly 4:00 PM. Those wishing to see the highlights roll over the block should be there by late morning.

The Quail, A Motorsports Gathering

The Bonhams auction is held in conjunction with this event. Please see *quaillodgeevents.com* for more.

Parking

One of the best parts about this auction is the ease of parking. Just follow the signs to the auction and park in the field west of the auction tents.

Auction Viewing (preview)

The Friday auction is preceded by two viewing days, and the preview schedule tends not to change much year to year. Please contact Bonhams for any updates or changes.

- Wednesday - 10:00 AM–6:00 PM
- Thursday - 9:00 AM–6:00 PM

Auction Sales

The auction continues to be run on Friday in conjunction with Quail.

- Friday - Automobilia starts at 9:30 AM
- Friday - Motorcars start at 11:00 AM

Bidder Registration

The price to enter the auction to watch or bid is the same. Bidders may register beforehand at *www.bonhams.com/quail* or onsite during the auction. If you wish to phone bid, absentee bid, or bid online, it doesn't cost you anything to register.

Admittance

- Admission for two people with no cost to register to bid $80
- VIP admission for two people with reserve seats & catalog $150

Bidder Registration

Admission is $80 and there is no additional fee to register as a bidder.

Contact Information
Bonhams San Francisco
220 San Bruno Avenue
San Francisco, CA 94103

Toll Free: (866) 869-3157
Phone: (415) 391-4000
Fax: (415) 391-4040
www.bonhams.com/quail
Email: *motors.us@bonhams.com*

Opposite: *Ferrari 365 GT 2+2 to the left of a Ferrari 330 GTC.*
Below: *1949 Talbot-Lago Type 26 Course Formula 1 racing car inside the Bonhams auction tent.*

Gooding & Company

There is little doubt that Gooding & Company does one thing and one thing really well at Pebble Beach: They offer and then sell the best cars on the planet and in the process, they set record price after record price. When asked what makes the auction at Pebble Beach special, David Gooding told us *"Gooding & Company's Pebble Beach Auctions have redefined motoring auction events by selling the world's most significant and valuable collector cars."* If you want to see the very best, Gooding & Company is the only place you need to visit.

Via Corsa Car Lover's Guide to Northern California

History

David Gooding is the founder and president of the California-based Gooding & Company. His 20 years in the business started with **Christie's International Motor Car Department** and he also served as president of **RM Auctions, Inc**.

GOODING

Today

Gooding & Company offers three annual public auctions. Each year begins with a January auction in Scottsdale, Arizona and a second auction each March at Amelia Island, Florida. The third is Pebble Beach.

Quick Stats

▶ Three exclusive auctions a year, all in the United States
▶ David Gooding is both the founder & president of Gooding

The Auction Setting

Tucked away at the northern end of Pebble Beach and just off the historical start/finish line of the Pebble Beach car races of the 1950s, the Gooding & Company auction is a vibrant but formal affair. Be prepared to see classy people and the best cars in Monterey here.

Highlight Sales

Gooding & Company continually sets record sales as they move forward from 2012. The auction company set 11 records at Amelia Island in 2012 alone, including $4.4 million for a 1973 Porsche 917 Can-Am Spyder.

Opposite: *1959 Fiat 642/RN-2 Ferrari Transporter sits at the front entry to Gooding & Company on Portola Road.*
Above: *1955 Ferrari 857 Sport*

Directions

From **Monterey by car:**

▶ South on SR 1 (Highway 1)
▶ Take Exit 399A direction Pacific Grove/ Pebble Beach
▶ Pass over SR 68 and continue straight
▶ Stop at guard station (fee paid here)
▶ Follow the 17-Mile Drive as it loops to the left and heads south
▶ Follow the 17-Mile Drive until you reach Portola Road. Straight on Portola Road.
▶ Gooding & Co. tent on your right

DOLLARS	$14,900,000
GBP	£9,089,000
EURO	€10,281,000
SWISS FRANC	11,771,000
YEN (x 100,	11, 00

Monterey Record!

As the saying goes *"You just had to have been there."* Before lot 18 rolled on to the stage, a 1957 Ferrari Testa Rossa, one could feel the excitement building around us. Of course it was standing room only, for what we all knew would be something special, but no one knew for sure exactly how special. Once the Ferrari roared on to the stage and bidding began, the car quickly jumped from $5 million to $10 million in just a blink and then to $11 million. About 14 minutes later, the crowd jumped to their feet and erupted in cheers to a historic $16.39 million dollar sale.

Above: *David Gooding sits to the right of auctioneer Charlie Ross as the hammer comes down on the sale of the Ferrari 250 Testa Rossa #0666 TR.*

Below: *1957 Ferrari 250 Testa Rossa*

Tips for Attendees

One cannot overdress for attending a Gooding & Company auction, and a spectator might even feel a little out of place in shorts and flip-flops. Crowds are heavy during the auction, but viewing days are casual and relaxed, with noticeably fewer people.

Parking

Other than Saturday night and Sunday, parking is mostly easy, and there are a number of dirt lots close to the auction on Stevenson Road.

Best Time to See Cars

Go as early in the week as possible and early in the day to photograph the cars without a lot of people.

Best Time to See Action

Gooding & Company does a good job featuring great cars on both Saturday and Sunday. If you visit Gooding & Company on Saturday night, arrive early, as parking can be a challenge.

Viewing

Generally speaking, these hours are somewhat consistent year after year. Please check *www.goodingco.com* for latest information.

- ▶ Wednesday - 10:00 AM–6:00 PM
- ▶ Thursday - 8:00 AM–6:00 PM
- ▶ Friday - 9:00 AM–5:00 PM
- ▶ Saturday - 9:00 AM–4:30 PM
- ▶ Sunday - 9:00 AM–5:30 PM

Auction

- ▶ Saturday - starts at 5:00 PM
- ▶ Sunday - starts at 6:00 PM

Admittance

- General Admission $40
- Catalog for two and $100
  admittance to all events
- Children under 12 Free

Bidder Registration

Admission for two with catalog and two reserved seats (subject to availability) is $200.

Contact Information

Gooding & Company

1120 Forest Avenue, Box 101
Pacific Grove, CA 93950-5145

On-Site Contact

Phone: (310) 899-1960
Fax: (310) 899-0930
www.goodingco.com
Email: *info@goodingco.com*

Above: *1967 Austin-Healey 3000 Mk III*
Below: *1931 Duesenberg Model J Long-Wheelbase Coupe "Whittell Coupe"*

Photo Tips

Time of day as well as sun or clouds will have an impact on your lighting. Ideally the best time to photograph the cars is on a cloudy day. Gooding & Company also has a policy that photographers must be escorted to the bidding platform to take photos and prohibits photographing guests. Please contact Gooding & Company for their current photo rules.

Mecum Auctions

The most recent addition to the Monterey auction scene is also the biggest. Mecum Auctions sell more cars nationwide per year than any of the other auction companies here on the peninsula. While most of these cars fall into the more common collectible, Mecum has offered a number of highly collectible rare cars, all pulling in high numbers. When Dana Mecum launched his Monterey auction, he stated "We are thrilled to launch the Monterey Auction and look forward to giving attendees a new event they're sure to never forget."

Via Corsa Car Lover's Guide to Northern California

History

Driven by the passion of the business, Mecum Auction president Dana Mecum founded his auction company more than 26 years ago. He has made a name for himself over the years by specializing in American Muscle, collector cars, and Corvettes. In spring 2008 he hit a milestone and sold their 50,000 car. In 2009, Mecum came to Monterey with an auction at the Monterey Hyatt and Del Monte Golf Course. Back then, it was a one-day auction with 200 cars held inside the Hyatt ballroom.

Today

Mecum holds over a dozen auctions around the United States selling everything from farm tractors to vintage Indy cars. Mecum in Monterey now sees strong sales each year.

Directions

From **Monterey by car:**
- Enter SR 1 (Highway 1)
- Take Exit 401A/Aguajito Road
- If exiting to the north, merge onto Mark Thomas Drive.
- If the Hyatt is your destination, turn right on Old Golf Course Road; otherwise follow signs
- If exiting to the south, left/south on Aguajito Road.
- Left on Mark Thomas Drive
- Follow signs to parking on the Del Monte Golf Course.

Opposite: *Auctioneer Mark Delzell offers the crowd a 1954 Kaiser Manhattan 4-door*
Above: *Two modified 1969 Chevrolet Camaros sit on the Del Monte Golf Course in the morning fog of Monterey*

The auction is now held inside a tent along the **Del Monte Golf Course** behind the Hyatt Hotel and the auction has grown from 200 cars to around 750. The large majority of the cars sell in a range us regular folks can afford, but that doesn't mean that Mecum ignores the "blue chip" collectibles seen at other auction companies. Each year their featured cars sell for many millions.

Quick Stats

- 750 Vehicles for sale in Monterey
- 15,000 vehicles sold per year
- Largest collector car auction company nationwide based on the number of cars sold

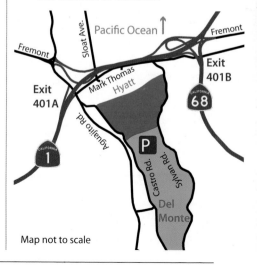

Map not to scale

Highlight Sales

- 2009 - 1965 Daytona Cobra Coupe #CSX2601 sold for $7.25 million; 2010 - 1967 Chevrolet Corvette L88 Convertible sold for $1.25 million
- 2011 - 1931 Miller Bowes Seal Fast Special Indy 500 winner for $2 million
- 2012 - 1972 Porsche 917/10 Spyder that sold for $5.83 million & 1908 Simplex 50 Speedcar Roadster for $2 million

The Auction Setting

As casual as can be. No suits and ties here. The auction tent is fairly small compared to the field of cars waiting outside on the golf course. Expect to walk a good distance in and around the auction/golf course.

Best Time to See Cars

Any time is good. Mornings might be foggy and a little chilly.

Tips for Attendees

Wear good shoes, as there is a lot of walking. Mornings and evenings are chilly, and a jacket is recommended.

Best Time to See Action

Saturday is the day the blue chips roll on to the block. All the top sales over the last years have all been auctioned off midway through the day around lot numbers 100 to 150.

Parking

Parking at the Hyatt is NOT allowed. Please follow traffic and parking instructions to the parking area to the south of the auction site.

Live Television

Unique to Mecum, this Monterey auction may be viewed on the **Discovery Channel Velocity** (*velocity.discovery.com*). Live coverage runs Thursday thru Saturday from 12 PM to 6 PM Pacific.

Vehicle Check-in

▶ Tuesday - 8:00 AM–6:00 PM
▶ Wednesday - 8:00 AM–6:00 PM

Preview & Auction

For each day, the gates open at 8:00 AM and the vehicle auction begins at 10:00 AM. Road Art is auctioned off 30 minutes before the vehicles.

▶ Thursday - starts at 8:00 AM
▶ Friday - starts at 8:00 AM
▶ Saturday- starts at 8:00 AM

Photo Tips

Undoubtably the Mecum Auction is held in the most natural setting of all the auctions. The green fields of the Del Monte Golf Course make for a rich backdrop for any level of photographer. Even when the auction is in full swing it is easy to snap photos of cars, as they are spread widely about the course. Morning fog is also a bonus if you arrive early enough.

Admittance

▶ General Admission   Free

Bidder Registration

Bidder registration is $100

Contact Information

Mecum Auctions
445 S. Main Street
Walworth, WI 53184-8261

Phone: (262) 275-5050
Fax: (262) 275-3424
www.mecum.com
Email: *info@mecum.com*

On-Site Contact (during auction)

Hyatt Regency Monterey
Del Monte Golf Course
1 Old Golf Course Road
Monterey, CA 93940

Opposite: *Friday's cars wait in the morning fog of the Del Monte Golf Course.*
Below: *Collector cars slowly making their way to the Mecum Auction tent.*

RM Auctions

Outshining all other auction houses with both their top quality collector cars and exotic locations, RM Auctions carries a global presence with auctions at such historic locations as on the banks of Lake Como in Italy, London, and of course Monterey. While bidders have long known of RM Auction's quality offerings in Monterey, it is also a highlight for attendees from all around the peninsula. For the casual spectator, there is no better place to simply hang out than outside the Portola Hotel lobby on Friday and Saturday night.

History

Rob Myers, the founder and chairman of RM Auctions, began his automotive career in 1976 with a single car garage restoration business and grew his company through out the 1980s by actively buying and selling collector cars. In 2012, the company's flagship Monterey sale posted exceptional results with a spectacular $96 million in total sales —a 20 percent increase from the 2011 sale generated by a smaller, more elite offering as RM continues to focus on the top tier of the collector car market. RM's top sale of the weekend and 2012 year was a 1968 Ford GT40 Gulf/ Mirage Lightweight Racing Car, used extensively as the camera car in the 24 Hours of Le Mans, which sold for $11 million to set a new world record as the most expensive American automobile ever sold at auction.

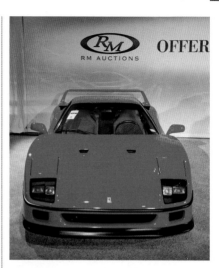

Directions

From **Monterey - Exit 339B by car:**

▶ North on SR 1 (Highway 1)
▶ Take Exit 339B /Munras Avenue north towards Monterey.
▶ Follow Munras Avenue north as it changes into Abrego Street and eventually becomes Washington Street.
▶ Left/west on Del Monte Avenue.
▶ The Portola Hotel is at the intersection of Alvarado Street and Del Monte Avenue.

Opposite: 1956 Ferrari 250 GT LWB Berlinetta 'Tour de France', 1955 Aston Martin DB3S, and a 1968 Ford GT40 Gulf/ Mirage Lightweight Racing Car
Above: 1991 Ferrari F40 #89441 sold for $715,000 in 2012

Today

RM Auctions is truly a worldwide presence with auctions currently in Phoenix, Amelia Island, Michigan, Monaco, Hershey, London, and Italy where they partner with the renowned **Concorso d'Eleganza Villa d'Este** on the banks of Lake Como. Today they are the largest auction house for quality automobiles and world wide functions.

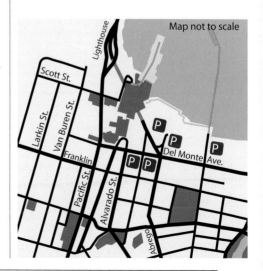

Portola Hotel & Spa

Just steps away from historic Fisherman's Wharf, the Portola Hotel & Spa is without a doubt the center of the action in Monterey on any given normal evening. Add the RM Auction, and the Portola Hotel becomes the single most important and fun "must attend" event for Friday and Saturday nights during the entire Monterey Car Week. You do not need be a guest of the hotel to visit the lobby or watch the cars enter the auction outside at the front of the hotel.

Contact Information

Portola Hotel & Spa
Two Portola Plaza
Monterey, CA 93940
Phone: (888) 222-5851
www.portolahotel.com
Email: *info@portolahotel.com*

Highlight Sales

In 2012, RM achieved a spectacular $96 million in total sales with top honors going to a 1968 Ford GT40 Gulf/Mirage Racing Car used extensively as the camera car in the film *Le Mans*.

The Auction Setting

The RM Auction is set up at the Portola Hotel with cars spread around both the lobby, the back courtyard, hotel pedestrian areas, and the conference center. While the preview days may be casual, the auction on both Friday and Saturday nights is elegant.

Tips for Attendees

The lobby of the Portola Hotel is open to the public and will have a number of high-end collectible cars on display. There are also cars in the pedestrian walkway to the east, and during the auction, cars will line up outside in front of the lobby prior to the auction. The cars located outside to the north in the hotel plaza require a RM preview ticket for entry.

Parking

There is plenty of parking inside the garages downtown, and payment is required. The city of Monterey has restrictions on most streets between 10:00 AM and 6:00 PM.

Best Time to See Cars

The best time to see the hotel lobby cars is during the preview days either really early in the morning or very late at night (lobby only).

Photo Tips

The sunlight dancing around the Portola hotel lobby each morning is already a photographer's dream, but nighttime is magical! In fact of all the auctions, the RM Auction is a photographer's dream come true, be it day or night. RM Auctions has asked photographers not to take pictures of the bidders or guests attending the RM Auction.

Auction Viewing (preview)

- ▶ Wednesday - 10:00 AM–6:00 PM
- ▶ Thursday - 10:00 AM–6:00 PM
- ▶ Friday - 10:00 AM–6:00 PM
- ▶ Saturday - 10:00 AM–6:00 PM

Auction Sales

- ▶ Friday - starts at 6:30 PM
- ▶ Saturday - starts at 6:30 PM

Admission to Preview

- ▶ Admission per person
  (preview only, not auction) $50

Bidder Registration

The auction is limited to registered
bidders and consignors.
Bidder admission for two (includes
event catalog) $300

Contact Information

RM Auctions Corporate Office
One Classic Car Drive
Blenheim, Ontario N0P 1A0
Canada

Toll Free: (800) 221-4371
Phone: (519) 352-4575
Fax: (519) 351-1337
www.rmauctions.com
Email: *info@rmauctions.com*

Location Information

Portola Hotel & Spa (opposite page)

Top Right: *RM Auctioneer Max Girardo*

Middle Right: *Left to Right, 1965 Shelby GT350, 1965 Shelby 427 Competition Cobra, 1964 Shelby 289 Competition Cobra*

Bottom Right: *A 1998 Mercedes-Benz CLK GTR sits between a 2004 Porsche Carrera GT and a 1998 Porsche 911 GT1 "Strassenversion"*

Russo and Steele

Now in a new location at the Old Fisherman's Wharf at Monterey Harbor, the Russo and Steele Collector Automobile Auction is now celebrating its 13th year. This high-energy auction is a great alternative to the more traditional auction houses around the peninsula. Visitors to Russo and Steele will see no stage and no separation between themselves and the collector cars and should walk away with a visceral and interactive experience. Be sure to visit this auction on both preview days and when it is underway to see the action.

History

The Russo and Steele Collector Automobile Auction were founded in 2001 by long-time Arizona auction personality **Drew Alcazar**. The focus was to bring a mix of high-end European sports cars ("Russo") and American Muscle ("Steele") to his auctions. In 2012, Russo and Steele moved to Fisherman's Wharf from the cozy but small Marriott ballroom. This move also means that spectators and bidders were able to see the cars out in the open instead of the garages that have housed the cars in the past.

Today

This auction is an alternative for those that find the traditional auctions boring. Russo and Steele says this about their format, "Highly interactive, visceral ground-level auction arena that provides cars with no separation from the buyers." Russo and Steele also holds auctions in January

Directions

From **Monterey - Exit 339B by car:**

▶ North on SR 1 (Highway 1)
▶ Take Exit 339B / Munras Avenue north towards Monterey.
▶ Follow Munras Avenue north as it changes into Abrego Street and eventually renames into Washington St.
▶ Left on Del Monte Avenue.
▶ Parking garages are on your left.
▶ Once parked, walk past the Portola Hotel & Spa and over the pedestrian bridge spanning the Lighthouse Avenue tunnel.
▶ The auction is at the Fisherman's Wharf by the ocean.

in Scottsdale, June in Newport Beach, and September in Las Vegas.

Quick Stats

▶ 250 automobiles in Monterey
▶ "Auction in the Round" format
▶ Moved from the Marriott to Fishermans Wharf in 2012

Opposite: Russo and Steele's new location at the Old Fisherman's Wharf.

Above: Collector cars line up to be auctioned.

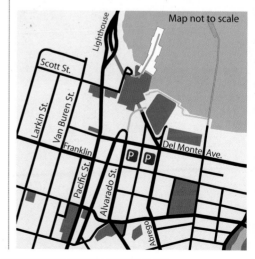

Highlight Sales

- 2012 - 1965 Shelby Cobra 289 - sold for $781,000
- 2011 - 1966 Ferrari 275 GTS - sold for $654,500
- 2010 - Shelby Cobra CSX2461 - sold for $649,000

The Auction Setting

The Russo and Steele Auction company is best known for its "Auction in the Round." For those who have never been to a Russo and Steele auction, there is no stage or proper auction block. Instead, the cars are rolled in as the crowd looks down on to the stage. People are welcome to look at the car up for auction.

Tips for Attendees

Once you find a parking spot, the rest is easy. The auction is really fun after 5:00 PM and many people stay late into the night. Forget the on site food vendors and eat at the Fisherman's Wharf instead.

Parking

Parking is a challenge on both Friday and Saturday night. Look for the large parking garage on the south side of Del Monte Avenue diagonal to the auction. If that is full, try the open lots a block or two further south. Parking on the street requires payment until 6:00 PM.

Best Time to See Cars

Daytime is great to preview the cars, but evening is more fun. It may be tough to look at the cars in the west lot, but the cars waiting to be auctioned off sit under a well lit tent.

Auction Viewing (Preview)

The Wednesday preview day is closed to the general public. The auction opens to the public on Thursday.

- Wednesday - 10:00 AM (closed to the general public)
- Thursday - 10:00 AM
- Friday - 10:00 AM
- Saturday - 10:00 AM

Auction Sales

- ▶ Thursday - 5:00 PM
- ▶ Friday - 5:00 PM
- ▶ Saturday - 5:00 PM

Admission to Preview

- ▶ One–day ticket $20
- ▶ Three–day ticket $55

Bidder Registration

Bidder registration & guest pass $150

Contact Information

Russo and Steele
5230 S. 39th Street
Phoenix, AZ 85040

Phone: (602) 252-2697
Fax: (602) 252-6260
www.russoandsteele.com
Email: *info@russoandsteele.com*

Location Information

Old Fisherman's Wharf
290 Figueroa Street
Monterey, California 93940

Opposite: "*Auction in the Round*"
Top Right: *Drew Alcazar*
Right: *1961 Nash Metropolitan Coupe is
ready for auction as the evening fog descends*

Photo Tips

The Russo and Steele auction really comes alive at night, both indoors and outside. Some skill and luck is needed to get clear long shots at night due to all the moisture in the air. Inside the auction tent, there is plenty of light and colors, so a high ISO camera is not really necessary. Because of the auction format, people are everywhere, so don't expect any clear shots.

Automobilia Monterey

Held early in the week, Automobilia Monterey is the kick-off event for all that follows. Based on the success in Europe of Retromobile and Techno Classica, Automobilia brings together the finest dealers of memorabilia and parts in North America. Expect to see 45-plus quality vendors offering authentic vintage parts (as no replicas or reproductions are allowed), one-of-a-kind hand-made sculptures, posters, hand-made resin model cars, and more. In fact all vendors must sell automotive-related items—no timeshares or jewelry companies here!

Via Corsa Car Lover's Guide to Northern California

History

Originally founded by enthusiast **Tony Singer** in 2002, Automobilia Monterey is the event that has kicked off the madness in Monterey every year since.

Today

Tony still runs Automobilia Monterey as well as the collector website *vintageautoposters.com*. Every year, he donates a portion of proceeds, plus all money raised from the silent auction to the **Monterey County Rape Crisis Center**.

The Setting

When visitors arrive at the 9,000 sq ft Grand Ballroom inside the Embassy Suites, one might think this will be a short visit. Once you talk to the vendors and explore their offerings, you will spend a few hours here at least.

Schedule

- Tuesday - 10:00 AM–6:00 PM
- Wednesday - 10:00 AM–7:00 PM

Location Information

Embassy Suites Monterey
1441 Canyon Del Rey
Seaside, CA 93955
Phone: (831) 383-1115
www.embassysuites.com

Directions

From **Monterey:**

- Head north on SR 1
- Take exit 403
- Right/south on Canyon Del Ray Blvd.
- Embassy Suites is at the right

Admission

- One-Day Ticket $15
- Two-Day Ticket $20

Contact Information

Spyder Enterprises, Inc.
12290 Saddle Road
Carmel Valley, CA 93924

Phone: (831) 659-1551
Fax: (831) 659-5335
www.automobiliamonterey.com
Email: *tony@automobiliamonterey.com*

Opposite: *Porsche Sculpture by renowned artist* **J. Paul Nesse**
Above: *"The Finish Line" is one of many vendors offering memorabilia*

Barnyard Ferrari Event

By Saturday afternoon, most people have experienced most of what the Monterey Car Week has to offer. By now, most people think that all that is left is the Pebble Beach Concours the next day. Well, no. There is the Barnyard Ferrari Event. But you are dead-tired and have sore feet. Leave them at the door and head to the Barnyard for a casual, quiet, and relaxing event offered during Monterey. Did I mention they have food prepared by eight different Barnyard restaurants and locally grown wine from about a dozen different wineries?

History

Many years ago, the well-known retail store Khaki's Men's Store used to host a Ferrari event in front of their premise. When they moved, The Barnyard Shopping Village Carmel picked up the ball and now hosts a new Ferrari event not far from the original location.

Today

The Ferrari Owners Club, in conjunction with the Barnyard Shopping Village, holds a casual Saturday afternoon gathering, with proceeds donated to the **JDRF** (Juvenile Diabetes Research Foundation).

When & Where

- Saturday, 4:00 PM–7:00 PM
- The Barnyard Shopping Village
- Cost is $32 in advance or $40 on the day of the event

Opposite: A Ferrari F355 GTS and a new Jaguar XJ 4-door in the distance

Top: The Barnyard Shopping Village is a 75,000 sq ft retail center offering visitors eight restaurants, four galleries, and 34 retail stores.

Above: Chardonnay by Ventana Vineyards of Monterey

Contact Information

The Barnyard Shopping Village
3618 The Barnyard
Carmel, CA 93923

Phone: (831) 624-8886
or 831-515-6403
Fax: (831) 622-0923
www.thebarnyard.com
Email: *info@thebarnyard.com*

Directions

From **Monterey:**

- Head south on SR 1
- Left/east on Carmel Valley Road
- South on Carmel Rancho Blvd. and follow the signs.

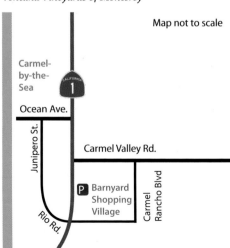

Carmel-by-the-Sea Concours on the Avenue

As a regular of the Monterey Car Week, I thought I had seen it all. Then I went to the Carmel-by-the-Sea Concours on the Avenue. Yes, I was impressed by the wonderful cars (who wouldn't be?), but then I saw the "Tiffany blue." Being married, I've come to both love and loathe this unmistakable color. After passing all the cars I should have been photographing, my first photo of the day was a cellphone picture of the awards table sent to my wife. It is now my wife's dream to enter a car into this concours and win an award. I can live with that.

Via Corsa Car Lover's Guide to Northern California

History

When Doug Freedman and his wife Genie were visiting Carmel-by-the-Sea in 1987, he thought to himself that Ocean Avenue would be the perfect place to hold a Concours. It had something for everyone—shopping, restaurants, and a perfect backdrop for collector cars. In 2001, he started working on making his dream come true, and in 2007, it came to fruition when the town of Carmel granted him permission.

Today

Now in its seventh year, the **Carmel-by-the-Sea Concours on the Avenue** is held the Tuesday prior to the **Pebble Beach Concours d'Elegance**. It is a casual and beautifully presented show that features an eclectic mix of muscle cars, hot rods, sports cars, and luxury cars. The awards for the cars that are allowed entry are marques from 1940 through 1973, with a special exception for Porsche and Ferrari automobiles through 1989. During the concours, shop windows are adorned with memorabilia and center stage (with the help of Tiffany & Company) is simply breathtaking.

Directions

From **Monterey:**
▶ Head south on SR 1.
▶ Right/west on Carpenter.
▶ Or Right/west on Ocean Avenue (not recommended)
▶ Parking should be available within a few blocks of Ocean Avenue in either direction.

Quick Facts
▶ First year of the show was 2007
▶ Today there are roughly 175–200 cars on display
▶ To date, over $200,000 raised for the Carmel Foundation
▶ Announcers are Ed Justice, Jr. (of the Justice Brothers), Michael T. Lynch, and Donald Osborne
▶ Concours covers the park and 18 blocks ("Concours Avenues")

Opposite: Ed Justice, Jr. to the left, and Michael T. Lynch on the right, interview Jim & Kathy Orsburn in their 1954 Kaiser Darrin Roadster #381 (They received 1st place in "America Sport" class)

Above: The absolutely stunning awards from the world-famous Tiffany & Company.

Setting

As a perfect precursor to the crowd-heavy events later in the week, this concours is really a treat. It is casual, fun, and beautiful. What's more is the automobile owners are friendly, all the local shops decorate their store windows, and a seat for lunch or dinner is a short wait. The cars in the concours are stunning examples of production cars, not the esoteric automobiles seen at Pebble Beach.

Tips for Entrants & Spectators

Application for entry opens in late December of the preceding year and closes June 15. To enter your car it costs $250 or greater and proceeds support the "Carmel Foundation." (founded in 1950 to benefit the senior citizens of Monterey Peninsula) *www.carmelfoundation.org.* Parking in Carmel is limited to two hours in spots close to Ocean Avenue, so plan accordingly, as you will want to stay the whole day.

Major Award Categories

▶ Multi-Marques 1940-1973

▶ Porsche 1948-1989

▶ Ferrari 1947-1989

Admission

▶ Spectators are free

▶ Entrants pay $250 plus

Top: *BMW Isetta "Courtesy Car"*

Middle Top: *Jaguars E-Type getting a last-minute detailing.*

Middle Below: *1959 Morgan Plus 4 Factory Lightweight.*

Left: *1966 Lola T70 #SL71-17 in front of 1969 McLaren M6B #50-17.*

Schedule

▶ Open to the public
10:00 AM–5:00 PM

▶ Staging of Cars
8:30 AM–11 AM

▶ Judging - 11 AM–2 PM

▶ Class Awards - 2:30 PM–3:45 PM

▶ Major Awards
3:45 PM–5:00 PM

Contact Information

Motor Club Events, LLC
2575 Peachtree Road NE, Suite 303
Atlanta, GA 30305

Phone: (404) 805-1650
Fax: (404) 237-2644
www.motorclubevents.com
Email: *info@motorclubevents.com*

Event Location:
Carmel-by-the-Sea
Concours on the Avenue
Ocean Avenue
Carmel-by-the-Sea, CA 93923

Top: *Ferrari 365 Daytonas lined up on Ocean Avenue just to the west of San Carlos Street.*

Right: *Porsche 356 Coupes, Convertibles, and Speedsters.*

Photo Tips

Downtown Carmel-by-the-Sea is the perfect backdrop for concours photographers with its lush colors, morning fog, and quaint cafés. Plus this event precedes the Pebble Beach Tour by two days and experiences much smaller crowds, hence a better chance to take unobstructed photos. I was able to shoot the photo to the right at f2 200mm early in the morning with help of a morning fog.

Concorso Italiano

For over a quarter of a century, Italian car enthusiasts have been served up the single best place to celebrate their respective marques: Concorso Italiano. Originally based at the Quail Lodge, the Concorso Italiano has seen a few changes in venue (some better than others) but generally retained its dedication to showcasing the very best from Italy. Today, Concorso Italiano has found a new home at the beautiful and lush Laguna Seca Golf Ranch just to the west of another favorite stop during this hectic weekend, Mazda Raceway Laguna Seca.

History

The Concorso Italiano was founded in 1985 by Frank and Janet Mandarano and held the first show in 1986 at Lake Tahoe with the first annual Concorso Italiano (called the **Concours Italiana Quail Lodge** back then) held at the **Quail Lodge Golf Club** in Carmel Valley in 1987. The show was renamed to the **Concorso Italiano** and remained at the Quail Lodge Golf Club through 2002.

In 2003 Concorso Italiano moved to the **Black Horse Golf Course,** with another move in 2008 to the Marina Municipal Airport to the north of Monterey. In 2009, Concorso Italiano found a new venue at the **Laguna Seca Golf Ranch,** and is the place to be on each Friday before the Pebble Beach Concours weekend.

Opposite: *Ferrari F50 reunion in 2011. The F50 in the foreground is the Ferrari F50 #001 owned by Art Zafiropoulo.*

Top Right: *Pagani debuts the V12 twin-Turbo Huayra to the U.S. market in 2012.*

Spectator Directions

From **Monterey by car:**

► Take SR 1/Cabrillo Highway north from Carmel or south from Seaside.
► Exit 401B onto SR 68/Salinas Highway east towards Salinas.
► You will pass the Monterey Peninsula Airport to the north/left.
► Drive 6 miles on SR 68
► Turn left/north on Pasadera Road into the Laguna Seca Golf Ranch. Follow signs.

Participant Directions

From **Monterey by car:**

► Follow the signs and enter Concorso on York Road to the west of the event.

Del Monte
Fremont
California 1
California 218
Monterey Peninsula Airport
General Jim Moore
Canyon Del Rey
South Boundary Road
South Boundary Road
California 68
York
York Rd.
Laguna Seca Golf Ranch
P
Pasadera

Map not to scale

Today

In 2013, Concorso Italiano celebrated its 28th annual event. While the focus is and has always been Italian cars and motorcycles, other marques are welcome.

Quick Stats

▶ First Concorso was in 1986
▶ 800–1,000 Italian cars on display
▶ Be sure to look for the Concorso Italiano "Black & White" display. It is a crowd favorite!

Location

The Laguna Seca Golf Ranch is an 18-hole resort-style golf course. The course was designed by Robert Trent Jones Senior & Junior in 1970 and the signature hole is #15 and a par 5. Overall the course and its oak-studded hillsides providing breathtaking views and landscapes for this world-class event.

Where to Begin

The heart of the show is centered around a small stage and grandstands. All the major awards, guest speakers, and fashion show happen at the stage, so arrive early if you would like a seat; otherwise, it is standing room only!

The Centerpiece Display Cars

Each Concorso Italiano has a magnificent display of centerpiece cars. These are often some of the rarest cars on the planet and change year to year.

Top Left: *Heading home after a long day.*
Middle Left: *Lamborghini Gallardos.*
Bottom Left: *Concorso Wine Garden*

Displaying Your Car

If you are displaying your car, you need to arrive between 6:00 AM and 9:00 AM. If you arrive after 9:00 AM, you will be asked to park in the spectator lot. You will be allowed to leave at 5:00 PM and not before.

Schedule (subject to change)

- Show hours are from 9:00 AM to 5:00 PM
- Marque presentations are in the morning
- Fashion show follows lunch
- Early afternoon begins with Special Feature Presentations
- Best of Marque and Best of Show awards follow the Special Presentations

Above: *2012 Bertone Nuccio prototype*
Below: *Jay Leno is featured on the cover of "Carmel Magazine."*
Bottom: *Jay Leno talks to crowds at Concorso Italiano.*

Tickets

Two categories—Spectator & Display

Spectator

- General admission (pre-event) $150
- General admission (day of event) $175
- CI Club Package $325
- CI Club Package includes admission, VIP parking, entrance into the CI Club pavilion, and lunch.
- Children 12 and under are free with a paying adult

Jay Leno

Jay Leno, a longtime car enthusiast and visitor to Monterey and Concorso Italiano, received the "La Bella Macchina" award in 2009 in recognition of his contributions to both Concorso Italiano and the hobby of car collecting. If you aren't a late night viewer, try catching him on the Internet at *www.jaylenosgarage.com*.

Display (a Car at Concorso)

Registration price per vehicle (**NOT** accepted on the day of the event).
- $150 (Italian)
- $200 (non Italian)

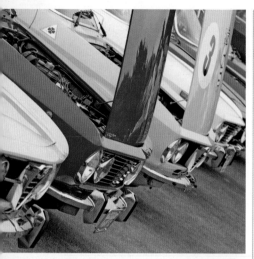

Featured Marques

First off, this is not a glorified Ferrari show. Yes, there are a lot of Ferraris, but the true beauty of this show is in the diversity of all Italian marques.

Among the major manufacturers represented (this includes motorcycles and scooters, too) are Abarth, Alfa Romeo, De Tomaso, Ferrari, Fiat, Iso & Bizzarrini, Lamborghini, Lancia, and Maserati. Marque awards are also given to special coachwork. A visitor may also expect each Concorso Italiano to showcase smaller automobile companies known for very limited production, such as Pagani Automobili.

If that isn't enough, a number of designers are also featured, including Bertone, Italdesign-Guigiaro, Pininfarina, Touring, and Zagato.

Unlike some other shows, Concorso Italiano is really a show for the people about the people. You do not need to own a multimillion dollar garage queen to win an award, nor do you need to own a 50-year-old car just to gain admittance. In fact most of the fields of cars are regular Italian production automobiles or motorcycles available at your local dealer.

It must be added that without the help and coordination of everyone from the **Abarth Enthusiasts Worldwide** to the **Iso & Bizzarrini Owner's Club** as well as the many car clubs, a show of this magnitude would never be possible.

Top: *The Alfa Romeo GTVs out in force thanks in part to the Alfa Romeo Owners Club and Alfa Romeo Association of Northern California.*

Above: *Concorso invited Maserati Ghibli owners to celebrate their 45th birthday.*

Spectator Tips

As with most large events, traffic is a problem. Spectators should arrive early and stay late (or leave early, as in 3:00 PM) to avoid sitting on Highway 68. There is plenty of parking, but watch out for the high curbs when driving on the golf course paths. If you are interested in the lunch, pre-purchase your tickets.

Contact Information

Concorso Italiano
8318 197th Street SW
Edmonds, WA 98026

Phone: (425) 742-0632
Fax: (425) 742-0764
www.concorso.com
Email: *ci@concorso.com*

Event Location:
Laguna Seca Golf Ranch
10520 York Road
Monterey, CA 93940

Top: *The very popular Friday afternoon fashion show draws huge crowds!*

Above: *A Ferrari Enzo sits at the Meguiar's pavilion. Meguiar's is a long-time-sponsor of the Concorso.*

Below: *Lunchtime at Concorso Italiano!*

Concours d' LeMons

J ust about everyone agrees that the Pebble Beach Concours d'Elegance brings out the very best automobiles in the world. So isn't it natural that there is a concours for the very worst? Thanks to Alan Galbraith, there is such a show and rally. But before all these much-maligned lemons are simply disregarded as corporate incompetence, it should be noted that in a recent running of the Pebble Beach Tour d'Elegance Presented by Rolex, six of their automobiles broke down, while every single lemon finished its equally long rally, albeit missing a few parts.

History

Way back in 2007, or maybe 2008, after another running of "24 Hours of LeMons," **Alan Galbraith** paid the race founder **Jay Lamm** the ultimate compliment by noting that his race had successfully lowered the standard of professional endurance racing everywhere, much to their mutual delight. It was then that Alan thought a new concours might be in order. So in 2009, the Concours d'LeMons debuted at Toro Park in Salinas.

Today

Now in its new location in Seaside and sponsored by Hagerty, the Concours d'LeMons and rally is a refuge for all those unwanted and homeless cars.

Contact Information

Alan Galbraith
Phone: (916) 207-4645
www.concoursdlemons.com
Email: *agalbraith@ concoursdlemons.com*

Event Location:
Laguna Grande Park
1249 Canyon Del Rey Blvd.
Seaside, CA 93955

Saturday concours from 10:00 AM to 1:00 PM with rally to follow.

Directions

From **Monterey:**
- Head north on SR 1.
- Take exit 403.
- Right/south on Canyon Del Ray Blvd.
- Embassy Suites is at the southwest corner of Del Monte Ave. and Canyon Del Ray Blvd.

Opposite: *Mindy Kindelberger's 1970 Subaru 360 Deluxe sedan leads the 2012 Tour of LeMons as the winner of the 2nd annual "Search for America's Sweetest LeMon".*

Top Right: *Yet more junk*

Right: *Awards for the "Worst of Show"*

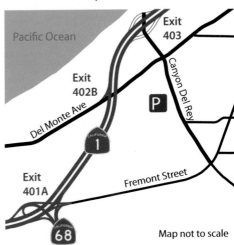

Map not to scale

Legends of the Autobahn

Some old-timers lament that the charm that used to be the Monterey Car Week is gone. Corporations and high ticket prices and such. Perhaps they have yet to visit the Legends of the Autobahn. This one-day show is open to four German marques, namely Audi, BMW, Mercedes-Benz, and Porsche and organized by volunteers at each of their respective car clubs. Spectator entry is free, parking is easy, and the cars on display could be anything from a Mercedes-Benz 300 SL to a BMW concept car. Plus, there is German beer on tap.

History

Founded in 2009 as a "German alternative" to the other more Italian-themed car shows on the Friday prior to the Pebble Beach Concours d'Elegance, this show has grown exponentially in the years since its inception. Originally just a BMW-led show, Porsche and Mercedes-Benz joined in 2010 and finally Audi in 2012.

Today

The format of the event looks and acts like any visitor would expect. Judging of cars takes place in the morning and awards are given in the afternoon. What sets this event apart from all others is that this is a combined effort made by four car clubs. Each club judges its own marque and awards cars based on its own club rules. Any given participant must belong to the respective club of the car they wish to display. There will be a "Best of Show" award selected by a group of celebrity judges. Of course, owners may pass on judging and enter their car for display in the Corral parking.

The Legends of the Autobahn currently fields several hundred cars for both judging and display. Cooperation between these clubs has made this event possible:

- **ACNA** - Audi Club of North America
- **BMWCCA** - BMW Car Club of America
- **MBCA** - Mercedes-Benz Club of America
- **PCA** - Porsche Club of America

Directions

From **Monterey:**
- South on SR 1 (Highway 1)
- Left/east on Carmel Valley Road
- Travel 1.1 miles to the east.
- Right/south on Rio Road
- Spectator parking is in the asphalt parking lot next to the Community Church of the Monterey Peninsula.

Opposite: *Class trophies*
Top Right: *Spaten! A beer from Munich, Germany dating back to 1397*

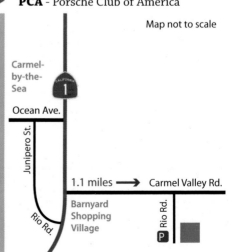

Map not to scale

Carmel-by-the-Sea

Ocean Ave.

Junipero St.

1.1 miles → Carmel Valley Rd.

Rio Rd.

Barnyard Shopping Village

Rio Rd.

Location

Rancho Canada Golf Club is open to the public and offers two 18-hole courses over 4,366 acres. The property formally named "Rancho Canada de la Segunda" was once an 1839 Mexican land grant.

Concept Cars

In 2011, crowds were wowed by the BMW 328 Homage concept car and 2012 saw the Zagato Roadster Concept debut to the public.

Displaying Your Car

First, join the respective club for your marque, then fill out their application linked on the event website *www. legendsoftheautobahn.org*.

Tips for Spectators

So far, this show hasn't drawn the massive crowds seen elsewhere. Take advantage of this, and visit this event before the masses know about it!

Schedule

Friday Schedule:

- ▶ 7:00 AM Registration opens
- ▶ 7:00 AM–9:00 AM Cars placed on field and in corral
- ▶ 10:00 AM–12:00 PM Judging in all classes
- ▶ 12:00 PM–1:00 PM Luncheon
- ▶ 1:30 PM–3:00 PM Awards Ceremony
- ▶ 3:00 PM–4:00 PM Have fun & socialize

Participants (subject to change)

- ▶ Judged $60
- ▶ Judged - late (after July 31) $75
- ▶ Display only $30
- ▶ Display only - late (7/31) $40

Participants may also buy
- ▶ Breakfast Buffet
- ▶ Luncheon
- ▶ VIP Luncheon

Spectator Admission

- Spectators   Free!
- Parking donation at the
  Community Church of
  the Monterey Peninsula $10

Contact Information

Please refer to the event website listed below for all information about the Legends of Autobahn event.

Event Website:
www.legendsoftheautobahn.org

Event Location:
Rancho Canada Golf Club
4860 Carmel Valley Road
Carmel, CA 93923
Phone: (800) 536-9459
www.ranchocanada.com

Audi
Audi Club North America -
Golden Gate Chapter
www.audiclubgoldengate.org

BMW
BMW Car Club of America
www.bmwcca.org

Mercedes-Benz
Mercedes-Benz Club of America
www.mbca.org

Porsche
Porsche Club of America
www.pca.org

Opposite: *A mix of BMW, Mercedes-Benz, and Porsches on display in the Corral*

Top Right: *1961 Mercedes-Benz 300 SL Roadster awaits judging*

Right: *The 2011 BMW 328 Hommage Concept Car, celebrating 75 years since the debut of the BMW 328*

The Little Car Show

Bigger is better? Not according to these guys! Welcome to what could be described as the cutest and littlest car show in Monterey. Founded in 2010 and sponsored by Marina Motorsports, each year features a vehicle theme and entry is limited to the first 100 cars. There are some definitions to "small," however. The show only allows those with a 1,601-cc engine or smaller as well as electric cars. Crowd favorites are the BMW Isettas, Messerschmitts, and Mini Coopers. But really, all the cars in this show are great and the owners friendly.

Admission

▶ Spectators   Free

▶ Display   Free

▶ Donations are welcome either to benefit the Pacific Grove Library, Pacific Grove Youth Center, and Veterans Transition Center.

Schedule

Held Wednesday prior to the Pebble Beach Concours d'Elegance

▶ Setup 11:00 AM

▶ Show 12:00 PM–5:00 PM

Contact Information

Marina Motorsports, Inc.
P.O. Box 1200
Marina, CA 93933

Phone: (831) 484-1966
www.marinamotorsports.org
Email: *jam@redshift.com*

Event Location:
Lighthouse Avenue between Fountain Avenue and 16th Street.

Directions

From **Monterey:**

▶ Head northeast on Lighthouse Avenue.

▶ Follow for roughly 1 mile into Pacific Grove.

▶ Left/south on Forest Avenue.

Opposite: *1956 Aircraft Tug with Chrysler Hemi hosting the Little Car Show banner*

Top Right: *Joe Palazzolo's handmade Tipo 2002 with a 200cc air-cooled engine*

Above Right: *1955 BMW Isetta 300 owned by Joey Garello of Pebble Beach*

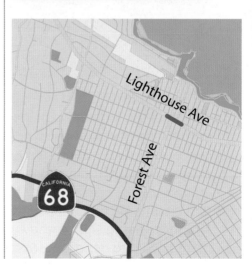

Pacific Grove Concours Auto Rally

This long-established event in Pacific Grove has remained one of the Monterey Car Week's best-kept secrets. Founded in 1995 and having enjoyed nearly two decades of success, this concours and rally brings out enthusiasts and spectators for a casual Friday alternative to the more hectic and crowded shows around the peninsula. During the concours, both spectators and participants are welcome to indulge in both the local restaurants and shops lining Lighthouse Avenue. Remember, this is a fundraising event to benefit the youths of the community!

History

The Pacific Grove Concours Auto Rally was founded in 1995 and has been organized by the Pacific Grove Youth Action, Inc. (PGYA) and the Pacific Grove Rotary. To date, they have raised over $175,000 for the youths of the community. These funds have helped benefit the PG Youth Center, the City of Carmel Police Athletics Program, the City of Carmel Mayor's Fund, and the Pacific Grove High School Driver's Training Scholarships. In 2012, the featured marque was Volkswagen and 2013 is celebrating the 100th anniversary of Aston Martin.

Today

As in past years, the Concours Auto Rally is held on the Friday afternoon and evening prior to the Pebble Beach Concours d'Elegance. The event draws 200 cars and over 8,000 spectators for the show and subsequent rally. The day ends with a barbecue dinner for both spectators and participants at the historic **Chatauqua Hall**, located at Central Avenue at 16th Street in Pacific Grove.

Admission

- Spectators   Free
- Rally only $75
- Rally plus BBQ dinner $90
- BBQ Dinner only $20

Directions

From **Monterey:**
- Head northeast on Lighthouse Avenue.
- Follow for roughly 1 mile into Pacific Grove.
- Left/south on Forest Avenue.

Opposite: *MG TF and a BMW E30 M3 parked on Lighthouse Ave. at the Pacific Grove Concours Auto Rally*

Schedule

Held the Friday prior to the Pebble Beach Concours d'Elegance.

- 1:00 PM–5:30 PM
  Concours on Lighthouse Avenue
- 6:00 PM
  Rally begins
- 7:00 PM
  Barbecue dinner
- 8:00 PM
  Raffle & Awards Presentation

Contact Information

Pacific Grove Concours Auto Rally
Pacific Grove Youth Action, Inc.
P.O. Box 51453
Pacific Grove, California 93950

Phone: (831) 372-6585
Fax: (831) 372-8159
www.pgautorally.org
Email: *pgautorally@gmail.com*

Event Location:
Lighthouse Avenue in downtown Pacific Grove - staging at Forest Ave.

Château Julien - Dine in DiVine

For two evenings a year, guests have the rare opportunity to attend Château Julien Wine Estate's "Dine in DiVine." For this special occasion, the winery arranges the cars and cocktail party outside in a courtyard amongst their lush landscape and Sangiovese vines as guests indulge on hors d'oeuvres and their Chardonnay and Merlot wines while watching the sunset. The dinner that follows is inside their wine storage room, or chai (pronounced "shay"), with guests sitting under open-beam cathedral ceilings and surrounded by 1,000 oak barrels.

History

Started in 2009 and originally held outside amongst the vines, Château Julien moved their "Dine in DiVine" into their barrel room, or "chai," in 2012, thus turning a romantic, chilly night into a much warmer and happier experience. Be sure to arrive early to check out the cars on display.

Admission

- ▶ Club Members/Car Entrants $85
- ▶ Per Guest $95
- ▶ Per Guest - after July 31 $105

Schedule - Wednesday & Thursday

- ▶ 5:30 PM–6:30 PM
  Car viewing and cocktails
- ▶ 6:30 PM - Dinner in the Chai

Contact Information

Château Julien Wine Estate
8940 Carmel Valley Road
Carmel, CA 93923

Phone: (831) 624-2600
Fax: (831) 624-6138
www.chateaujulien.com
Email: *info@chateaujulien.com*

Directions

From **Monterey:**

- ▶ Head south on SR 1 (Highway 1)
- ▶ Left/east on Carmel Valley Rd.
- ▶ Follow road for 5.1 miles
- ▶ Just past Scheffer Rd., turn right into the entry for Château Julien

Opposite: dine inside their chai
Top Right: *Tesla at Château Julien*
Above Right: *Fisker featured in 2012*

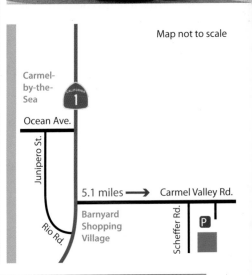

Map not to scale

Carmel-by-the-Sea

Ocean Ave.

Junipero St.

Rio Rd.

5.1 miles →   Carmel Valley Rd.

Barnyard Shopping Village

Scheffer Rd.

P

A Motorsports Gathering

The Quail, A Motorsports Gathering

Topping out at $450 per person, **The Quail, A Motorsports Gathering** is one of the most expensive events during the Monterey Car Week. What do people get for such a high price? Small crowds (limited to 3,000), outstanding cars, wine tasting, and a gourmet lunch. Anyone wishing to attend needs to purchase their tickets many months in advance as they do sell out each year. Each year also brings new featured marques and themes to the show. If price isn't an issue and you plan ahead, this is the place to be on Friday.

Directions

From **Monterey:**

- ▶ South on SR 1 (Highway 1)
- ▶ Left/east on Carmel Valley Road
- ▶ Travel two miles to the east
- ▶ Right/south on Rancho San Carlos Rd.

Above: *50th Anniversary of the Jaguar E-Type was celebrated in 2011*

Admission

- ▶ Advance tickets via lottery $550

Schedule - Friday

Held the Friday prior to the Pebble Beach Concours d'Elegance.

- ▶ 10:00 PM–4:00 PM

Contact Information

Peninsula Signature Events
8000 Valley Greens Drive
Carmel, CA 93923

Phone: (831) 620-8879
signatureevents.peninsula.com
Email: *thequail@quaillodge.com*

Event Location:
Quail Lodge & Golf Club
8000 Valley Greens Drive
Carmel, CA 93923

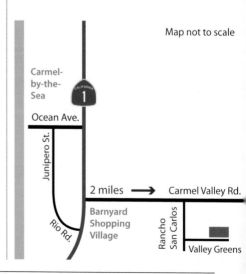

Map not to scale

Motorworks Revival

Gordon McCall's Motorworks Revival at the Monterey Jet Center

The evening revival was founded by Gordon McCall in 1992 as pioneers of the aircraft and automotive luxury lifestyle experience and have been producing their exclusive annual event for the past 22 years. Now bring in some VIPs, corporate sponsors, and some racing legends and you have an event unparalleled anywhere else in Monterey. While the ticket prices may seem high, proceeds from the event benefit the California Highway Patrol's 11-99 Foundation. The event draws roughly 3,000 people and covers roughly six acres of hangar and tarmac. Cocktail attire is the norm.

Admission

▶ Tickets $325

Schedule—Wednesday Evening

Held the Wednesday prior to the Pebble Beach Concours d'Elegance.

▶ 5:00 PM–10:00 PM - guests enjoy dinner and wine

Directions

From **Monterey:**

▶ Head north on SR 1 (Highway 1)
▶ Exit 401A
▶ Merge onto Mark Thomas Dr.
▶ Right/east on Garden Rd.
▶ Left/north on Skypark Dr.

Above: *A Boeing F/A-18F Super Hornet sits behind a Lamborghini Gallardo*

Contact Information

McCall Events, Inc.
395 Del Monte Center #330
Monterey, CA 93940
www.mccallevents.com
Email: *info@mccallevents.com*

Event Location:
Monterey Jet Center
300 Skypark Drive
Monterey, CA 93940

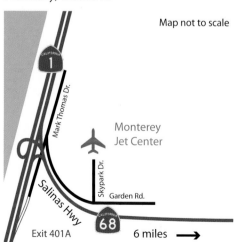

Map not to scale

Rolex Monterey Motorsports Reunion

With the support of the Pebble Beach Concours d'Elegance, the Monterey Historic Automobile Races were born in 1974. The vision of Steve Earle has since turned into the premier North American vintage race weekend. Where else can spectators see half a dozen Ferrari 250 GTOs rip past along a straightaway or see Porsche 917s tackle the famed Corkscrew? Each year brings a new theme and featured marque to the Monterey Peninsula and yet another reason for us all to return to see these legends in action.

History

In 1970, Steve Earle founded General Racing, Inc. (*www.generalracing.com*) *"to encourage the restoration, preservation and the use of historic sports and racing cars."* Once founded, he began to work on creating an event that *"would unite former racing greats with enthusiastic amateurs who owned some of the rare motorcars that once graced road courses worldwide."*

The Monterey Historic Automobile Races debuted in 1974 with a field of 66 cars and a handful of spectators. Back then, a spectator could buy a ticket to both the historic races and the Pebble Beach Concours d'Elegance for just $10! Because of both spectator and participant interest, the 1975 event was expanded to two days. 2009 saw the last event run by Steve Earle. The name change in 2010 to the **Rolex Monterey Motorsports Reunion** and it is now run exclusively by **SCRAMP** (Sports Car Racing Association of the Monterey Peninsula).

Directions

From **Monterey via CA 68 by car:**

- ▶ Take California Highway 1/ Cabrillo Highway north from Carmel or south from Seaside.
- ▶ Exit 401B onto SR 68/Salinas Highway east towards Salinas.
- ▶ Drive 7 miles on SR 68.
- ▶ Turn left/north on B Road and into the Laguna Seca Recreational area.
- ▶ See page 207 for more parking information.

Opposite: *1963 Ferrari 250 GTO chassis 4293GT tackles the exit of turn 4 at Mazda Raceway Laguna Seca.*

Today

Counting what is now known as the "Pre-Reunion" on the weekend preceding the Monterey Car Week, the event that was just a day now spans a total of seven. The Reunion proper begins with registration on the Wednesday, with Thursday and Friday consisting of practice and qualifying. Saturday and Sunday see 550 cars take to the track in 16 race groups. Each year since its inception has had a featured marque, and that tradition continues. 2013 celebrates the Chevrolet Corvette and, if tradition holds, 2014 should be Ferrari. SCRAMP is still producing the event.

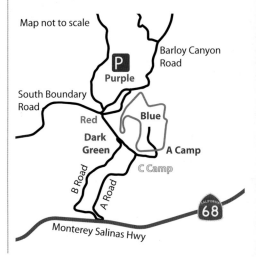

Map not to scale

Barloy Canyon Road

P Purple

South Boundary Road

Red

Blue

Dark Green

A Camp

C Camp

B Road

A Road

68

Monterey Salinas Hwy

Rolex Race Schedule

Saturday

▶ 1:00 - 1:20 Rolex Race 1A
Pre 1940s Sports Racing and Touring

▶ 1:25 - 1:45 Rolex Race 2A
1927-1951 Racing Cars

▶ 1:50 - 2:10 Rolex Race 3A
1955-1962 GT Cars

▶ 2:15 - 2:35 Rolex Race 4A
1960-1968 Sports Racing USRRC

▶ 2:40 - 3:00 Rolex Race 5A
1963-1966 GT over 2500cc

▶ 3:10 - 3:30 Rolex Race 6A
IMSA GT, GTX, AAGT, GTU, GTP

▶ 3:35 - 3:55 Rolex Race 7A
1955-1961 Sports Racing over 2000cc

▶ 4:00 - 4:20 Rolex Race 8A
1966-1972 Trans-Am

Sunday

▶ 1:00 - 1:20 Rolex Race 1B
1955-1961 Sports Racing under 2000cc

▶ 1:25 - 1:45 Rolex Race 2B
1958-1963 Formula Junior Cars

▶ 1:50 - 2:10 Rolex Race 3B
1966-1984 F1

▶ 2:15 - 2:35 Rolex Race 7B
1961-1966 GT Cars under 2500cc

▶ 2:45 - 3:05 Rolex Race 5B
1947-1955 Sports Racing & GT

▶ 3:10 - 3:30 Rolex Race 6B
81-89 FIA Champ & IMSA GTP/GTO

▶ 3:35 - 3:55 Rolex Race 4B
1970-1979 Sports Racing under 2000cc

▶ 4:00 - 4:20 Rolex Race 8B
Weissach Cup

▶ 4:45 Awards Ceremony

Photo Tips

There are many great spots for photos. The control tower looking down on the start/finish, the west-facing grandstands looking towards turn 4, and of course the hill looking down onto the Corkscrew. Bring a polarizing filter and a long lens —at least a 200mm. For good blur, shoot at 1/125 second and work down to 1/30 second as your panning skills improve.

Top Left: 1970 Porsche 908/3 #908-03004 leads the 1968 Porsche 908 #908-010 out of the Corkscrew.

Left: 1972 McLaren M20 #M20/2 owned by the National Automobile Museum in Reno on display at Mazda Raceway Laguna Seca.

Opposite: *A lone Ferrari 250 GTO passes under the pedestrian tire bridge.*

Quick Facts

- Nearly 1,000 requests are made for the 550 entries available
- In 1991, there was no featured marque, but rather a salute to Juan Manuel Fangio
- Television coverage by SPEED

Pre-Reunion

Saturday and Sunday prior to the Monterey weekend is the "Pre-Reunion." Open to the public and tickets only at the gate, there are discounts for ticket-holders for the Rolex Monterey Motorsports Reunion.

Parking Information

There are three points of entry into the track.

- Main Gate–Enter off of SR 68 and head north on A road.
- South Boundary–Best way to enter is to head north on York and east on South Boundary to the public purple parking lots.
- Watkins Gate–North on Reservation Road just to the west of Salinas. West at Barloy Canyon Road and follow road west to the public purple parking lots.

Tickets

3-Day Advance	$130
3-Day Gate	$150
2-Day Advance	$110
2-Day Gate	$130
Friday Advance	$50
Friday Gate	$70
Saturday Advance	$80
Saturday Gate	$100
Sunday Advance	$60
Sunday Gate	$80
Premier Pit Row Suite	$510
3-Day Flagroom	$375/$80 youth

Contact Information

Mazda Raceway Laguna Seca
1021 Monterey-Salinas Highway
Salinas, CA 93908

Tickets: (800) 327-7322
Office: (831) 242-8201
Fax: (831) 333-4700
www.mazdaraceway.com
Email address:
Tickets: *Tickets@MazdaRaceway.com*

Will Call for Tickets

Embassy Suites Hotel
1441 Canyon del Rey
Seaside, CA 93955
Phone: (831) 393-1115

Pebble Beach

Where to Begin

The Pebble Beach Concours d'Elegance was founded by enthusiasts in 1950 and remains the driving force behind todays event. For more information about Pebble Beach Resorts, visit *www.pebblebeach.com*.

Related Events

The Pebble Beach Concours d'Elegance is more than just the beautiful cars on the fairway of the 18th hole at the **Pebble Beach Golf Links**. It is a number of related events brought to you by the Pebble Beach Concours over the course of Pebble Beach Automotive Week.

Pebble Beach Motoring Classic

The ultimate road trip leaves from Seattle and covers 1,500 miles on the ten-day trek to Pebble Beach. A maximum of 30 collector cars are accepted. On the Wednesday prior to the Concours, the cars arrive in Pebble Beach and are on display in front of The Lodge at Pebble Beach for a few hours in the afternoon.

Pebble Beach Tour d'Elegance Presented by Rolex

See page 214 for more

Pebble Beach Auctions Presented by Gooding & Company

See page 160 for more

Opposite: 1930 Bentley Speed Six H.J. Mulliner Drophead Coupé of The Hon. Sir Michael Kadoorie. 2nd place in class.

Pebble Beach RetroAuto™

Stop by this exhibitor area in the days preceding the Concours.

- ▶ 10:00 AM–5:00 PM Friday and Saturday
- ▶ 8:00 AM–6:00 PM Concours Sunday

Automotive Fine Arts Society

The **AFAS** tent is located beside the Concours show field. Respected automotive artists exhibit their works. A ticket to the Concours is required to visit the tent. See *www.autoartgallery.com*.

Pebble Beach Concours d'Elegance

This is the Concours everyone is talking about when you simply hear someone say "Pebble Beach." Our coverage begins on page 218.

Related Companies

Pebble Beach Company Foundation

The primary charitable partner for funds raised at the Concours.

The Lodge at Pebble Beach

The lodge at Pebble Beach Resorts has hosted the Concours since 1950. Resort reservations may be reached at (800) 654-9300.

Pebble Beach Golf Links

The famed 543-yard, Par 5 18th hole is often referred to as "the greatest finishing hole in all of golf" and is open to the public 364 days a year.

A Brief History of the Pebble Beach Road Races

Founded in 1950 as an SCCA-sanctioned race, the first **Pebble Beach Road Race** featured four groups of race cars and drew almost 150 participants over the years. 20,000 to 30,000 spectators would line the course to get a glimpse of the everything from Aston Martins to OSCAs.

On April 22, 1956, during the **Del Monte Trophy Race** (reserved for the modified race cars over 1500cc), **Ernie McAfee** lost control of his Ferrari 121 LM near turn 6 and perished in the accident. Today visitors may (slowly) drive most of the original course. There have been some changes over the years to turns 4 & 6 and a portion of the track is now used for parking (between turns 3 & 4).

Top: *Lap one of the 1956 Modified over 1500cc Pebble Beach Road Race. Ernie McAfee (in the blue Ferrari 121 #0546LM) is in between the Austin-Healey of John Tanner and the Kurtis Kraft of Lou Brero.*

Quick Facts

▶ Phil Hill holds the lap record for the 2.1-mile course at 1:31

▶ The shorter 1.8-mile course was used in 1950. The course was lengthened to 2.1 miles in 1951

▶ Carroll Shelby won the 1956 race in Ferrari 750 Monza #0510M, Phil Hill was 2nd in Ferrari 860 Monza #0604M, Jack McAfee third in a Ferrari 857 S #0588M

Photos on Opposite Page

1   *Right-hand turn from Sombria Lane onto Drake Road*

2   *Looking west down Drake Road, spectators would see the cars racing towards them.*

3   *Ernie McAfee memorial on the west side of Forest Lake Road.*

4   *The finish line on Portola Road as it appears today.*

Photo #4, Far Right: *The 1955 Ferrari 410 SuperAmerica of John La Barbera & Lynn Gabriel heads to the finish line of the 2009 Pebble Beach Tour d'Elegance.*

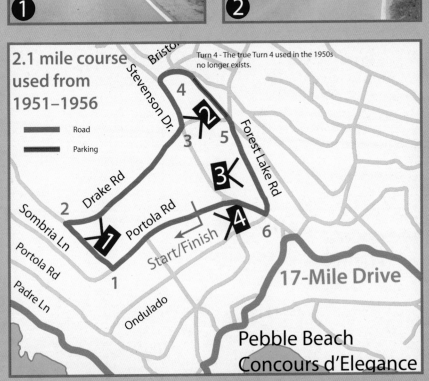

2.1 mile course used from 1951–1956

Turn 4 - The true Turn 4 used in the 1950s no longer exists.

Road

Parking

Bristol

Stevenson Dr.

Drake Rd

Sombria Ln

Portola Rd

Padre Ln

Portola Rd

Ondulado

Start/Finish

Forest Lake Rd

17-Mile Drive

Pebble Beach Concours d'Elegance

Ernie McAfee
1917-
1956

FINISH

Entering Pebble Beach

Getting into and out of the Pebble Beach Concours d'Elegance is straight-forward and easy if you plan ahead and follow a few tips. It is best to enter Pebble Beach via the **Pacific Grove** or **Highway 1** gates. The gate in Carmel is best for those with parking passes. As you enter Pebble Beach, show your ticket to the Concours as you pass the gate attendant.

Parking on the Coastline

Park in the lot to which the attendants are directing visitors. If you are tempted to get closer and find an empty parking spot in a closed lot, the Coastline buses ferrying spectators to the Concours will not stop to pick you up and will pass you by!

Arriving at the Concours

Shuttles are available from the Coastline Bus Stop to the Concours drop off point, but most people walk down to the show (it's the walk back that hurts). There is plenty to see on the way down through the corporate sponsors as well as Pebble Beach RetroAuto™ and the MidAmerica Motorcycle Auction.

Entry into the Concours

Visitors with tickets enter the Concours after walking past the concept cars and down the stairs. Remember to grab a copy of your Pebble Beach Program on your way in. Returning to your car is done the exact same way as you arrived, just walk back up the hill to the Coastline Bus stop.

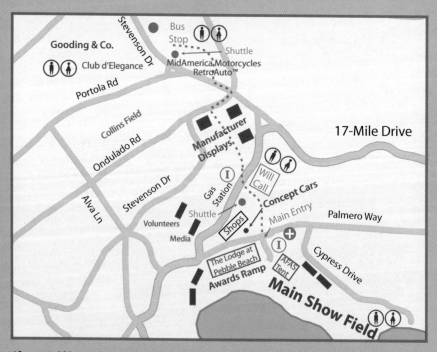

Above: *Pebble Beach Event Map*   **Opposite:** *Coastline Bus Stop*

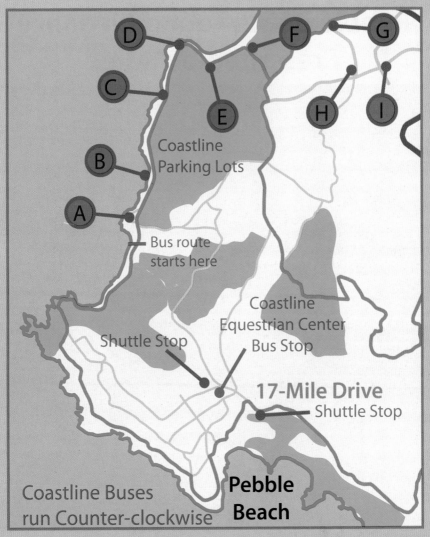

Coastline
Parking Lots

Bus route
starts here

Coastline
Equestrian Center
Bus Stop

Shuttle Stop

17-Mile Drive
Shuttle Stop

Coastline Buses
run Counter-clockwise

Pebble Beach

The first bus returning to the parking areas will leave the Coastline Bus Stop at 10:00 AM. The last bus returning to your designated parking area will leave the Coastline Bus Stop at 6:00 PM.

In addition to the parking inside Pebble Beach, there is now a shuttle service is available for $20 per person round trip leaving from the front of the Carmel Plaza on Ocean Avenue in Carmel. Service starts at 8:30 AM and ends at 6:00 PM.

Pebble Beach Tour d'Elegance Presented by Rolex

Getting up close to admire the beautiful automobiles at the Pebble Beach Concours d'Elegance is great, but what may be better is seeing these same great cars in action during the Pebble Beach Tour d'Elegance Presented by Rolex. This is an excellent opportunity for all automotive enthusiasts to watch and listen as these collector cars are driven around the Monterey Peninsula. For the entrant, it is a wonderful opportunity to drive their collector car and also a chance to split a tie when judged during the Pebble Beach Concours d'Elegance.

History

The Pebble Beach Tour d'Elegance was founded in 1998 as a complimentary event to the Pebble Beach Concours d'Elegance. It has given the Concours entrants a chance to create a "museum in motion" and drive their historic cars along Monterey's most scenic roads. Successful completion of the Tour is also used in the judging process during the Pebble Beach Concours d'Elegance.

Today

Held on the Thursday prior to the Concours, the Tour has become a favorite amongst both entrants and the 10,000 plus spectators, who line almost the entire 70-mile route (many of whom arrive hours in advance to see the cars). At the end of the Tour, each entrant is awarded a green ribbon which can be seen on Sunday on each entrant's windshield. Rolex has presented the Tour since its inception and continues their support to this day. The route changes from time to time, so please see page 217 and check for changes to the route when you arrive in Monterey.

Quick Facts

- In the event of a tie during the Pebble Beach Concours d'Elegance, the car that successfully completes the Pebble Beach Tour d'Elegance Presented by Rolex gets the win.
- Trip is 70 miles long.
- Over 150 historic vehicles took part in 2012.
- The Pebble Beach Tour d'Elegance is presented by Rolex.

Opposite: The 1925 Rolls-Royce Phantom I Barker Sports Torpedo Tourer of The Hon. Sir Michael Kadoorie, the 2012 winner of the Maharaja Rolls-Royce class, leads the 1934 Rolls-Royce Phantom II "Star of India" Thrupp & Maberly All Weather of Yuvraj Saheb Mandhatasinh Jadeja of Rajkot on Highway 1 heading to Big Sur.

Top: 1938 Packard 1601 Eight Graber Cabriolet of Paul E. Andrews Jr., the 2011 class winner of the American Classic Open enters downtown Carmel-by-the-Sea for lunch at Devendorf Park in Carmel.

Above: 1931 Alfa Romeo 6C 1750 Gran Sport Aprile Spider Corsa of Mercurio S.r.l., the 2012 second-place winner in the European Classic: Sports Racing class on Highway 1 returning from the turn around point at the Ripplewood Resort in Big Sur.

Photo Tips

I've used every lens from a 14mm to 300mm to capture photos, but a single 24mm–70mm zoom lens would work just fine. Most of the spots to see the cars are close to the road, negating the need for a telephoto. Using a slow shutter speed (around 1/30 to 1/60) may create desired blur, but will lose the scenic background, especially when facing the Pacific Ocean.

Schedule

▶ **7:00 AM–8:00 AM**
Cars line up near the Equestrian Center off Portola Road.

▶ **8:00 AM**
Tour departs in two groups for their 70-mile journey.

▶ **11:30 AM–Noon**
Tour arrives in Carmel taking a left from Junipero Street onto Ocean Avenue to park.

▶ **Noon–2:00 PM**
Cars displayed on Ocean Avenue.

▶ **2:00 PM–2:30 PM**
Tour returns to Pebble Beach.

▶ **3:00 PM**
Tour concludes and participants toast with champagne.

Above: *The 1938 Mercedes-Benz 540K Sports Tourer of William Parfet, 2011 third place winner in the Mercedes-Benz 380K through 770K class, slowly drives into downtown Carmel-by-the-Sea for their traditional lunch.*

Left: *1962 Ferrari 250 GTO of Scuderia DiBari, LLC draws large crowds during lunch in downtown Carmel-by-the-Sea. This Ferrari GTO won both the 2011 Ferrari 250 GTO class and the Most Elegant Sports Car Trophy.*

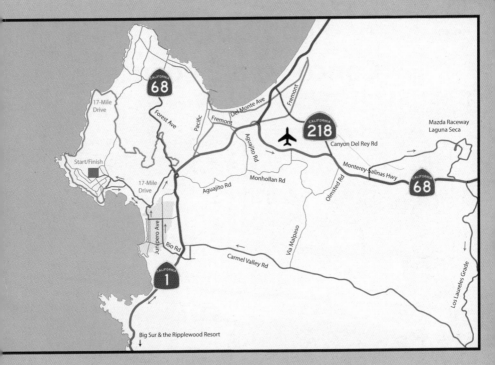

Viewing the Tour

Watching the Pebble Beach Tour d'Elegance is for many a lot more exciting than seeing the cars a few days later on the fairway of the 18th hole at Pebble Beach. For starters, you get to hear these cars as they roar by and often the owners at the wheel wear period clothes and eagerly wave to the crowd lining the streets. Here is how to get the most out of the experience.

The Tour leaves in two groups with each group escorted by California Highway Patrol on motorcycles. Each group is spaced several minutes apart and it is possible to see one group return from Big Sur as another group heads south. Whatever spot you choose, arrive at least an hour early, as traffic is unpredictable.

Four main sightseeing areas

▶ **17-Mile Drive & Carmel Valley**
In 2013, the cars will head east on SR 68 and run a lap on Mazda Raceway Laguna Seca. The Los Laureles Grade is a steep and scenic road.

▶ **Highway 1 to & from Big Sur**
Very popular place to see and hear the cars. Lots of places to park with scenic views. However, there is a lot of additional traffic with hard-to-reach viewing spots to look west.

▶ **Carmel-by-the-Sea**
Very crowded and very popular. Walk south along Junipero Avenue away from town for fewer people.

▶ **Portola Road - Start/Finish**
Great place to see the cars finish up. Plus a chance to stop by Gooding & Company afterwards. Remember to park legally no matter where you go!

Pebble Beach Concours d'Elegance

Who could have possibly imagined back in 1950 that the field of less than 30 automobiles and the handful of spectators would evolve into the best-known Concours d'Elegance in the world? Back then, the Pebble Beach Concours displayed cars fresh from the dealer showrooms, but today the Concours exhibits the very best pre-war and post-war classics. The cars on the 18th fairway of the Pebble Beach Golf Links are not only some of the rarest automobiles, but also some of the best preserved and most accurately restored cars anywhere.

History

On Sunday, November 5, 1950, the San Francisco Region of the SCCA sponsored four races to take to the local streets around Pebble Beach. The races kicked off at noon and weaved a 1.8-mile clockwise lap around the tree-lined streets. Phil Hill won both the 25-lap **Pebble Beach Cup** and the 12-lap **Monterey Unlimited Race Class** in his Jaguar XK120 #670138. For one dollar, visitors could watch the races and visit the Pebble Beach Concours d'Elegance down the road at the **Beach Club.** Fewer than 30 cars appeared that day. In April 1952, the Concours moved to the lawn next to the **Del Monte Lodge** (now named **The Lodge at Pebble Beach**). The tragic death of Ernie McAfee in 1956 moved the races to a newly built Laguna Seca in 1957, but the Pebble Beach Concours has continued ever since.

In 1974, the **Monterey Historic Automobile Races** (see page 204)
debuted at Laguna Seca, and spectators are offered discounted tickets for $10 for admission to both the Monterey Historic Automobile Races and the Pebble Beach Concours d'Elegance. In the ensuing decades, the Concours has gained international status as one of the most competitive shows and coveted awards.

Opposite: *Edward Herrmann and Jay Leno interview 102-year-old Margaret Dunning of Plymouth, Michigan about her 1930 Packard 740 Custom Eight Roadster as she receives the Classic Car Club of America Trophy - a special Pebble Beach Concours d'Elegance award*

Above: *Directional signs are hard to miss and help visitors navigate the event*

Today

The Pebble Beach Concours d'Elegance is firmly planted in the third Sunday in August. So set your calendars! Today the Pebble Beach Concours d'Elegance draws more than 200 entrants from roughly 30 states and a dozen countries. As of 2013, over 16 million dollars have been raised to benefit over 60 charities in the Monterey Peninsula. 2012 alone saw $1.25 million dollars raised.

Quick Stats

- ▶ Artists have created posters for each new Concours since 1950.
- ▶ With nine wins, Bugatti takes the lead with the most Concours "Best of Show" awards
- ▶ Since 1999, actor and personality Edward Herrmann has been the "Master of Ceremonies"
- ▶ 600 volunteers support the Concours
- ▶ 1,000-plus media professionals
- ▶ Collective experience of the Concours judges is over 1,500 years.

What to Wear

There is an informal dress code for attending the Concours. Men wear khaki pants and blue blazers and women wear hats, the more elegant the better. Call it "Resort Casual" or "Wealthy Casual." Of course visitors are allowed entry wearing cut-off jeans, but why do that? This is an elegant affair. Remember it is cold in the early morning and warm past noon, so layer your clothes.

Tips

- ▶ Visitors are allowed entry with blankets and small chairs
- ▶ There is food and drink available inside the Concours, albeit a limited menu.
- ▶ The earlier you arrive, the smaller the crowd, and the better the chance for unobstructed photos
- ▶ During the show, The Tap Room and the Gallery Restaurants are open to the public, as is the Pebble Beach Market.

Corporate Sponsors

Infiniti, as well as many others, are corporate sponsors of the Concours. They maintain pavilions on the **Peter Hay Golf Course** and host events over the preceding days ranging from "Ride & Drives" to tastings and receptions.

Concept Cars

As visitors walk to the Concours, roughly 20 concept cars will grace the putting green. Many North American and world debuts happen here, with each new year bringing a glimpse of cars to come.

Master of Ceremonies

Edward Herrmann has been the "Master of Ceremonies" since 1999. While most may know him as an Emmy and Tony Award-winning actor, some may also remember he won his class with his 1929 Auburn Boattail Speedster in the 2001 Concours d'Elegance.

The Judges

150 men and women volunteer for the rolls of Class and Honorary Judges. Many judges have decades of experience and a few judges have nearly 40 years of experience on the field. The collective experience of the judges on the field during the Sunday Concours is over 1,500 years. The Chief Judge of the Concours is Chris Bock.

Ribbons

Look for ribbons on the windshields of the entrants!

- ▶ Blue–First in Class
- ▶ Red–Second in Class
- ▶ White–Third in Class
- ▶ Green Ribbon–Completed Tour

Entry applications are due in January prior to the August show. Those interested should send an email to *entries@pebblebeachconcours.net*

Below: *The Pebble Beach Concours d'Elegance at 12 noon on Sunday*

Class Listing

The 2013 Class listing

A	Antique
B	Simplex
C	American Classics
D	Lincoln Custom Coachwork
E	Aston Martin Centennial
F	Vanvooren Coachwork
G	Duesenberg
H	Rolls-Royce
I	Mercedes-Benz
J	European Classics
L-1	Prewar Preservation
L-2	Postwar Preservation
M-1	Ferrari Grand Touring
M-2	Ferrari Competition
N	Lamborghini
O	Postwar Sports Racing + Touring
P	Porsche 911 through 1978
U	BMW 507
V-1	Prewar Open-Wheel Race Cars
V-2	Indianapolis Roadsters
X	French Motorcycles
Z	Alfa Romeo 8C Tour of Rockies

Best of Show Award

To be named Best of Show, entrants must first win their class. Then, using a simple tally of the independent and secret ballots cast by the Chairman, the Chief Judge, the Chief Honorary Judge, the Chief Class Judges, the Honorary Judge Team Leaders, and select Class Judges, a winner is selected. The Best of Show Award is a perpetual award that is maintained at The Lodge at Pebble Beach.

Class Awards

First, Second and Third in Class winners are selected by Class Judges based on originality, authenticity, and proper and excellent preservation or restoration.

Elegance & Special Awards
Generally selected by special committees of Honorary Judges.

Elegance Awards

For styling, design and presentation. There are four Elegance Awards.

J.B. & Dorothy Nethercutt
Most Elegant Closed Car
Most elegant closed car. The Nethercutts won the top award, Best of Show, a record-setting six times.

Gwenn Graham
Most Elegant Convertible
Gwenn Graham was involved in founding the Pebble Beach Concours d'Elegance.

Most Elegant Open Car
Awarded to the most elegant open car. An open car has no windows, though it may have side curtains, as compared to a convertible, which generally has roll-up windows.

Strother MacMinn
Most Elegant Sports Car
Awarded to the most elegant sports car present. MacMinn was a respected automotive designer, instructor, and historian who served for years as Chief Honorary Judge of this Concours.

Special Awards

Alec Ulmann Trophy
Most exciting Hispano-Suiza present.

Ansel Adams Award
Most desirable touring car of its era. The renowned photographer was a Honorary Judge at this Concours.

Art Center College
of Design Award
Best use of new technology in its era that is considered to have had the greatest impact on car design today.

Briggs Cunningham Trophy
Most exciting open car present.

Chairman's Trophy
Most deserving car present as selected by the Chairman.

Charles A. Chayne Trophy
Most advanced engineering of its era.

Opposite: Pebble Beach Concours d'Elegance Best of Show Trophy

Classic Car Club of America Trophy
Most significant classic car present.

Dean Batchelor Trophy
Most significant hot rod, when hot rods are on the show field.

Elegance in Motion Trophy
To qualify for this award, a car must have successfully completed the Pebble Beach Tour d'Elegance.

Enzo Ferrari Trophy
Best Ferrari present.

FIVA Trophy
Best preserved and regularly driven prewar and postwar cars.

The French Cup
Most significant car of French origin.

Gran Turismo Trophy
Balances both artistic beauty and performance at the highest level.

Lincoln Trophy
The most significant Lincoln present.

Lorin Tryon Trophy
Recognizes an automotive enthusiast who has contributed significantly to the Pebble Beach Concours d'Elegance.

Lucius Beebe Trophy
The Rolls-Royce considered most in the tradition of Lucius Beebe, an early judge at the Concours.

Mercedes-Benz Star of Excellence Award
Most significant Mercedes-Benz.

Mille Miglia Trophy
Most significant car eligible to participate in the Mille Miglia.

Montagu of Beaulieu Trophy
Most significant British car.

The Phil Hill Cup
Awarded to a significant race car. Phil Hill (1961 Formula 1 Champion) won the Pebble Beach Road Races in 1950, 1953, and 1955 and the Pebble Beach Concours d'Elegance on multiple occasions.

Revs Program at Stanford Trophy
Most historically significant automobile.

Road & Track Trophy
Awarded to the car that the editors of that magazine would most like to drive.

Tony Hulman Trophy
Most significant open-wheel race car present. Hulman owned the Indianapolis Motor Speedway for decades.

The Vitessen Elegance Trophy
Recognizes the car that best embodies both excellence in performance and elegance in design.

Tickets

General Admission tickets include admission, parking, coastline bus transfers, and a copy of the Event Program. Children under the age of 12 years are admitted free of charge.

Per Person   **$225/$275 (day of)**

Club d'Elegance tickets include a VIP Patron Badge (your admission to the Concours), VIP parking (one per group), and shuttle service from Club tent at Equestrian Center to and from show field.

In addition, Club d'Elegance ticket holders receive a copy of the Event Program, a Concours Poster signed by the poster artist, and a Special Commemorative Gift (a dash plaque like the one provided to each Concours entry). There is also a full buffet breakfast served from 9:00 AM to 11:00 AM and an elegant buffet lunch from 11:00 AM to 2:00 PM. Plus there is wine, a cash bar, executive restrooms, and a coat and package check (no need to carry the Concours program with you!). Club d'Elegance is held at the Equestrian Center next to the Gooding & Company auction.

Per Person   **$600 (advance only)**

Top: *The windshield of the 1923 Bugatti Type 23 Brescia Lavocat Marsaud of Giuseppe Redaelli, Varese, Italy. The car sports a green ribbon for participating in the Tour d'Elegance and the blue ribbon for the 2011 Chairman's Trophy.*

Middle: *Period Bentley overalls*

Left: *1928 Mercedes-Benz 680S Saoutchik Torpedo of Berthold Albrecht, Essen, Germany and recipient of the 2012 Mercedes-Benz Star of Excellence Award.*

Schedule

- 7:00 AM - Lawn opens to Entrants, VIPs, Judges, & Media
- 8:30 AM - Judging commences
- 10:30 AM
  Field opens to spectators
- 1:30 PM – 5:00 PM
  Awards are presented on stage

Contact Information

Pebble Beach Concours d'Elegance
200 Clock Tower Place, Suite 205A
Carmel, CA 93923

Mailing Address:
PO Box 222860
Carmel, CA 93922

Phone: (831) 622-1700
Fax: (831) 622-9100
Email: *info@pebblebeachconcours.net*

Concours Tickets
Call (877) 693-0009 or online at
tickets.theconcoursstore.com

- General admission & U.S. Club d'Elegance tickets mailed in July.
- International Club d'Elegance tickets at Will Call.

Future dates

- 2013 – Sunday, August 18
- 2014 – Sunday, August 17
- 2015 – Sunday, August 16
- 2016 – Sunday, August 21
- 2017 – Sunday, August 20

Top: *The Ferrari 250 GTO/64 of Gregory Whitten, Bellevue, Washington, sits in the foreground of additional Ferrari 250 GTOs.*

Right: *2012 Concept Cars—Rolls-Royce Phantom Coupé Aviator Collection sits in front of the Lamborghini Urus.*

Goodguys Hot Rod Week & West Coast Nationals

Goodguys is well known in the hot rod and custom car world as the premier event promoter, holding dozens of events across the country ranging from "cruise-Ins" to swap meets to AutoCross. Of all these events, there is but one held in their own backyard. Call it a hometown event if you will. The "West Coast Nationals" is a full-week extravaganza usually starting on the Monday after the Monterey Car Week, drawing entrants and spectators from around the country to shop, show off, and have a good time.

Goodguys West Coast Nationals

Started in 1987, The Goodguys West Coast Nationals Presented By Flowmaster now draws over 3,500 hot rods, customs, classics, muscle cars, and trucks. Attendance at the Alameda Fairgrounds in Pleasanton hits 70,000 spectators.

The week starts out with the annual Goodguys Hot Rod Week, a four day cruise around the San Francisco Bay to visit area shops and businesses, followed by the Thursday Kick Off Party at the Pleasanton Hilton.

Friday Night is their Hot Rod Bash & Dance Party and Saturday Night's Party & Dance follows with the crowning of America's Most Beautiful Street Road Award, all at the Pleasanton Hilton.

Spectators at the Fairgrounds will enjoy their Swap Meet, Mini-Engine Display, Model & Pedal Car Show, Indoor Cushman Display, Pinstripers Brush Bash & Auction, Goodgals Arts & Crafts Gallery, Tether Car Races, Nitro Thunderfest, and More!

Location

Hilton Pleasanton at the Club
7050 Johnson Drive
Pleasanton, CA 94588
Phone: (925) 463-8000
www.hilton.com

Alameda County Fairgrounds
4501 Pleasanton Avenue
Pleasanton, CA 94566
Phone: (925) 426-7600
www.alamedacountyfair.com

Contact Information

Goodguys Rod & Custom Assoc.
Phone: (925) 838-9876
www.good-guys.com

Schedule

2013 Hot Rod Week
August 19 to August 22

2013 West Coast Nationals
August 23 to August 25

- ▶ Friday, 8:00 AM–5:00 PM
- ▶ Saturday, 8:00 AM–5:00 PM
- ▶ Sunday, 8:00 AM–3:00 PM

Vehicle Event Registration

Preregistration closes 2 weeks prior

▶ Goodguys Silver Member	$20
▶ Goodguys Gold Member	$35
▶ 3-Day "Show & Shine" price for Preregistration Member	$45

Spectator Admission & Pricing

▶ General Admission	$18
▶ Kids (ages 7–12)	$6
▶ Kids (ages 6 & under)	FREE
▶ Parking	$8

Opposite & Above: *Hot rods at sunset at the Hilton Hotel in Pleasanton, CA*

Goodguys' Hot Rod Week

Hot Rod Week

Usually held on the first Monday after the Monterey Car Week, the Goodguys Hot Rod Week is a four-day romp around the San Francisco Bay and Sacramento to see hot rod shops, museums, and private collections. The locations visited change year to year, but popular spots are revisited every few years.

Know Before You Go

Check *www.good-guys.com* for the exact dates and just show up in the back parking lot of the Hilton in Pleasanton at 8:00 AM. There is no need to sign up in advance and no fee is required when participating. Many of the popular destinations featured in their Hot Rod Week appear here over the next several pages.

Andy's Tee-Shirts
1960 Arnold Industrial Place
Concord, California
94520-5318
Phone: (925) 825-8911
www.andystees.com

Campbell Automotive Restoration
260 Cristich Lane, #A1
Campbell, CA 95008-5416
Phone: (408) 371-5522
www.campbellautorestoration.com

CTR Motors
950 N. Canyon Parkway
Livermore, CA 94551
Toll Free: (866) 252-7486
www.ctrmotors.com

Dominator Street Rods
4130 Commercial Drive
Tracy, CA 95304
Phone: (209) 830-4314
www.dominatorusa.com

Gambino Kustoms
645 Horning Street Unit #N
San Jose, CA 95112
Phone: (408) 561-5744
www.gambinokustoms.com

A full-service hot rod shop offering
custom bodywork, chassis fabrication,
sheet metal fabrication, and more.

Goodies Speed Shop
527 Charcot Avenue, Suite 331
San Jose, CA 95131
Phone: (408) 295-0930
Toll Free: (800) 994-0930
www.goodies-speedshop.com

Parts and service for everything
from basic maintenance to racetrack
preparation.

East Bay Muscle Car Facility
560 Valdry Court, Unit B4
Brentwood, CA 94513
Phone: (925) 516-2277
www.eastbaymusclecars.com

Hall Fabrications and Racing
5418 Gateway Plaza Drive
Benicia, California 94510
Phone: (707) 747-1289
www.hallfabracing.com

Hot Rod Bill's Street Rod Shop
648 Fairfax Drive
Oakdale, CA 95361
Phone: (209) 847-4803
www.hotrodbills.com

Hot Rod Plus
21801 Plummer Street
Chatsworth, CA 91311
Phone: (818) 341-6598
www.hotrodsplus.com

Hot Rod Service Company
1090 Florence Way
Campbell, CA 95008
Phone: (408) 529-5944
www.hotrodservice.com

Lazze Metal Dreams
1051 Serpentine Lane, Suite #500
Pleasanton, CA 94566
Phone: (925) 461-2961
www.lazzemetalshaping.com

Moal's Auto Metal Works
937 E. 12th Street
Oakland, CA 94606
Phone: (510) 834-9066
www.moal.com

Monterey Speed & Sport
Don Orosco
10 Harris Court, Suite B-1
Monterey, CA 93940
Phone: (831) 649-0890
www.montereyspeedandsport.com

Mustangs Plus
2353 N Wilson Way
Stockton, CA 95205
Phone: (209) 944-9977
www.mustangsplus.com

Pacific Coast Customs
5757 Napa-Vallejo, Hwy. 29
American Canyon, CA 94503
Phone: (707) 224-4011
www.pacificcoastcustoms.com

Roy Brizio Street Rods
505 Railroad Avenue
South San Francisco, CA 94080
Phone: (650) 952-7637
www.roybriziostreetrods.com

For more than 20 years, Roy Brizio has constructed some of the best hot rods in the industry. His client list includes celebrities such as Eric Clapton and Reggie Jackson. His shop has built more than 300 turn-key hot rods using a simple philosophy of "quality first." In 2013, his 1927 Ford Track T Roadster was voted "America's Most Beautiful Roadster".

Sanderson Headers
517 Railroad Avenue
South San Francisco, CA 94080
Phone: (650) 583-6617
www.sandersonheaders.com

Next door to Roy Brizio Street Rods is Sanderson Headers. Since 1964 they have been manufacturing and installing headers and complete exhausts for both hot rods and trucks. Their products fit primarily cars and trucks by Chevrolet, GMC, and Ford, and their specialty headers fit most custom-bodied hot rods. They also offer gaskets and bolts.

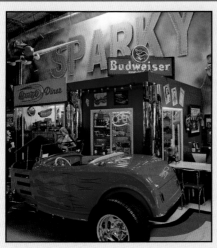

Sparky's Hot Rod Garage
975 Industrial Road, Suite A
San Carlos, CA 94070
Phone: (650) 400-5810
Email: *Sparky@SparkysHotRodGarage.com*
www.sparkyshotrodgarage.com

Joe "Sparky" Bullock has opened up his private garage and collection for both tours, events, and parties. The key word here at Sparkys is "party." It doesn't matter if you want to hold a children's birthday party, car club meeting, rock concert, or watch professional ballroom dancers, Sparky can accommodate!

Rootlieb Vintage Auto Sheet Metal
815 Soderquist Road
Turlock, CA 95380
Phone: (209) 632-2203
www.rootlieb.com

Revolution Rod & Custom
3737 1st Street
Livermore, CA 94551
(925) 447-7637

Street Rods Plus
400 N. Cluff Avenue
Lodi, CA 95240
Phone: (209) 334-0617

Top of the Hill Performance Center
410 Longfellow Court
Livermore, CA 94550
Phone: (925) 449-3330
www.topofthehillpc.com

Vern Tardell's "Flathead Ranch"
464 Pleasant Avenue
Santa Rosa, CA 95403
Email: sales@verntardel.com
www.verntardel.com

Speed Nymph Garage
1325 Old Bayshore Highway, Suite 10
San Jose, CA 95112
Phone: (408) 289-1750
www.speednymph.com

The Speed Nymph Garage is the private collection of Dennis "Captain Fun" Varni. Dennis is a veteran of the Bonneville Salt Flats and set a record in 2011 with a 330.874 mph run and again in 2012 with a 334.260 mph run both in his Joe Casanova-built Bonneville 909 Streamliner E/BGS. The Speed Nymph Garage is closed to the public, but occasionally opens its doors to the Goodguys Hot Rod Week and others. Contact the Speed Nymph Garage for dates.

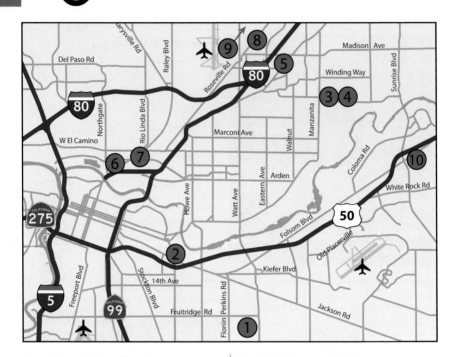

1 Alston's Chassisworks
8661 Younger Creek Dr.
Sacramento, CA 95828
Phone: (916) 388-0288
www.cachassisworks.com
Chassis for Hot Rods

3 R/C Country Hobbies
6011 Folsom Blvd.
Sacramento, CA 95819
Phone: (916) 731-5868
www.rccountryhobbies.com
Diecast collectibles & toys

3 American Pastimes Hot Rod Shop
7637 Fair Oaks Blvd.
Carmichael, CA 95608
Phone: (916) 944-6600
www.americanpastimes.com
Parts, engines, exhausts

4 Rods R Us
7637 Fair Oaks Blvd.
Carmichael, CA 95608
Phone: (916) 830-0038
www.rodsrusonline.com
Full-service shop & builds

6 Sherm's Custom Plating
2140 Acoma Street
Sacramento, CA 95815
Email: *kelly@shermsplating.com*
www.shermsplating.com
Custom plating bumpers & more

5 Blue Collar Customs
4824 Amber Lane
Sacramento, CA 95841
Phone: (916) 338-4327
www.bluecollarcustoms.com
A full-service hot rod shop

8 The Gearhead Garage
5780 Roseville Road, Suite B
Sacramento, CA 95842
Phone: (916) 481-3040
www.gearheadcars.com
Restoration & maintenance

7 So-Cal Speed Shop Sacramento
1715 Del Paso Blvd.
Sacramento, CA 95815
Phone: (916) 924-9744
www.socalsac.com
Founded in 1946 in Burbank by Alex
Xydias. Today sells cars and clothes.

10 Sacramento Vintage Ford
2484 Mercantile Drive
Rancho Cordova, CA 95742
Phone: (916) 853-2244
Toll Free: (888) 367-3100
www.vintageford.com
Mail order parts, retail store,
1950s diner, and showroom

9 Roseville Rod & Custom
9600 Antelope Oaks Court, Unit B
Roseville, CA 95747
Phone: (916) 784-3931
www.rosevillerodandcustom.com
Custom hot rod shop

Canepa

Call it what you will, a state-of-the-art restoration facility or a race car preparation center, there is nothing else in Northern California that holds a candle to Canepa. Tucked away in the unassuming town of Scotts Valley, Canepa is a 70,000 sq ft display of the very best work that can be done to restore, rebuild, modify, race prepare, or even federalize a vehicle. We say "vehicle" and not "sports car," because Canepa also builds some of the very best race transport trucks seen in pit rows and paddocks across the country.

Via Corsa Car Lover's Guide to Northern California

History

Bruce Canepa founded Canepa over 30 years ago and it has become a leader in engineering, product design, engineering, restoration, and race preparation. He is particularly well known for his federalization of the venerable Porsche 959 supercar.

Today

Canepa is a multi-faceted automotive organization that includes Canepa Design and Canepa Motorsports. Canepa provides exceptional automobiles to collectors worldwide, as well as performing Pebble Beach level restorations on historically important vehicles. Canepa is renown for expertly combining sophisticated design and superb craftsmanship in creating personalized sports cars, hot rods, SUVs, and motorcycles; as well as concept, prototype, and production vehicles. Canepa Motorsport is the racing arm of Canepa, and is a recognized leader in vintage racecar restoration, preparation, and support.

Directions

From **San Francisco:**

- ▶ South on US 101
- ▶ West on SR 85 direction Santa Cruz
- ▶ Exit 11A and merge onto SR 17 south direction Santa Cruz.
- ▶ Drive a winding 16.6 miles until Scotts Valley.
- ▶ Exit 5 onto Granite Creek Road/ Scotts Valley Drive and head south.
- ▶ Canepa is roughly ½ mile on the left side of the road.

Opposite: *Porsche 959s are imported and serviced at Canepa.*

Porsche 959

Since being part of team that created the "Show and Display" legislation to bring cars like these to the US, Canepa has developed the technology to not only make this supercar street legal, but has worked with Porsche AG to continue their technological development. The Canepa Stage 2 conversion brings the horsepower up to 610 and while being California smog legal.

Quick Facts

- ▶ 70,000 sq ft facility
- ▶ Bruce Canepa is often spotted driving at the Rolex Monterey Motorsports Reunion.

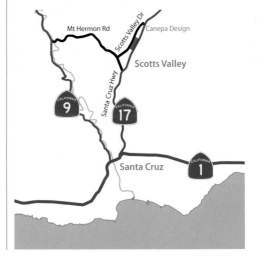

Contact Information

Canepa
4900 Scotts Valley Drive
Scotts Valley, CA
Phone: (831) 430-9940
Fax: (831) 430-9941
www.canepa.com

Top: *Porsche 959 in for service*
Above: *State of the art restoration shop*

Tours

Group tours are available and must be booked in advance. Tours of the facility are also available during their annual open house held in conjunction with the Monterey Car Week. Their website updates with weekly "Canepa Shop Walk" videos to highlight the latest happenings.

Awards

Canepa has earned seven first-place awards over the years

▶ 1955 Mercedes-Benz 300SL Gullwing—Hillsborough Concours
▶ 1962 Mercedes-Benz 300SL Roadster—Palo Alto Concours
▶ 1967 Cobra 427 Beverly Hills Concours
▶ 1969 Porsche 917-K—Marin Sonoma Concours d'Elegance
▶ 1970 Lola T70 Mk3B Can Am Hillsborough Concours
▶ 1972 Porsche 917-10 Class win at Pebble Beach Concours d'Elegance in 2009
▶ 1983 Lancia LC2 Prototype San Francisco Presidio Concours

Cars & Coffee

New this year is the Canepa Cars & Coffee. Join Canepa from 8:00 AM to 12:00 PM on the second Saturday of the month from April through October.

Open House

The annual Canepa Open House is held Monday either prior to or after the Monterey Car Week. Please check with Canepa for exact times.

Bruce Canepa

Bruce Canepa was born and raised in Santa Cruz. As a youngster, he worked in the family dealership learning mechanical, fabrication, body and paint. By the age of 12, his father had taught him to drive everything from a Ford Model A to a truck.

In 1978, he started racing professionally in IMSA and Trans-Am and placed 3rd overall in the 1979 annual "24 Hours of Daytona" co-driving a Porsche 935. He has been awarded the title "Rookie of the Year" and "Most Improved Driver" in three different race categories.

Canepa Motorsports Museum

On the second floor of Canepa is the Canepa Motorsports Museum. It is open to the public and free to enter. The cars on display are part of Bruce Canepa's personal collection, and each car has been chosen for its unique contribution to the history of the sport. Visitors will see Can-Am, NASCAR, Sprint Cars, and Le Mans race cars.

According to Bruce Canepa, his museum is "Dedicated to the spirit of automotive competition, and the celebration of engineering excellence."

Top: Canepa Motorsports Museum

Middle Top: 1969 Porsche 917-015 is frequently seen at various historic races around the country.

Middle Lower: 1961 Estes Sprinter and winner of the 1964 USAC National Championship.

Right: 1975 Porsche 917-10 - 017. The Porsche placed third in the 1975 German Interserie Championship.

Death Valley

Death Valley is the hottest, driest, and lowest place in North America. It is also one of the most beautiful. While there is no denying that this is the land of extremes, its beauty and landscape have been showcased in popular media in everything from blockbuster movies to car magazines. As many already know, Death Valley National Park is an unofficial testing ground for car manufacturers testing new models against these harsh environments. But don't go there to spy a new car, go there for the beauty.

Elevations

Lowest Point—Badwater Basin is 282 feet below sea level.

Highest Paved Road—Dante's View at 5,475 ft (movie location for the first viewing of Mos Eisley in 1977 blockbuster *Star Wars IV: A New Hope*).

Highest Point—Telescope Peak at 11,049 feet is located in the Paramint Mountain range to the west of Badwater.

Temperatures

The highest recorded temperature of 134° F was in July 1913 and the highest ground temperature of 201° F was recorded in July 1972 at Furnace Creek. But what makes it so hot and dry? First off, Death Valley National Park is a long, narrow basin surrounded by high mountain ranges. The air pressure from the low elevation and steep mountains trap the heat, and an effect known as "rainshadow" keeps Death Valley dry.

Hazards

The extreme heat is just one of many hazards in Death Valley. There are hundreds of open mines, flash floods, and all sorts of dangerous creatures. In summertime, plan on drinking at least one gallon of water per day and bring several days of extra food and water in case of trouble.

Opposite: Heat shimmering off a Death Valley road in summertime.

Above Right: A caution sign near Stove Pipe Wells offers visitors to the sand dunes a very real warning about the dangers of heat.

Right: Typical desert playa!

Roads

There are roughly 230 miles of paved roads and 1,500 miles of dirt roads.

Entrance Fees

7-day pass - 1 vehicle	$20
Annual pass	$40

Contact Information

Furnace Creek Visitors Center
Phone: (760) 786-3200
www.nps.gov/deva

For places to stay, see "Death Valley" on page 276

Popular Sites

Furnace Creek Area—The lowest point in North America is 200 square miles of salt flats known as **Badwater Basin** (at 282 feet below sea level). The **Harmony Borax Works** is a 19th-century plant that popularized the use of mule teams. **Dante's View** is a popular place for a scenic view, and **Zabriskie Point** (also a popular 1970s cult movie of the same name) is a popular place to see and photograph sunrises and sunsets.

Racetrack Playa— One of the more fascinating sites is the "**Racetrack.**" This dry lake bed or basin is where rocks mysteriously slide in near linear or wandering paths, leaving long tracks behind them. No one has seen these rocks move and there are a number of theories as to how and why they move. Visiting the Racetrack is not easy, and a four-wheel drive vehicle is recommended.

Scotty's Castle—Tour the 1920s Spanish mansion made famous by Walter "Death Valley Scotty" Scott and hear stories about his claims to have discovered a fictitious gold mine of fabulous wealth! It is important to note that there is no gasoline at Scotty's Castle, but snacks and drinks are available. There are house tours and underground tours, with house tours led by National Park Service Interpreters dressed in period clothes from 1939. To book a tour in advance (recommended) call (877) 444-6777 or visit *www.recreation.gov*. Prices start at $15 for adults.

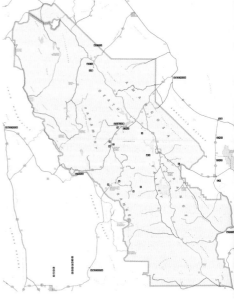

Above Left: *A Volvo press car on the two-wheel drive "20 Mule-Team Trail".*

Bottom Left: *A paved road during a dust storm, near Stove Pipe Wells.*

Chat with Brenda Priddy

In summer, Death Valley National Park becomes a hotbed (excuse the pun) of activity for car manufacturers wishing to test secret new product in the harshest environment possible, which, of course, attracts the automobile "spy" photographer. There is none better than Brenda Priddy, who chatted with us about her adventures in Death Valley. For more information, see *www.brendapriddy.com*.

VIA CORSA: Why do manufacturers love to test in Death Valley?

BRENDA PRIDDY: A couple of reasons. One is the extreme heat and the other is because of the extreme elevation changes.

VC: Now we know it's hot there, but what kind of temperature changes do you see?

BP: The official temperatures are taken at Furnace Creek at probably 120 °F or 122 °F, and I've recorded it well over 130 °F in the shade.

VC: Can you give me an idea of what it is like to spend time in that?

BP: Well, it is not necessarily bad on a normal day. If there is a breeze or a strong wind, it truly feels like there is a furnace blowing at you, and you can hardly breathe. If there is no wind, you can almost tolerate it. Oh, and if you get too much sun and get a sunburn, any sun touching you can be agonizing.

VC: So obviously summer is the season to test the cars, but it's also the worst season for tourists to visit Death Valley.

BP: Yes, there are a lot of hazards for tourists in the summer. Unfortunately, it seems that every year, tourists go climbing sand dunes and they don't bring enough water in the heat of the day and they don't realize how hot it really is.

VC: So being a seasoned traveler there, what do you recommend people do in case they are tempted to visit in the summer?

BP: Well it is very easy to get heat exhaustion or heat stroke in a climate like that so the main thing is to have a lot of water with you. Be hydrated before you go and stay hydrated the entire time, even if you don't feel thirsty, as in a dry climate you don't sweat a lot, so it can really catch you off guard. Let people know where you are going to be. Make sure your tank is full of gas before you head out. And don't try to do the hikes you read about in the books, as those are not meant for the summer. And even some of the off-road excursions that you might be tempted to do are not recommended for summer because if you have a breakdown, the roads are not heavily traveled.

VC: What are some of the rewards of working in Death Valley?

BP: It is a beautiful place! There is almost every color in the rocks that you can imagine. There is a place called Scotty's Castle that has some wonderful tours. It is a beautiful place to drive through or for hiking. There is a lot of wildlife. The place has coyotes, bobcats, and snakes, so you do have to be a little careful. If you are driving through, there is so much to look at, so if the kids are in the back seat and have the DVD player on, turn it off. Have them look out the window.

VC: So if you are not photographing cars in Death Valley, what else do you like to photograph?

BP: The landscape is amazing and there are some ghost towns. But mostly it is the landscape and Scotty's Castle. That is a photographer's dream! You want to give yourself at least one full day in the park. You won't see everything but you'll be able to see the basics!

Fantasy Junction

About Fantasy Junction

Since 1976, Bruce Trenery has offered "Blue-Chip" collector cars to the public. It is not uncommon for visitors to see around 50 cars available for purchase at any given time. Their focus is on classic cars and not the new, straight-off-the-dealership showroom kind of cars. They are open to the public from 9:30 AM to 5:30 PM six days a week.

Directions

From **San Francisco:**

▶ Head east on I-80.
▶ Merge onto I-580 direction Hayward.
▶ Exit immediately to MacArthur Blvd. towards San Pablo Avenue
▶ Left onto Peralta/Emory Street
▶ Fantasy Junction is on your right.

Above: *Fantasy Junction showroom*

Contact Information

Fantasy Junction
1145 Park Avenue
Emeryville, CA 94608
Phone: (510) 653-7555
www.fantasyjunction.com

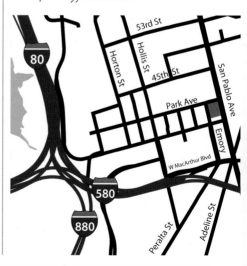

My Hot Cars

About My Hot Cars

Originally opened in 1989 as Kassabian Motors, owner Brad Kassabian has since renamed it to My Hot Cars and moved to Livermore. Their focus is on American Muscle.

Hours

- ▶ Mon.–Fri.   10:00 AM–7:00 PM
- ▶ Saturday   10:00 AM–6:00 PM
- ▶ Sunday   10:00 AM–5:00 PM

Directions

From **San Francisco:**
- ▶ Head east on I-580.
- ▶ Take Exit 50 in Livermore.
- ▶ Head straight through the intersection and pass Airport Blvd.
- ▶ Dealership is on your right.

Above: *Muscle for sale at My Hot Cars*

Contact Information

My Hot Cars, Inc.
2476 Nissen Drive
Livermore, CA 94551
Phone: (925) 292-0922
www.myhotcars.com

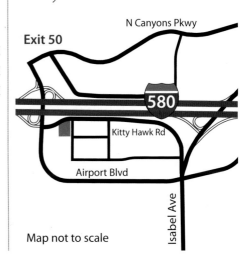

Reiff's Gas Station

I normally don't like surprises during photo shoots but when someone says to me after I thank them and am walking out their door, "Ya know, I think you should check this other place out too," I have to stop and say, "Tell me more!" Reiff's Garage was more than just a surprise, it was an absolute delight. It is really great to see what one man's passion for his hobby, as well as a pretty good imagination, can create. Mark Reiff took seven years to build his station in this quiet residential neighborhood and has shared it with over 10,000 people since.

Via Corsa Car Lover's Guide to Northern California

About Reiff's Gas Station & Museum

Woodland native Mark Reiff bought his first antique gas pump in 1999, and the rest is as they say, history. Today, Mark's entire house resembles a 1950s gas station and diner on the outside and is an automotive museum now hosting dozens of antique gas pumps (and much, much more) on the inside. Mark welcomes visitors to stop by and check out his place. Fill up beforehand, as his gas station pumps are for show only.

Tours & Events

Museum tours are by appointment and Mark requests a $7 per person donation. He also hosts an annual "Street Bash Vintage and Custom Car Show" on the 2nd Saturday in June.

Contact Information

Reiff's Gas Station Museum
52 Jefferson Street
Woodland, CA 95695
Phone: (530) 666-1758
www.reiffsgasstation.com
Email: *mark@reiffsgasstation.com*

Directions

From **San Francisco:**

▶ Head north on I-80 direction Sacramento.
▶ North on SR 113 direction Woodland
▶ Exit 36 onto Gibson Road.
▶ West on Gibson Road for 1.8 miles.
▶ Right/north on West Street.
▶ Right/east on Jefferson Street.
▶ Gas Station is on your right.

Opposite: *Mark's 1956 Chevy Tow Truck*
Above: *A 1956 Oldsmobile, a faux railroad crossing, and a crashed plane.*

Movie Locations

Notable Movies

Long before the movie **Bullitt** set the standard for the epic car chase, the roads and hills of San Francisco have been a popular place to feature cars on film. The website *www.imdb.com* shows over 4,000 titles having been filmed in the San Francisco area, but here are the automotive highlights.

A Jitney Elopement (1915)
This silent movie with Charlie Chaplin features a brief drive.

The Lineup (1958)
A 1957 Plymouth is chased by police in this largely unknown film through the Presidio and Golden Gate Bridge Park.

Vertigo (1958)
No chase, but lots of scenic drives and highlights of landmarks.

The Love Bug (1968)
Herbie heads down Lombard Street.

THX-1138 (1971)
Modified Lola T70 Mk IIIs race at 140 mph through the Caldecott Tunnel and Posey Street Tubes to freedom.

What's up, Doc? (1972)
A comical car chase around downtown San Francisco with a run down Lombard Street in a Volkswagen Bug.

Magnum Force (1973)
The chase down Vermont Street between 20th & 22nd Streets is reminiscent of Lombard Street's turns.

Opposite: 1000 Lombard Street

The Enforcer (1976)
This third installment in the "Dirty Harry" series features a number of cars driving around San Francisco.

Foul Play (1978)
Tony Carlson (Chevy Chase) and Gloria Mundy (Goldie Hawn) race against the clock in a comical spin through San Francisco.

The Presidio (1988)
A night time car chase adds a new spin on things as police chase an 1986 Lincoln, resulting in sparks, gunfire, and explosions.

The Dead Pool (1988)
In the fifth "Dirty Harry" installment, Harry Callahan (Clint Eastwood) is chased by a remote-control car around Potrero Hill.

Basic Instinct (1992)
Nick Curran (Michael Douglas) in his Ford Mustang chases a Lotus Esprit SE through Telegraph Hill at night.

Jade (1995)
In one scene David Corelli (David Caruso) loses its brakes in his Ford Mustang and barely escapes with his life. Later, Corelli starts chasing a 1992 Ford Thunderbird in his 1994 Ford Taurus at The Palace Hotel and weaves through Chinatown, Nob Hill, and the Marina District.

The Rock (1996) Stanley Goodspeed (Nicolas Cage) in a Ferrari F355 Spider chases John Mason (Sean Connery) in a H1 Hummer. In the end, the Ferrari is totaled by a street trolley.

American Graffiti

American Graffiti (1973)

The plot of this "coming of age" movie follows multiple story lines of a group of teenagers over a single pivotal evening in their lives. Based on and inspired by George Lucas's youth cruising in Modesto, California, the movie was a success for Lucas and nominated for five Academy Awards in 1974. *American Graffiti* was filmed in sequence over 29 days during the summer of 1972. A number of the cars that appeared in the film still survive and are periodically displayed by their respective owners.

Cast & Crew

Produced by Francis Ford Coppola
Directed by George Lucas
Written by George Lucas, Gloria Katz, and Willard Huyck

Richard Dreyfuss........Curt Henderson
Ron Howard................. Steve Bolander
Paul Le Mat.......................John Milner
Charlie M. Smith...Terry "Toad" Fields
Cindy Williams........Laurie Henderson
Candy Clark...............Debbie Dunham
Mackenzie Phillips...................... Carol
Wolfman Jack...................Disc Jockey
Harrison Ford.......................Bob Falfa
Suzanne Somers........ Blonde in T-Bird

Petaluma

Founded as a ranch in 1836, today Petaluma is home to roughly 58,000 residents and a wonderful historic downtown. Back in 1972, when *American Graffiti* was filmed, almost all of the outdoor nighttime photography took place in and around Petaluma. Here is your walking guide to several movie locations. The map to these locations is on the next page.

Above: *George Lucas on the set of American Graffiti.*

Scene: *Curt sees blonde in T-Bird*
Time into movie: *12:10 (as seen on DvD)*
Camera Icon: *#1 (see page 254)*
Where: *Petaluma Boulevard North & Washington Street*

Scene: *Terry Field hits car behind him*
Time into movie: *16:10*
Camera Icon: *#2 (see page 254)*
Where: *Petaluma Boulevard North & Washington Street*

Opposite: *John Milner and Bob Falfa sit at the intersection of Western Avenue and Petaluma Blvd. North and prepare to drag race north. It is worth noting that in the finished film, the cars have their headlights turned on and appear in the reverse order. See camera icon #9 on page 254 for the film location.*

Above: *Mel's Drive-In opened in 1985 on Lombard Street in San Francisco.*
Mel's Drive-In
2165 Lombard Street
San Francisco, CA 94123
(415) 921-3039
www.melsdrive-in.com

Scene: *Car salesman in giant rocking chair tries to sell Terry Field a new car.*
Time into movie: *16:58*
Camera Icon: *#3 (see page 254)*
Where: *320 Petaluma Boulevard North*

Scene: *Terry tempts Bob Falfa to race.*
Time into movie: *30:00*
Camera Icon: *#4 (see opposite page)*
Where: *Petaluma Blvd. N. at Western Ave.*

Scene: *Curt & Pharaohs park by Arcade.*
Time into movie: *1:03:05*
Camera Icon: *#8*
Where: *Mary Street*

Scene: *Milner and Falfa drag race*
Time into movie: *1:12:40*
Camera Icon: *#9*
Where: *Petaluma Blvd. North*

Scene: *Curt stands in road.*
Time into movie: *44:11*
Camera Icon: *#5*
Where: *Western Avenue & Kentucky Street*

Scene: *Curt sits on hood of car watching TV*
Time into movie: *52:35*
Camera Icon: *#6*
Where: *145 Kentucky Avenue*

Scene: *Police car gets totalled.*
Time into movie: *1:19:50*
Camera Icon: *#10*
Where: *23 Petaluma Blvd. North*

Scene: *Milner & Carol prank girls in car.*
Time into movie: *59:06*
Camera Icon: *#7*
Where: *Western Avenue*

Opposite: *Each black camera icon corresponds with a given movie location. Colored arrows indicate the direction of travel and match numbers. Most of the camera placements are approximations.*

Scene: *Milner jumps from car.*
Time into movie: *1:37:47*
Camera Icon: *#11*
Where: *Petaluma Blvd. North & Water St*

Scene: *Milner rescues Terry & Debbie*
Time into movie: *1:31:47*
Camera Icon: *#12*
Where: *Water Street*

Bullitt

Bullitt

In the movie *Bullitt*, Frank Bullitt (Steve McQueen) is a San Francisco police lieutenant fighting organized crime in San Francisco, but most people don't know that. What people do know is that this film set the benchmark for car chases. This epic chase used two 1968 Ford Mustang 390 GT 2+2 Fastbacks and two 1968 Dodge Charger R/T 440s on loan from the Ford Motorcar Company and has every filmmaker since trying (usually not very successfully) to copy the intensity of this film.

Cast & Crew

Produced by Philip D'Antoni
Directed by Peter Yates

Steve McQueen................Frank Bullitt
Jacqueline Bisset.........................Cathy
Robert Duvall......................Weissberg

Stunt driving done by **Bud Ekins** in the Ford Mustang and by **Bill Hickman** in the Dodge Charger. Bill Hickman would later drive in the movies *The French Connection* (1971) and *The Seven-Ups* (1973).

(In the following pages, we have traced out almost the entire chase with maps, photos, and approximate duration)

Opposite: 2008 Ford Mustang Bullitt roaring down Taylor Street and jumping the intersection at Union Street
Above: 1968 Dodge Charger R/T 440 roaring down Taylor Street and jumping the intersection at Union Street during filming

Location 1

Hit men see Frank Bullitt pull onto York Street. They make an illegal U-turn and follow. They pause at the intersection of York Street and Peralta Avenue and then continue up York Street.

► Cesar Chavez -> illegal U-Turn -> York -> Peralta -> York
  (Scene lasting roughly 58 seconds)

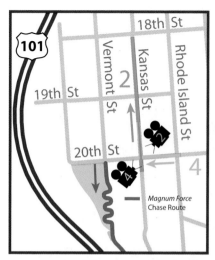

Location 3

Chase between Bullitt and hit men speeds up on Columbus Avenue.

- Filbert -> Columbus -> Chestnut -> Leavenworth
  (lasting roughly 83 seconds)

Location 2

Hit men drive along Kansas Street heading north. They spot Bullitt in their rearview mirror.

- Kansas St - 20th St -> 18th St
  (lasting roughly 20 seconds)

Location 5

Bullitt is forced to back up and smokes the tires in the process.

- Lombard -> Larkin -> Chestnut
  (lasting roughly 23 seconds)

Location 4

Bullitt chases hit men. Both take a right turn onto Kansas Street from 20th Street.

- 20th St -> Kansas St
  (lasting roughly 11 seconds)

Location 6

In-car camera footage of Bullitt taking a left turn up Jones Street.

- Chestnut -> Jones
  (lasting roughly 9 seconds)

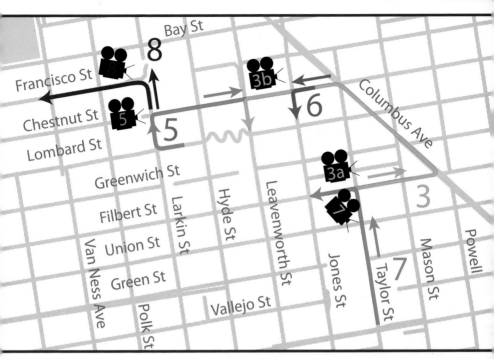

Location 7

In the most iconic part of the chase, both cars travel north on Taylor Street (and pass a green Volkswagen Bug four times!). Several cameras from different angles were used to capture cars going down the street. See the original film photo and the 2008 retake on page 252

▶ Taylor -> Filbert
(lasting roughly 57 seconds)

Location 8

Dodge Charger loses two hubcaps.

▶ Larkin -> Francisco
(lasting roughly 17 seconds)

Location 9 (not on map)

High-speed chase west on Marina Blvd.

▶ Francisco -> Laguna -> Marina
(lasting roughly 57 seconds)

Location 10 (not on map)

Chase heads west past John McLaren Park

▶ Olmstead -> University -> Mansell
(lasting roughly 12 seconds)

Location 11 (not on map)

Multiple shots in both directions until end

▶ Guadalupe Canyon Parkway
(lasting roughly 200 seconds)

Presidio

History

For more than 200 years, the Presidio was a military base with the U.S. Army using the base from 1846 to 1994. In 1996, the Presidio Trust was formed by Congress and charged with preserving the park and its buildings. For more on the Trust or the Park Service, see *www.presidio.gov* and *www.nps.gov/prsf/index.htm*.

Today

Visitors are welcome to hike, bike, and picnic in the park. Other amenities include a golf course, playgrounds, restaurants and cafes, and The Presidio Visitor Center, located on the Main Post. Visitors may also spend the night in one of 22 rooms and suites at the Inn at the Presidio (see *www.innatthepresidio.com*).

Movies filmed at the Presidio

The popular internet website *www.imdb.com* lists over 50 titles that used the Presidio as a film location. The better-known films include *Foul Play (1978)*, *A View to a Kill (1985)*, *Presidio (1988)*, *The Game (1997)*, and *The Spy Next Door (2010)*.

Quick Facts

▶ Native Americans have called the Presidio home for nearly 10,000 years

▶ Presidio is 1,480 acres

▶ More than half of the 700+ buildings are historic properties

Opposite: *A rainy day is not enough to stop some visitors from strolling the grounds of the Presidio.*

Above: *Yoda statue at the Letterman Digital Arts Center.*

Right: *Map of the Presidio*

Tip for Families

The **Walt Disney Family Museum** is a 40,000 square foot state of the art museum dedicated to the life of Walt Disney. Located on the Main Post of the Presidio, families may enjoy interactive galleries, a learning center, a museum store, and a *Fantasia*-themed movie theater.

Walt Disney Family Museum
104 Montgomery Street
The Presidio San Francisco,
CA 94129
Phone: (415) 345-6800
www.waltdisney.org

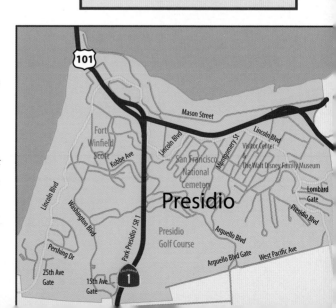

Driving Northern California

I could spend a lifetime driving around Northern California looking for great roads, so I did one better. I asked someone who has spent a lifetime driving around Northern California for his recommendations. The late Martin Swig, the founder of the California Mille, obliged me and provided 15 years' worth of routes. In this section, there is a spread about the California Mille, a brief interview with Martin, and five of the routes the Mille has taken over the years. Martin said he didn't have a favorite drive, stating they are all great. But after a little prodding, he admitted that State Route 1 north of San Francisco was special to him.

The Drives

The mileage for each drive is a few hundred miles and is meant to be a full-days drive and the contact information for lodging at both the starting and finishing location is listed. Before you leave, please map out your drive in detail as our maps are not accurate enough to provide each possible turn and detour.

What to Bring

Emergency supplies, water, coolant, and perhaps a AAA Card. A number of these drives are in remote locations, and cell service will not work.

When to Go

Aside from Sierra Nevada, these drives may be done year-round. The winter months are the wettest with summer producing heavy traffic.

Opposite: A 1953 Nash-Healey overlooking the rocks along Van Damme Beach near the Little River Inn along State Route 1

Precautions

Drive defensively! Expect to see wild animals, rocks on the road, and slippery road surfaces. Roads constantly change due to construction, weather, and debris. Keep your eyes up and speeds down.

Gasoline

Gas Stations are few and far between, with diesel fuel even harder to find, especially along State Route 1. Fill up with gas at every opportunity.

Emergency Numbers

California Highway Patrol
Emergency calls: 911
www.chp.ca.gov

American Automobile Assoc. (AAA)
Phone: (800) 922-8228
Monday–Friday 7:00 AM–9:00 PM
Saturday 7:00 AM–7:00 PM
calstate.aaa.com

California Mille Rally

History

After a run in the 1982 Italian Mille Miglia with John Lamm of *Road & Track*, Martin Swig was hooked on the Mille. In 1991, he founded the **Amici americani della Mille Miglia** (American Friends of the Mille Miglia) otherwise known as the California Mille. After 22 years leading the Mille, Martin passed away.

Today

Under the guidance of his two sons, David and Howard, the California Mille continues and grows, as both have inherited their father's love of cars. 2013 saw the largest field of entrants to date, and the future of the California Mille seems secure.

Above: *1957 AC Ace-Bristol Zagato owned by Jim Feldman*

Martin Swig

Of all the people who have voiced their support of this guidebook, the late Martin Swig was one of *the* most enthusiastic. He granted us this interview and supplied all the routes for driving in Northern California.

Never short of stories, Martin shared this one with us on how he was introduced to cars: *"My dad was in the wholesale food business and among other things, they had a milk receiving plant in Manchester, California (near Eureka). We went up there one time in 1947 with my dad. I was 13 years old, and I had learned how to drive. My dad had a 1946 Chrysler six-cylinder, and his manager up there (at the plant) had a 1946 Chevrolet and I got to drive the Chevrolet. I learned how much difference there was between the well-sprung agile Chevrolet and a big soggy Chrysler. It was the beginning of my car education."*

Schedule

The starting point is always at the **Fairmont Hotel** (*www.fairmont.com*) in Nob Hill, followed by four days covering 1,000 miles of beautiful roads in Northern California. The Mille is always held in April with each successive year's event taking a new route.

The entry is limited to roughly 60 classic cars built prior to January 1958. Contact Dan Radowicz at (415) 479-9940 for more information on entering the event.

Contact Information

Amici americani della Mille Miglia
154 Mitchell Boulevard
San Rafael, CA 94903

Phone: (415) 479-9950
Email: *info@californiamille.com*
www.californiamille.com

A Chat with Martin Swig

Via Corsa: *Do you have a favorite drive?*

Martin Swig: *It's very tough to beat State Route 1 north of San Francisco for about 150 miles. Everyone talks about SR 1 south of Carmel, but as you go further north, it is far less populated so the traffic is light. It is tough to imagine a better drive.*

VC: *Favorite destination spots?*

MS: *I don't care about that. You know how they say "Getting there is half the fun?" No, getting there is way more than half the fun. I like the process of getting there.*

VC: *If not in a classic car, what new car would you take on State Route 1?*

MS: *It's pretty hard to beat a Miata or Boxster or a Subaru BRG. Anything light and balanced.*

VC: *What about a Mercedes-Benz S-Class or BMW 7 Series?*

MS: *Why would you want to drive a Country Club Poser Limousine on a fun road?*

VC: *Do you have any tips for new drivers?*

MS: *You don't know the road, so be ready for rocks that have fallen down off the hillside. Try to be alert and be ready for anything. You might not be the hero driver you think you are.*

Above: *The late Martin Swig is interviewed about his 1925 Lancia Lambda, Series five at the 2011 Concorso Italiano.*

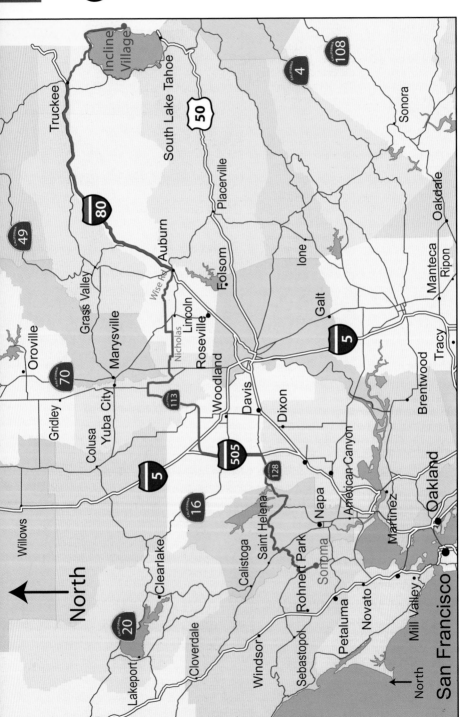

2004 California Mille—Day 4

This four-day rally took participants from San Francisco to Mendocino along State Route 1 for the first night. Day two headed north along the coast to Ferndale and east to Redding. The third day brought drivers and passengers to Lake Tahoe. The drive ends in Sonoma.

Starting Point

Hyatt Regency Lake Tahoe Resort
111 Country Club Drive
Incline Village, NV 89451
Phone: (775) 832-1234
laketahoe.hyatt.com

Ending Point

Sonoma Mission Inn
100 Boyes Blvd.
Sonoma, CA 95476
Phone: (707) 938-9000
www.fairmont.com/sonoma

Directions

- Leave Hyatt and turn left/west on State Route 28—6.7 miles
- North onto State Route 267/ North Shore Blvd.—12.3 miles
- West on Interstate 80—69.4 miles
- Exit 116 on to Ophir Rd. and turn right—0.9 mile
- At "Y" turn onto Wide Rd. and follow to the west—11.4 miles
- South on Dowd Rd.—8.8 miles

- West onto Nicolaus Rd. —10.7 miles
- North on SR 99—9.3 miles
- West on SR 113—21.2 miles
- At "Y" go west on E-10 direction Zamora—9.8 miles
- South on SR 505—16.9 miles
- Exit 11 in Winters
- West on SR 128—37.4 miles
- Left/south on Silverado Trail —3.2 miles
- West on Oakville Crossroad —2.6 miles
- South onto SR 29—0.3 mile
- West on Oakville Grade—10.9 miles
- South on SR 12—5.2 miles
- Right at Boyes Blvd. to Sonoma Mission Inn

Top Right: *Lake Tahoe in the Spring*

Right: *Sonoma Mission Inn is a popular destination for car clubs and rallies. This shot is of the "Scuderia Rampage" Rally.*

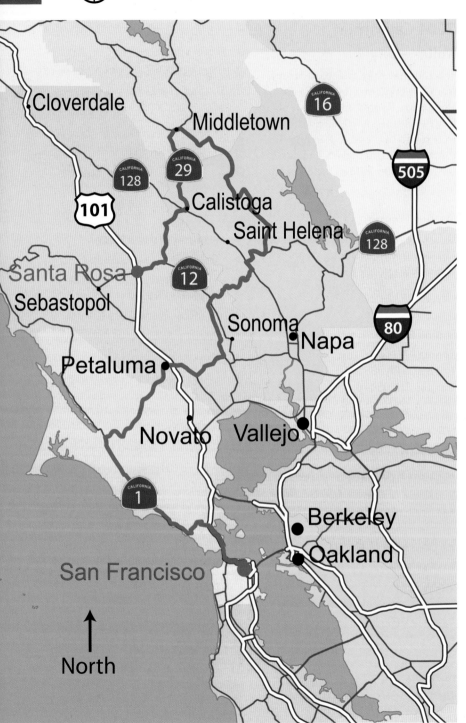

2005 California Mille—Day 1

The first day of this rally started with a loop around wine county hitting Napa, Lake, and Sonoma Counties. This is a great drive for someone spending a few days around Wine Country.

Starting Point

Fairmont Hotel
950 Mason St.
San Francisco, CA 94108
Phone: (415) 772-5000
www.fairmont.com/san-francisco

Ending Point

Fountaingrove Inn
101 Fountaingrove Pkwy.
Santa Rosa, CA 95403
Phone: (707) 578-6101
www.fountaingroveinn.com

Below: *Trinity Road connects State Route 12 in Sonoma to State Route 29 in Napa*

Directions

- North on U.S. 101
- Take Exit 445B & west on Highway 1
- North on State Route 1—28 miles
- East on Point Reyes-Petaluma Rd. —15 miles
- South on Lakeview St.—4.2 miles
- East on Stage Gulch Rd.—5 miles
- North on Arnold Dr.—9 miles
- North on Sonoma SR—0.6 mile
- East on Trinity Rd.—11.3 miles
- North on State Route 128—0.2 mile
- East on Oakville Grade—2.5 miles
- North on Silverado Trail—3.1 miles
- East on Sage Canyon Rd.—3.8 miles
- North on Chiles Pope Valley Rd. —31 miles
- West on SR 29—15.5 miles
- North on State Route 128—1 mile
- South on Petrified Forest Rd. —11.5 miles
- West on SR 12 into Santa Rosa

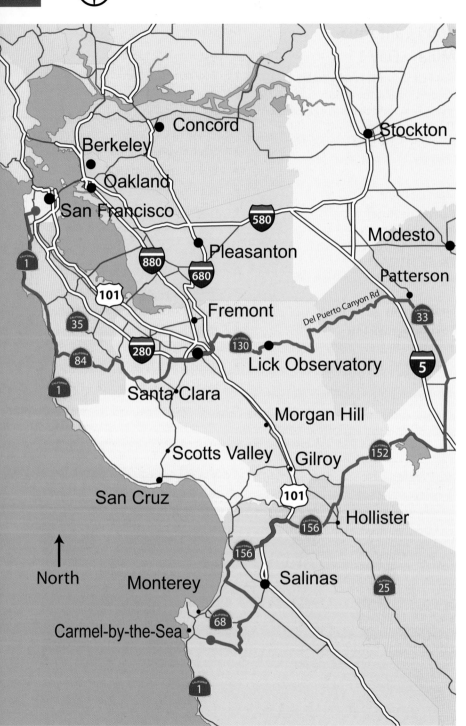

2009 California Mille—Day 1

The 2009 Mille headed south on the first day zigzagging between the coast and inland roads. Day one climbed Mt. Hamilton and passed the Lick Observatory and dropped down into Carmel Valley for the evening.

Starting Point

Fairmont Hotel
950 Mason St.
San Francisco, CA 94108
Phone: (415) 772-5000
www.fairmont.com/san-francisco

Ending Point

The Quail Lodge
8205 Valley Greens Drive
Carmel, CA 93923
Phone: (831) 620-8860
www.quaillodge.com

Directions

- ▶ Head south on SR 1 at any point in San Francisco—roughly 29 miles
- ▶ East on SR 84—8.1 miles
- ▶ East on Pescadero/Alpine Rd. —8.5 miles
- ▶ South on SR 35/Skyline Blvd. —6.3 miles
- ▶ North on SR 9 direction Saratoga —7.1 miles
- ▶ East on I-280 direction San Jose and follow north as I-680—6.6 miles
- ▶ Exit 1D east onto Alum Rock Rd. and buy gas here—next station 90 miles
- ▶ East on Alum Rock Rd.—2.1 miles
- ▶ East on SR 130/ Mt. Hamilton Rd. —18 miles
- ▶ Stop and look at the Lick Observatory!
- ▶ Continue east 18 more miles to Del Puerto Canyon Rd.
- ▶ East on Del Puerto Canyon Rd. —24 miles
- ▶ South on SR 33—30 miles
- ▶ West on SR 152—26 miles
- ▶ West on SR 156—17.3 miles
- ▶ South on SR 156/US 101—20 miles
- ▶ Exit 336 west back onto SR 156
- ▶ South on SR 156/SR 1—10.3 miles
- ▶ Exit 410 onto Reservation Rd.
- ▶ East on Reservation Rd.—9 miles
- ▶ West on SR 68—5.8 miles
- ▶ South on Los Laureles Grade Rd. —5.8 miles
- ▶ West on Carmel Valley Rd.—6 miles
- ▶ The Quail Lodge is on the south side of the road

Above: *Sunset along California State Route 1 near Half Moon Bay*

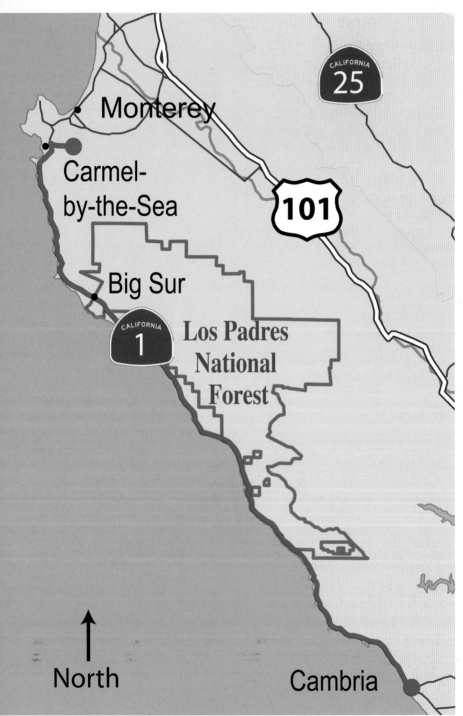

Monterey

Carmel-
by-the-Sea

Big Sur

Los Padres
National
Forest

CALIFORNIA 25

101

CALIFORNIA 1

North

Cambria

2009 California Mille—Day 2

This 100-mile round trip on State Route One south of Carmel is the drive everyone should take once. This scenic run up and down the coast is best not hurried. Take every opportunity you can to stop along the side of the road to admire the views!

Starting/Ending Point

The Quail Lodge
8205 Valley Greens Drive
Carmel, CA 93923
Phone: (831) 620-8860
www.quaillodge.com

Lunch

Cambria Pines Lodge
2905 Burton Drive
Cambria, CA 93428
Phone: (805) 927-4200
www.cambriapineslodge.com

Below: *Ocean views along California State Route 1.*

Directions

▶ Head west on Carmel Valley Rd. —3.1 miles

▶ South on SR 1 / California State Route 1—25 miles

▶ Stop at Nepenthe for a snack or coffee. Nepenthe is located at 48510 Highway One, Big Sur, CA 93920 Phone: (831) 667-2345 (*www.nepenthebigsur.com*)

▶ Continue on Highway 1/SR 1 south for another 68 miles to Cambria for lunch.

Above: *One of the many beaches along California State Route 1 south of Carmel*

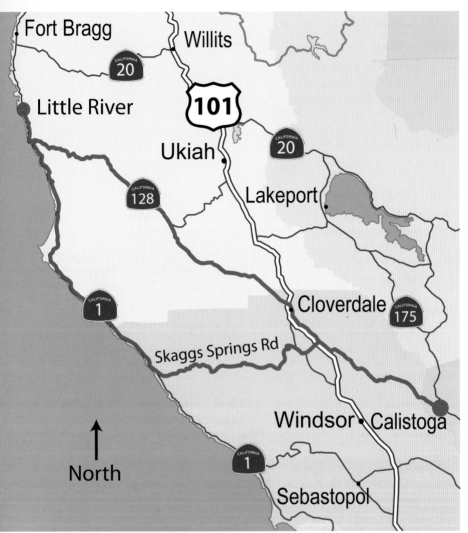

Fort Bragg

Willits

CALIFORNIA **20**

Little River

101

Ukiah

CALIFORNIA **20**

CALIFORNIA **128**

Lakeport

CALIFORNIA **1**

Cloverdale

CALIFORNIA **175**

Skaggs Springs Rd

↑ North

Windsor • Calistoga

CALIFORNIA **1**

Sebastopol

Above: *1939 BMW 328 during the 2011 California Mille.*

Above: *The other Pebble Beach off State Route 1 in Sonoma County.*

2011 California Mille—Day 2

The second day of the 2011 rally covered Martin Swig's favorite drive in all of Northern California.

Starting/Ending Point

Solage Calistoga
755 Silverado Trail
Calistoga, CA 94515
Phone: (707) 226-0800
www.solagecalistoga.com

Lunch

Little River Inn
7901 California 1
Little River, CA 95456
Phone: (707) 937-5942
www.littleriverinn.com

Directions

▶ Head west on SR 128—24.8 miles

▶ West on Canyon Rd.—2.2 miles

▶ North on Dry Creek Rd.—5 miles

▶ South on Skaggs Springs Rd. —34.4 miles

▶ North on SR 1—57.1 miles

Lunch at Little River Inn

▶ South on SR 1—7.3 miles

▶ East on SR 128—55 miles

▶ South on Cloverdale Blvd.—2.8 miles

▶ Cross over US 101 to the east

▶ South on Asti Rd.—8.1 miles

▶ South on SR 128—23 miles

Top: *The 2011 California Mille near the Albion Cove heading south on State Route 1.*

Middle: *1939 Jaguar SS at Little River Inn.*

Right: *Redwoods in Navarro River Redwoods State Park along SR 128.*

Additional Race Tracks

Dirt Ovals—Track Locations

American Valley Speedway
204 Fairgrounds Road
Quincy, CA 95971
www.americanvalleyspeedway.com

Antioch Speedway
1201 W. 10th Street
Antioch, CA 94509
www.antiochspeedway.com

Calistoga Speedway
1435 N. Oak Street
Calistoga, California 94515
Phone: (707) 942-5111
www.calistogaspeedway.org

Chowchilla Speedway
1000 S. 3rd Street
Chowchilla, CA 93610
Phone: (415) 320-7889
www.chowchillaspeedway.net

Cycleland Speedway
47 Nelson Road
Chico, CA 95965
Phone: (530) 342-0063
www.cyclelandspeedway.com

Delta Speedway
1658 S. Airport Way
Stockton, CA 95206
Phone: (408) 595-8922
www.deltaraceway.com

Dixon Speedway
4975 Rio Dixon Road
Dixon, CA 95620
www.facebook.com/dixon.speedway

Lemoore Raceway
1750 Highway 41
Lemoore, CA 93245
Phone: (559) 924-2536
www.lemooreraceway.com

Marysville Raceway Park
1468 Simpson Lane
Marysville, CA 95901
Phone: (530) 743-1327
www.marysvilleracewaypark.com

Ocean Speedway
2601 E. Lake Avenue
Watsonville, CA 95076
Phone: (831) 662-9466
www.oceanspeedway.com

Orland Speedway
Glenn County Fairgrounds
221 E. Yolo Street
Orland, CA 95963
www.orlandspeedway.info

Petaluma Speedway
100 Fairgrounds Drive
Petaluma, CA 94953
Phone: (707) 763-7223
www.Petaluma-Speedway.com

Placerville Speedway
100 Placerville Drive
Placerville, CA 95667
Phone: (530) 626-3680
www.placervillespeedway.com

Plaza Park Raceway
700 S. Plaza Street
Visalia, CA 93277
Phone: (559) 651-5114
www.plazaparkraceway.com

Silver Dollar Speedway
2357 Fair Street
Chico, CA 95928
Phone: (530) 891-6535
www.silverdollarspeedway.com

Siskiyou Motor Speedway
1750 Fairlane Road
Yreka, CA 96097
www.siskiyoumotorspeedway.com

Thunderbowl Raceway
Tulare Fairgrounds
215 Martin Luther King Jr. Avenue
Tulare, CA 93274
Phone: (559) 688-0909
www.thunderbowlraceway.com

Asphalt Oval—Track Locations

All American Speedway
800 All America City
Roseville, CA 95678
Phone: (916) 786-2025
www.allamericanspeedway.com

American Quarter Midget Association
Prairie City OHV Park
13300 White Rock Road
Rancho Cordova, CA 95742
www.aqma.org

Lakeport Speedway
401 Martin Street
Lakeport, CA 95453
Phone: (707) 279-9577
www.lakeportspeedway.com

Madera Speedway
1850 Cleveland Avenue
Madera, CA 93637
Phone: (559) 673-7223
www.racemadera.com

Shasta Speedway
1890 Briggs Street
Anderson, CA 96007
Phone: (707) 349-6998
www.shastaspeedway.com

Stockton Speedway
4105 N. Wilson Way
Stockton, CA 95205
Phone: (209) 466-9999
www.stockton99.com

Ukiah Speedway
Redwood Empire Fairgrounds
1055 N. State Street
Ukiah, CA 95482
Phone: (707) 279-9577
www.ukiahspeedway.com

Asphalt Drag Strips—Track Locations

Redding Drag Strip
Redding Municipal Airport
6030 Old Oregon Trail
Redding, CA 96003
Phone: (530) 241-8185
www.reddingdragstrip.info

Sacramento Raceway Park
5305 Excelsior Road
Sacramento, CA 95827
Phone: (916) 363-2653
www.sacramentoraceway.com

Samoa Drag Strip
Eureka Municipal County Airport
900 New Navy Base Road
Samoa, CA 95564
www.samoadragstrip.com

Airports

Monterey Regional Airport
Phone: (831) 648-7000
www.montereyairport.com

Oakland Int. Airport
Phone: (510) 563-3300
www.oaklandairport.com

Sacramento Int. Airport
Phone: (916) 929-5411
www.sacramento.aero

San Francisco Int. Airport
Phone: (650) 821-5000
www.flysfo.com

San Jose Int. Airport
Phone: (408) 392-3600
www.flysanjose.com

Airlines

AeroMexico
Phone: (800) 237-6639
www.aeromexico.com

Air Canada
Phone: (888) 247-2262
www.aircanada.com

Air France
Phone: (800) 237-2747
www.airfrance.com/us

Air New Zealand
Phone: (800) 262-1234
www.airnewzealand.com

Alaska Airlines
Phone: (800) 252-7522
www.alaskaair.com

American
Phone: (800) 433-7300
www.aa.com

British Airways
Phone: (800) 247-9297
www.britishairways.com

Cathay Pacific
Phone: (800) 233-2742
www.cathaypacific.com

China Airlines
Phone: (800) 227-5118
www.china-airlines.com

Delta
Phone: (800) 221-1212
www.delta.com

Frontier
Phone: (800) 432-1359
www.flyfrontier.com

Hawaiian Airlines
Phone: (800) 367-5320
www.hawaiianair.com

Japan Airlines
Phone: (800) 525-3663
www.ar.jal.com/en

JetBlue
Phone: (800) 538-2583
www.jetblue.com

KLM
Phone: (800) 225-2525
www.klm.com

Korean Air
Phone: (800) 438-5000
www.koreanair.com

Lufthansa
Phone: (800) 645-3880
www.lufthansa.com

Philippine Airlines
Phone: (800) 435-9725
www.philippineairlines.com

SAS
Phone: (800.221-2350
www.flysas.com

Singapore Airlines
Phone: (800) 742-3333
www.singaporeair.com

Southwest
Phone: (800) 435-9792
www.southwest.com

Sun Country
Phone: (800) 359-6786
www.suncountry.com

Swiss Int. Air Lines
Phone: (877) 359-7947
www.swiss.com

United
Phone: (800) 864-8331
www.united.com

United Express
Phone: (800) 864-8331
www.united.com

US Airways
Phone: (800) 428-4322
www.usairways.com

Virgin Atlantic
Phone: (800) 821-5438
www.virgin-atlantic.com

Rental Car Agencies

Alamo Rent A Car
Phone: (888)233-8749
www.alamo.com

Avis Rent-A-Car
Phone: (800) 633-3469
www.avis.com

Budget Rent A Car
Phone: (800) 218-7992
www.budget.com

Dollar
Phone: (866) 434-2226
www.dollar.com

Enterprise
Phone: (800) 261-7331
www.enterprise.com

Fox
Phone: (800) 225-4369
foxrentacar.com

Hertz Corporation
Phone: (800) 654-3131
www.hertz.com

National Car Rental
Phone: (877) 222-9058
www.nationalcar.com

Thrifty Car Rental
Phone: (877) 283-0898
www.thrifty.com

AAA

American Automobile
Association Northern
California
Phone: (888) 937-5523
calstate.aaa.com

Emergency Services

Police   911
Highway Patrol (CHP) 911
  Non-emergency
  (800) 835-5247
Fire   911
Information   511

California Highway Patrol

601 N 7th Street
Sacramento, CA 95831
Phone: (800) 835-5247
www.chp.ca.gov

Northern Division (101)
2485 Sonoma Street
Redding, CA 96001-3026
Phone: (530) 225-2715

Valley Division (201)
2555 First Avenue
Sacramento, CA 95818
Phone: (916) 731-6300

Central Division (401)
5179 North Gates Avenue
Fresno, CA 93722-6414
Phone: (559) 277-7250

Coastal Division (701)
4115 Broad Street, #B-10
San Luis Obispo, CA
93401-7963
Phone: (805) 549-3261

Inland Division (801)
847 E. Brier Drive
San Bernardino, CA
92408-2820
Phone: (909) 806-2400

Park Service

National Park Service
www.nps.gov

California Department of
Parks & Services
www.parks.ca.gov

Monterey County Parks
www.co.monterey.ca.us

Death Valley
www.nps.gov/deva

Napa County Parks
www.napaoutdoors.org

San Francisco Parks
www.sfrecpark.org

Sonoma County Parks
parks.sonomacounty.ca.gov

Traffic Reports

California Dept. of
Transportation
Phone: (800) 427-7623
www.dot.ca.gov
(Call this toll free number for traffic updates)

San Francisco Chronicle
www.sfgate.com/traffic

511 San Francisco Bay
511.org

Interstate 5
www.drivei5.com

Interstate 80
www.idrive80.com

Death Valley

Places to Stay

Furnace Creek Inn & Ranch Resorts
Phone: (760) 786-2345
furnacecreekresort.com

Stovepipe Wells Village
Phone: (760) 786-2387
escapetodeathvalley.com

Panamint Springs Resort
Phone: (775) 482-7680
www.deathvalley.com/psr

Restaurants

Bad Water Saloon
Phone: (760) 786-2387
escapetodeathvalley.com

Amargosa Opera House Restuarant
Phone: (760) 852-4441
amargosa-opera-house.com

Visitors Center

Furnace Creek Visitors Center
Phone: (760) 786-3200
www.nps.gov/deva

Napa

Welcome Centers/ Cambers of Commerce

Calistoga Chamber of Commerce
Phone: (707) 942-6333
www.calistogavisitors.com

Napa Chamber of Commerce
Phone: (707) 226-7455
www.napachamber.org

Napa Welcome Center
600 Main Street
Napa, CA 94559
Phone: (707) 260-0106
www.visitnapavalley.com

Napa Train

1275 McKinstry Street
Napa, CA 94559
Phone: (707) 253-2111
www.winetrain.com

Places to Stay

Calistoga Ranch
580 Lommel Road
Calistoga, CA 94515
Phone: (855) 942-4220
www.calistogaranch.com

Meadowood Napa Valley
900 Meadowood Lane St. Helena, CA 94574
Phone: (877) 963-3646
www.meadowood.com

Silverado Resort and Spa
1600 Atlas Peak Road
Napa, CA 94558
Phone: (800) 532-0500
www.silveradoresort.com

Solage Calistoga
755 Silverado Trail
Calistoga, CA 94515
Phone: (707) 226-0800
www.solagecalistoga.com

Villagio Inn & Spa
6481 Washington Street
Yountville, CA 94599
Phone: (707) 944-8877
www.villagio.com

Restaurants

(summary of notable ones)

Ad Hoc
6476 Washington Street
Yountville, CA 94599
Phone: (707) 944-2487
www.adhocrestaurant.com

Bottega
6525 Washington Street
Yountville, CA 94599
Phone: (707) 945-1050
botteganapavalley.com

French Laundry
6640 Washington Street
Yountville, CA 94599
Phone: (707) 944-2892
www.frenchlaundry.com

Gott's Roadside
933 Main Street
St. Helena, CA 94574
Phone: (707) 963-3486
www.gotts.com

Morimoto Napa
610 Main Street
Napa, CA 94559
Phone: (707) 252-1600
morimotonapa.com

Press
587 St. Helena Highway
St. Helena, CA 94574
Phone: (707) 967-0550
www.pressnapavalley.com

Redd Restaurant
6480 Washington Street
Yountville, CA 94599
Phone: (707) 944-2222
www.reddnapavalley.com

Hospitals

Queen of the Valley
1000 Trancas Street
Napa, CA 94558
Phone: (707) 252-4411
www.thequeen.org

St. Helena Hospital
10 Woodland Road
St. Helena , CA 94574
Phone: (707) 963-3611
www.sthelenahospitals.org

Sonoma

Welcome Centers/ Cambers of Commerce

Sonoma Visitor's Bureau
453 1st Street East
Sonoma, CA
Phone: (707) 996-1090
www.sonomavalley.com

Sonoma Chamber of
Commerce
Phone: (707) 996-1033
www.sonomachamber.org

Places to Stay

Bodega Bay Lodge & Spa
103 Coast Highway One
Bodega Bay, CA 94923
Phone: (888) 875-2250
www.bodegabaylodge.com

Above: French Laundry in Yountville, CA

Fountaingrove Inn
101 Fountaingrove Pkwy.
Santa Rosa, CA
Phone: (707) 578-6101
www.fountaingroveinn.com

Little River Inn
7901 California 1
Little River, CA 95456
Phone: (707) 937-5942
www.littleriverinn.com

Duchamp Hotel
421 Foss Street
Healdsburg, CA 95448
Phone: (800) 431-9341
www.duchamphotel.com

Sonoma Mission Inn
100 Boyes Blvd.
Sonoma, CA 95476
Phone: (707) 938-9000
www.fairmont.com/sonoma

Restaurants

Cafe La Haye
140 E. Napa Street
Sonoma, CA 95476
(707) 935-5994
www.cafelahaye.com

El Dorado Kitchen
405 1st Street West
Sonoma, CA 95476
(707) 996-3030
www.eldoradosonoma.com

Harvest Moon Cafe
487 1st Street West
Sonoma, CA 95476
(707) 933-8160
harvestmooncafesonoma. com

Above: *Tin Lizzies of The Tin Lizzie Inn*

"There is no better way to see and be seen as you drive through Yosemite National Park. You can choose either a Roadster or Touring Car."
- Tin Lizzy Inn

Tin Lizzy Inn offers -
1915 Touring
1922 Touring
1926 Touring
1928 Model A Touring
1929 Model A Roadster

Sierra Nevada

Places to Stay

Tin Lizzie Inn
7730 Laurel Way
P.O. Box 63
Fishcamp, CA 93623
Phone: (866) 488-6877
www.tinlizzieinn.com
www.driveamodelt.com

Lake Tahoe Resort Hotel
4130 Lake Tahoe Blvd.
S. Lake Tahoe, CA, 96150
Phone: (866) 767-0278
www.tahoeresorthotel.com

Hyatt Regency Lake Tahoe
111 Country Club Drive
Incline Village, NV 89451
Phone: (775) 832-1234
laketahoe.hyatt.com

Monterey

Chambers of Commerce/ Welcome Centers

Monterey Peninsula
Chamber of Commerce
30 Ragsdale Dr., Suite 200
Monterey, CA 93940
Phone: (831) 648-5360
www.mpcc.com

Monterey County Convention & Visitors Bureau
765 Wave Street
Monterey, CA 93940
Phone: (877) MONTEREY
www.seemonterey.com

Fisherman's Wharf
www.montereywharf.com

Places to Stay

Casa Munras
700 Munras Avenue
Monterey, CA 93940
Phone: 831.375.2411
HotelCasaMunras.com

Hyatt Regency & Spa
1 Old Golf Course Road
Monterey, CA 93940
Phone: (831) 372-1234
monterey.hyatt.com

Monterey Marriott
350 Calle Principal
Monterey, CA 93940
Phone: (831) 649-4234
www.marriott.com

Monterey Plaza
400 Cannery Row
Monterey, CA 93940
Phone: 800-334-3999
montereyplazahotel.com

Portola Hotel & Spa
Two Portola Plaza
Monterey, CA 93940
Phone: (888) 222-5851
www.portolahotel.com

Restaurants

Crabby Jim's Seafood
25 Fisherman's Wharf
Monterey, CA 93940
Phone: (831) 372-2064
crabbyjimsmonterey.com

Fish Hopper Restaurant
700 Cannery Row
Monterey, CA 93940
Phone: (831) 372-8543
www.fishhopper.com

Grotto Fish Market
42 Old Fisherman's Wharf
Monterey, CA 93940
Phone: (831) 372-3769
www.grottofishmarket.com

Isabella's
60 Wharf 1
Monterey, CA 93940
Phone: (831) 375-3956
isabellasonthewharf.com

Monterey Fish House
2114 Del Monte Ave.
Monterey, CA 93940
Phone: (831) 373-4647

Old Fisherman's Grotto
39 Fisherman's Wharf
Monterey, CA 93940
(831) 375-4604
oldfishermansgrotto.com

Other Activities

Glass Bottom Boat Co.
90 Fisherman's Wharf #1
Monterey, CA 93940
Phone: (831) 372-7151

Princess Whale Watching
Fisherman's Wharf
Monterey, CA 93940
Phone: (831) 372-2203
montereywhalewatching. com

Monterey Bay Aquarium
886 Cannery Row
Monterey, CA 93940
Phone: (831) 648-4800
montereybayaquarium.org

Museum of Monterey
5 Custom House Plaza
Monterey, CA 93940
Phone: (831) 372-2608
museumofmonterey.org

Monterey Bay Kayaks
693 Del Monte Avenue
Monterey, CA 93940
Phone: (831) 373-5357
montereybaykayaks.com

A B Seas Kayaks
Phone: (831) 647-0147
www.montereykayak.com

Police

Non-Emergency
(831) 648-7006

Laundry

Monte Vista Laundry
23 Soledad Drive
Monterey, CA 93940

Carmel / Carmel Valley

Chambers of Commerce

Carmel Chamber of
Commerce
Phone: (831) 624-2522
www.carmelcalifornia.org

Visitor Center
Phone: (800) 550-4333
On San Carlos between
5th & 6th

Places to Stay

Blue Sky Lodge
10 Flight Road
Carmel Valley, CA 93924
Phone: (831) 659-2256
www.blueskylodge.com

Briarwood Inn
San Carlos St. & 4th St.
Carmel, CA 93923
(800) 999-8788
briarwood-inn-carmel.com

Carmel Country Inn
Dolores St. at 3rd Ave.
Carmel, CA 93923
Phone: (800) 215-6343
www.carmelcountryinn.com

Carmel Valley Ranch
1 Old Ranch Road
Carmel, CA 93923
(831) 625-9500
www.carmelvalleyranch.com

Coachman's Inn
San Carlos St. & 7th St.
Carmel, CA 93921
(831) 624-6421
www.coachmansinn.com

Cypress Inn
Lincoln St. & 7th St.
Carmel, CA 93921
(831) 624-3871
www.cypress-inn.com

Hyatt Carmel Highlands
120 Highlands Drive
Carmel, CA 93923
Phone: (831) 620-1234
highlandsinn.hyatt.com

The Quail Lodge
8205 Valley Greens Drive
Carmel, CA 93923
Phone: (831) 620-8860
www.quaillodge.com

Tally Ho Inn
Monte Verde & 6th St.
Carmel, CA93921
Phone: (800) 652-2632
www.tallyho-inn.com

Restaurants

Carmel's Bistro Giovanni
San Carlos St. & 5th Ave.
Carmel, CA 93921
(831) 626-6003
threecarmelrestaurants.com

Casanova
5th Ave. & San Carlos
Carmel, CA 93921
Phone: (831) 625-0501
casanovarestaurant.com

Em Le's
(Try the French Toast!)
Dolores St. & 5th Ave.
Carmel, CA 93921
Phone: (831) 625-6780
www.emlescarmel.com

Flaherty's Seafood Grill
6th Ave. near Dolores
Carmel, CA 93923
(831) 625-1500
www.flahertysseafood.com

Forge in the Forest
Junipero St. & 5th Ave.
Carmel, CA 93923
(831) 624-2233
www.forgeintheforest.com

Hog's Breath Inn
San Carlos & 5th Ave.
Carmel, CA 93923
Phone: (831) 625-1044
www.hogsbreathinn.net

Il Fornaio
Ocean Ave. & Monte Verde
Carmel, CA 93921
Phone: (831) 622-5100
www.ilfornaio.com

Other Activities

Carmel Mission Basilica
3080 Rio Road
Carmel, CA 93923
Phone: 831-624-1271
www.carmelmission.org
*The Carmel Mission Basilica
offers Catholic services and a
museum/store*

Newspapers

Carmel Pine Cone
www.pineconearchive.com

Monterey County Weekly
montereycountyweekly.com

Carmel Visitors Guide
www.carmelcalifornia.org

Pebble Beach

The Lodge at Pebble Beach
1700 17-Mile Drive
Pebble Beach, CA 93953
Resort Reservations
Phone: (800) 654-9300
www.pebblebeach.com

The Inn at Spanish Bay
2700 17-Mile Drive
Pebble Beach, CA 93953

Casa Palmero at
Pebble Beach
1518 Cypress Drive
Pebble Beach, CA 93953

Restaurants at the Lodge -

Stillwater Bar & Grill
Phone: (831) 625-8524

The Tap Room
Phone: (831) 625-8535

The Bench
Phone: (800) 654-9300

Gallery Cafe
Phone: (831) 625-8577

The Terrace Lounge
Phone: (831) 625-8524

Highway 1 - south

Places to Stay

Cambria Pines Lodge
2905 Burton Drive
Cambria, CA 93428
Phone: (805) 927-4200
cambriapineslodge.com

Ventana Inn & Spa
48123 Highway One
Big Sur, CA 93920
Phone: (831) 667-2331
www.ventanainn.com

Restaurants

Deetjen's Big Sur Inn &
Restaurant
48865 California 1
Big Sur, CA 93920
Phone: (831) 667-2377
www.deetjens.com

Nepenthe
48510 California 1
Big Sur, CA 93920
Phone: (831) 667-2345
www.nepenthebigsur.com

Point Lobos
State Reserve

Highway 1
Carmel, CA 93922
www.pointlobos.org
*This State Reserve is located
only 3.5 miles south of the
town of Carmel.*

Sacramento

Places to Stay

The Citizen Hotel
926 J Street
Sacramento, CA 95814
Phone: (916) 492-4460
www.jdvhotels.com

Hyatt Regency Sacramento
1209 L Street
Sacramento, CA 95814
Phone: (916) 443 1234
sacramento.hyatt.com

Larkspur Landing
Sacramento
555 Howe Avenue
Sacramento, CA 95825
Phone: (916) 646-1212
www.larkspurhotels.com

San Francisco

Places to Stay

Fairmont Hotel
950 Mason Street
San Francisco, CA 94108
Phone: (415) 772-5000
*www.fairmont.com/
san-francisco*

Four Seasons Hotel
757 Market Street
San Francisco, CA, 94103
Phone: (415) 633-3000
www.fourseasons.com

InterContinental
888 Howard Street
San Francisco, CA 94103
Phone: (888) 811-4273
*intercontinentalsanfrancisco
.com*

Mandarin Oriental
222 Sansome Street
San Francisco, CA 94104
Phone: (415) 276 9888
mandarinoriental.com

Omni San Francisco Hotel
500 California Street
San Francisco, CA 94104
Phone: (415) 677-9494
www.omnihotels.com

The Ritz-Carlton
600 Stockton Street
San Francisco, CA 94108
Phone: (415) 296-7465
www.ritzcarlton.com

The St. Regis
125 3rd Street
San Francisco, CA 94103
Phone: (415) 284-4000
stregis.com/SanFrancisco

Tourist Attractions

Alcatraz Island

This 22-acre island managed by the U.S. Park Service is open to the public (*www.nps.gov/alca*). The private ferry company Alcatraz Cruises is under contract with the National Park Service to provide tickets and transportation. Day Tickets -

Adult	$30
Juniors 12–17	$30
Children 5–11	$18.75
Seniors 62+	$28.25
Children 0–4	Free
Family Tickets—	
2 adults/2 children	$90.25

See *alcatrazcruises.com*

AT&T Park

Home of the San Francisco Giants, this stadium runs events all year long.
24 Willie Mays Plaza
San Francisco, CA 94107
Phone: (415) 972-2000
sanfrancisco.giants.mlb.com

Chinatown

The largest Chinatown outside of Asia, and the oldest in all of North America, dates back to 1848. Chinatown runs along the north-south Stockton Street east of US 101. See
sanfranciscochinatown.com

Financial District

Located just to the north of Interstate 80 on the east side of San Francisco. The Financial District is home to many banks and law firms.

Fisherman's Wharf

One of the city's biggest tourist draws, the Fisherman's Wharf is still operating with commercial fishing vessels. The highlight of the year is the opening of the Dungeness Crab season in November.
www.fishermanswharf.org

Golden Gate Bridge

Visitors wishing to see the bridge may do so on the east side of the bridge between 5:00 AM and 6:30 PM. The total length is 8,980 feet and visitors may park at either end of the bridge in small lots.
www.goldengatebridge.org

Golden Gate Park

Not many people remember that back in 1952, 100,000 people crammed the park to watch the SCCA National Golden Gate. Today visitors to this 1,017-acre park may stroll a Japanese Tea Garden, The Conservatory of Flowers, and the San Francisco Botanical Garden.
www.golden-gate-park.com

Haight-Ashbury

Made famous in the 1960s for hippies and drugs, the intersection of Haight Street and Ashbury Street is a let down for tourists who expect to see Deadheads strolling about. See
www.haightshop.com

Presidio

See page 256

Lombard Street

San Francisco's most famous street is just a few blocks off US 101. Everyone needs to drive down Lombard Street once.

Nob Hill

Directly west of Chinatown and, along with Mount Davidson, Mount Sutro, Rincon Hill, Russian Hill, Telegraph Hill, and Twin Peaks is one of the original "Seven Hills" of San Francisco.

Pacific Heights

This scenic district offers great views of the San Francisco Bay and beautiful homes. Located between California and Lombard.

Getting Around

Public Transportation is operated by the San Francisco Municipal Transportation Agency (SFMTA). See *www.sfmta.com* for routes and fees as well as information on catching a cable car. Perhaps one of the most unusual ways to tour the city is with a 3-wheeler, 49cc, 2-stroke, engine Go Car. See *www.GoCarSF.com*.

Above: *Tour San Francisco with www.GoCarSF.com*

Cars & Coffee in Northern California

Eurosunday

www.eurosunday.net
Holds events around California on the third Sunday of each month.

Eurosunday—Silicon Valley
Konditorei
3130 Alpine Road #284
Portola Valley, CA 94025

Eurosunday—Modesto
Starbucks
3801 Pelandale Avenue
Modesto, CA 95356

Eurosunday—East Bay
Venue changes

Eurosunday—Sacramento
Venue changes

Canepa

4900 Scotts Valley Drive
Scotts Valley, CA 95066
April to October -
Second Saturday of each month
Phone: (831) 430-9940
www.canepa.com/news/calendar.html

Blackhawk Museum

3750 Blackhawk Plaza Circle
Danville, CA 94506
First Sunday of each month
Phone: (925) 736-2280
blackhawkmuseum.org/carsncoffee.html

Pebble Beach Sports Car Club

Del Monte Shopping Center
1410 Del Monte Center
Monterey, CA 93940
Second Saturday of each month
www.pebblebeachsportscarclub.com

Racing Organizations

Sports Car Club of America (SCCA)
San Francisco Region
P.O. Box 308
Willows, CA 95988
Phone: (888) 995-7222
www.sfrscca.org

National Auto Sports Association
PO Box 2366
Napa Valley, CA 94558
Phone: (707) 872-7223
www.www.nasanorcal.com

Recommended Reading

On the Road to Nowhere?
California's Car Culture
By R. C. Lutz

Wheels of Change from Zero to 600 M.P.H: The Amazing Story of California and the Automobile
By Kevin Nelson

60th Anniversary Book
The Pebble Beach Concours d'Elegance is covered from 1950 to the very latest results from 2009 and 2010.
www.theconcoursstore.com

Thanks for the Interviews!

Milt Brown
Mario Andretti
Tommy Kendall
Justin Bell
Brenda Priddy
Martin Swig

Map Credits

California Auto Museum—page 33
National Auto Museum—page 58
Palmaz Winery—top of page 109
Map Resources—pages 10, 11, 68, 112, 113, 262, 264, 266, 268, 270
Mazda Raceway Laguna Seca—page 119
Sonoma Raceway—page 125
Thunderhill Raceway—page 129
Pebble Beach Company—page 212, 217
Open Street Map data was used to build maps on pages 12, 13, 81, 85, 91, 93, 101, 105, 107, 111, 121, 127, 154, 155, 161, 165, 169, 173, 181, 185, 197, 191, 205, 211, 213, 232, 235, 240, 242, 243, 245, 250, 253—255, 257

Acknowledgements

Sabu Advani
Anne Arns
Michaela Bates
Lynda Benoit
Dan Boeschen
Tab Borge
Yale Braunstein
Diana Brennan
Kevin Buckler
Jennifer Capasso
Lorraine Carrigan
Amy Christie
Michael Coats
Bruce Cohn
Becky Contos
Felicia Denham
Margaret DeVore
Chris & Becky DeSmet-Sollecito
Melainie Dougherty
John Drummond
Shannon Ell
John Ficarra
Dawna Friedman
Alan Galbraith
Christine Giovingo
Michelle Gothan
Jannelle Grigsby
Kandace Hawkinson
Shawn Heffernan
Peter Hiller
Brett Johnson
Morris Kindig
Lasseter Family
Susan E. Lindsey
Amanda Lorren
Kelly Loski
Katherine McFadden
Tim McGrane
Cindy Mietle
Bill Millard
Amy Miller
Anna Miller
Natalie Minas
John Moulton
Christian Palmaz
Frank Patek
Brenda Priddy
Stephanie Quinn
Laura Rateaver
Joe Richardson
Patty Reid
Tony Singer
Brianne Spiersch
Jim Tinsley
David Woodworth
Jared Zaugg

Pebble Beach Resort Credits

Photo Credits

All photos are taken by Ron Adams unless noted below.

Hiller Aviation Museum—page 43
Monterey Auto Museum—pages 44, 45
Adobe Winery—bottom of page 73
Far Niente—page 93
Francis Ford Coppola Winery—page 96
LucasArts Clipandstill—poster of *Tucker: The Man and His Dream*—page 99
Darryl Woo—page 121
Tommy Kendall—page 124
Audi sportscar experience—page 132
Simeraceway Performance Driving Center—page 139
RM Auctions—top of page 175
Peter Hiller—page 191
Kevin Hulsey Photography—page 202
Rick Mukherjee—page 203
Klemantaski Collection—page 210
Photo by Mark Estes/ Used Courtesy of the Pebble Beach Concours d'Elegance—page 223
Brenda Priddy—all photos on pages 238, 239, 240
MPTVimages—page 248
American Graffiti—top of page 249
© Universal Studios. All Rights Reserved
Wes Allison—page 252
Corbis—page 253
Jim Smith courtesy of the Walt Disney Family Museum—page 257
Stefan Schmidthuber—
top of pages 19, 263
David Woodworth—top of page 277

Special Thanks

Our hats off to the late Martin Swig for sharing all his wisdom and routes of his California Mille over the years.

Also Available!

Via Corsa Car Lover's Guide to Southern Germany

Explore Southern Germany's rich automotive history and discover the culture and personalities that define it today. Exclusive interviews with Hans-Joachim Stuck, Derek Bell, Susie Stoddart, Sabine Schmitz, and Wolfgang Kaufmann. Coverage includes over two dozen automobile museums, specialty car tuners, the legendary Nürburgring and Hockenheimring racetracks, and the car manufacturers that made Munich, Stuttgart, and Ingolstadt famous. This is the ultimate travel guide for anyone who loves the car.

ISBN-13: 978-0982571019

Available online at *www.amazon.com*, *www.barnesandnoble.com*, and *www.motorbooks.com*.
Or by calling (800) 458-0454

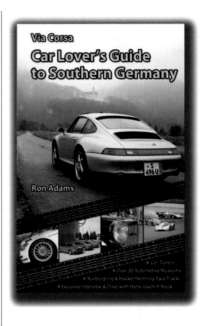

Coming Soon. . .

Via Corsa Car Lover's Guide to Southern California
Pocket size travel guidebook to Southern California

The Car Lover's Travel Magazine on Arizona
Travel magazine covering the events in Arizona

Watch *www.carloverstravel.com* for more information
